Unravelling
Research

D1354989

Unravelling Research

The Ethics & Politics
of Knowledge Production
in the Social Sciences

Edited by
Teresa Macías

Afterword by
Sherene H. Razack

Fernwood Publishing
Halifax & Winnipeg

Development editing: Fiona Jeffries
Copyediting: Sarah Michaelson
Cover design: Evan Marnoch
Printed and bound in Canada

Published by Fernwood Publishing
32 Oceanvista Lane, Black Point, Nova Scotia, B0J 1B0
and 748 Broadway Avenue, Winnipeg, Manitoba, R3G 0X3

www.fernwoodpublishing.ca

This book has been published with the help of a grant from the Federation for the Humanities and Social Sciences, through the Awards to Scholarly Publications Program, using funds provided by the Social Sciences and Humanities Research Council of Canada.

Fernwood Publishing Company Limited gratefully acknowledges the financial support of the Government of Canada, the Canada Council for the Arts, the Manitoba Department of Culture, Heritage and Tourism under the Manitoba Publishers Marketing Assistance Program and the Province of Manitoba, through the Book Publishing Tax Credit, for our publishing program. We are pleased to work in partnership with the Province of Nova Scotia to develop and promote our creative industries for the benefit of all Nova Scotians.

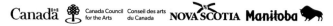

Library and Archives Canada Cataloguing in Publication

Title: Unravelling research: the ethics and politics of research in the social sciences / edited by Teresa Macías.
Names: Macías, Teresa, editor.
Description: Includes bibliographical references and index.
Identifiers: Canadiana (print) 20210354224 | Canadiana (ebook) 20210363223 | ISBN 9781773635231 (softcover) | ISBN 9781773635453 (PDF)
Subjects: LCSH: Social sciences—Research—Moral and ethical aspects. | LCSH: Social sciences—Research—Political aspects.
Classification: LCC H62 .U57 2022 | DDC 300.72—dc23

Contents

Acknowledgements

This book is the culmination of years of fruitful reflections and dialogue with colleagues. Among them are Lorena M. Gajardo, Vannina Sztainbok, Anne O'Connell, Harjeet Badwall and Donna Jeffery, who I am fortunate to work with and call my friends. Their continuous intellectual nourishment has been invaluable in helping keep this project alive and bringing it to fruition. Readers should not be surprised to see some of their names attached to chapters in this book. I would like to especially thank Sherene Razack for writing a brilliant and engaging Afterword. Her scholarship continues to influence and enrich mine as well as that of many of the contributors to this collection.

As with most intellectual endeavours, the effort and labour of producing a book like this one would not have been possible without the support of family. This is especially the case as much of that labour has been done during the difficult years of the COVID pandemic. The shift towards working from home entailed unforeseen adjustments for many of us, impacting us individually as well as our families. To my parents, Antonio and Prosperina Macías, with whom I share a home, I want to dedicate a special mention for the patience and care they have shown me. I thank my sister Maria Macías and her partner and children, Junior, Jarinca, Nicolas, Miila and Joshua, for their continued unconditional love. I want to thank my son Andres Macías for being my most important source of encouragement and a steadfast provider of laughter and hugs, and for bringing into our lives along with his partner Christina the newest addition to our family, baby Louisa Teresa, who has brought us all much joy.

I would also like to thank Catherine van Mossel, who copy edited the first draft of the manuscript, and Anna Lerner for her assistance with final formatting. Their work has proved invaluable. At Fernwood, I would like to acknowledge the work and assistance of Fiona Jeffries, Sarah Michaelson and all the rest of the staff who worked in the design, editing and final production of this book. I am particularly grateful to the anonymous reviewers for the generosity of their time and energy, their engagement with the multiple ideas contained in this book, and the gracious and constructive feedback that strengthened the collection.

Finally, I would like to thank the Federation for the Humanities and Social Sciences, the Awards to Scholarly Publications Program, and the Social Sciences and Humanities Research Council of Canada for the financial support they provided towards the publication of this book.

Permissions

I would like to thank the journal *Intersectionalities: A Global Journal of Social Work Analysis, Research, Polity, and Practice* for permission to reproduce early versions and selected sections of the following:

Harjeet Kaur Badwall. 2016. "Racialized Discourses: Writing against an Essentialized Story about Racism." *Intersectionalities: A Global Journal of Social Work Analysis, Research, Polity, and Practice* 5, 1.

Teresa Macías. 2016. "Between Violence and its Representation: Ethics, Archival Research, and the Politics of Knowledge Production in the Telling of Torture Stories." *Intersectionalities: A Global Journal of Social Work Analysis, Research, Polity, and Practice* 5, 1.

Anne O'Connell. 2016. "My Entire Life Is Online: Informed Consent, Big Data and Decolonial Knowledge." *Intersectionalities: A Global Journal of Social Work Analysis, Research, Polity and Practice* 5, 1.

Contributors

Leila Angod is assistant professor at the Institute of Interdisciplinary Studies at Carleton University. Her research examines how schools invite young people to enact racial and colonial orders, and how youth engage, resist and refuse these invitations. Her youth-centred and community-engaged projects include co-founding in:cite youth research journal.

Harjeet Kaur Badwall is associate professor at York University's School of Social Work in Toronto, Canada. Her areas of research focus on race, racism and whiteness in Social Work, racialized and gender-based violence, practice and theory connections, interlocking analysis of violence and oppression, post-structural theory, and Narrative therapy and practice. Harjeet worked in the anti-violence field for many years as a counselor, community organizer and activist.

Lorena M. Gajardo is a non-affiliated, independent scholar. Her scholarly interests include decoloniality, Latinx studies, pluriversality, the limits of extractive logics, and storytelling as research methodology.

Julia Elizabeth Janes is an assistant professor of Social Work at Memorial University of Newfoundland and Labrador, a first-generation scholar, second-generation settler, and guest on the unceded homelands of the Mi'kmaq and Beothuk. Julia's research interests are driven by the communities that she has collaborated with on social justice participatory action research projects, which explore the limits and possibilities of community/university alliances in the context of precarity in later life, arts-based activisms and methodologies, decolonizing practices and pedagogies.

Caitlin Janzen is a PhD candidate in Sociology at York University. Her current work applies a feminist psychoanalytic frame to analyze feminine forms of aggression in popular television and film. She has published in *Psychoanalysis, Culture & Society*, *Continuum*, and *Hypatia* and is a co-editor (along with Claire Carter and Chelsea Jones) of a forthcoming edited collection entitled *Contemporary Vulnerabilities: Reflections on Social Justice Methodologies.*

Brenda LeFrançois is a critical psychologist, social work educator and university research professor at Memorial University of Newfoundland.

Teresa Macías is associate professor at York University's School of Social Work, editor-in-chief of the journal *Intersectionalities: A Global Journal of Social Work Analysis, Research, Polity and Practice,* and co-editor with Sobia Shaikh and Brenda LeFrançois of *Critical Social Work Praxis* (Fernwood). Her research interests include human rights regimes, decoloniality, critical race theory, ethics, research methodology and critical education. She was born in Chile where she was a popular educator and a human rights and student activist. She currently lives with her family in Ontario, Canada.

Anne O'Connell is an associate professor in the School of Social Work, York University. Her work focuses on the colonial histories of poverty and connections to racial slavery, land theft, and genocidal/assimilationist polices that shore up white settler societies. Her research looks at how contemporary turns toward multiculturalism, apologies, and (informed) consent practices in institutions and government policies provide coherence to, and the entrenchment of, racial neoliberal capitalism.

Sherene H. Razack is a distinguished professor and the Penny Kanner endowed chair in Women's Studies in the Department of Gender Studies, UCLA. Her publications illustrate the thematic areas and anti-colonial, anti-racist feminist scholarship she pursues. Her most recent book is *Nothing Has to Make Sense: Upholding White Supremacy through Anti-Muslim Racism.*

Susan Strega, PhD, is professor emerita in Social Work, University of Victoria. She is the co-editor (with Sohki Aski Esquao [Jeannine Carriere]) of *Walking This Path Together: Anti-Racist and Anti-Oppressive Child Welfare Practice* (Fernwood), and the co-editor (with Leslie Brown) of *Research as Resistance: Revisiting Critical, Indigenous and Anti-Oppressive Approaches* (CSPI).

Vannina Sztainbok is an adjunct lecturer in the department of Social Justice Education, Ontario Institute for Studies in Education, University of Toronto. She has written on nation building and racism in South America, the fetishization of Blackness, and narratives of torture in the Southern Cone. Currently she is conducting research on race and organized abandonment during the COVID-19 pandemic, and the anti-fascist politics of the Black Uruguayan press in the 1930s.

Jijian Voronka is an assistant professor in the School of Social Work at the University of Windsor. She teaches primarily for their Disability Studies program, where she uses Critical Disability Studies perspectives to elucidate confluences of power that affect disabled people in everyday, community, and institutional life. Her current research explores disability inclusion strategies in health and social service systems; peer/survivor research methodologies in practice; sites of confinement in the age of deinstitutionalization; and teaching and learning through disability justice frameworks.

1

Introduction: Unravelling Research

Teresa Macías

The authors in this volume responded to an invitation to contribute to the scholarly literature on research ethics and the politics of knowledge production in the social sciences. I invited the authors to pick at the threads in the fabric of their own research, to let their research work unravel and, in the process reveal, render bare and, therefore thinkable, the very labour associated with knowledge production. Thus, the invitation was not to write conventional chapters on research ethics or methodology, nor to provide a guide for researchers seeking answers to the ethical and methodological challenges they confront. Rather, I asked the contributors to reflect on the thinking processes associated with the different stages of research work: the interpretative practices, the strategic negotiations, the methodological pitfalls, the theoretical voices, and even the mundane tasks associated with research. I encouraged the contributors to think of this work of unravelling research as an exercise in ethics, as well as a point of entry into a critical reflection on the ethics and politics of knowledge production informing and framing research work. I hoped that this process of unravelling research would reveal fissures, cracks, difficulties, dilemmas, challenges and lessons associated with the work of knowledge production within the social sciences.

This invitation was, foremost, a challenge to the authors to unsettle their own claims to knowledge, to expertise and to certainty. I asked them to dig, in a sort of archeological fashion (Agamben 2009), through the different layers of their research work in order to uncover those moments in which claims to knowing were the most precarious as well as those moments in which their commitment to ethical practices succeeded and/or failed. Though I did not name it as such, this was an invitation to engage in the kind of archeological vigilance that Agamben associates with inquiry in the social sciences and that he defines as a process of tracing research's "own trajectory back to the point where something remains obscure and unthematized" (2009, 8). Ultimately, I invited the authors to trace the histories of their own research: the moments in which curiosity led to questions and questions led to processes of enquiry, decisions about methodologies, methods, analytical frameworks, processes of dissemination, etc. In short, I asked the contributors to reveal the paradigms that inform their research: the "disciplinary matrixes" (Kuhn 1970) within which their studies are located, and within which certain questions and research practices become possible while others remain an impossibility.

The contributors' answers to my invitation do not disappoint. The chapters centre the authors' own research work as material foundation for analyses that stress the indivisibility of ethics, epistemology, methodology and politics. They situate themselves and their research work within historical and ongoing social power relations, and account for their positions as both members of the academy and of the communities on whom, and with whom, they do research. In doing so, the scholars in this book demonstrate a keen awareness of the colonial, historical, political, and institutional conditions that inform their work and that complicate their research labour. As Sherene Razack's Afterword observes, the contributors "make it their mission to find an ethical place to stand in social science research even as they acknowledge its impossibility and never stop worrying." Through the difficult labour of unravelling their own research, the authors offer bold paths towards ethical scholarly practice, as well as honest reflections on their misgivings about how research is practiced in dominant and mainstream research traditions, disciplines and institutions. Most importantly, the chapters enrich the field of research ethics by illuminating the challenges and negotiations that confront scholars and researchers who, due to race, gender, class, geographical origin, institutional location, labour precarity and histories of marginalization, labour at the margins of their disciplines and are often ignored in the mainstream research literature. In this way, the authors make timely contributions to the scholarly literature on epistemology, research methodology, and the ethics and politics of knowledge production at a time in which Canadian universities are contending with the many historical inequities that impact research and shape academic work.

It is important to recognize that my invitation to the authors carried a dangerous proposition. Unravelling research is risky for academics and researchers who labour at the margins of our disciplines, and who occupy precarious positions within historical global, racial, and transnational power relations. Despite recent efforts by Canadian universities to address racism and colonialism — through, for example, targeted hiring practices and the appointment of equity and diversity administrators — many of us continue to operate within hostile and structurally inequitable institutional, professional, disciplinary and political climates, and within materially problematic academic labour structures (see for example Canaan & Shumar 2008; Gill 2010; Giroux 2002). Within these contexts, our commitment to troubling conventional ways of knowing, and to unravelling our own research work can further unsettle our already precarious claims to disciplinary belonging and to academic respectability.

Unravelling research requires us to question the foundations of the disciplines to which we already precariously belong, and to think, speak and write against the grain of established conventions, practices, politics and conceptions of ethics. It also requires writing dangerously and subversively, to be un-disciplined (Mignolo 2015), to speak against what is unquestionably accepted, and to unsettle the very ground on which we already precariously stand. As the chapters in this volume demonstrate, the work of unravelling research leads to the troubling of knowledge claims, to the disruption of traditional approaches to studying social phenomena, to the historization and politization of methodology and knowledge, and to an exploration of the conditions that make knowledge possible (Agamben 2009, 93). Unravelling research also involves revealing what Mignolo (2009, 162) calls the "apparatus of enunciation," which determine what counts as knowledge and what knowledge counts within established geo-historical and geopolitical systems of knowledge production. Furthermore, unravelling research means engaging in a process of interrogation which aims, as Foucault (2005, xxiii) observes, to discover

> on what basis knowledge and theory [become] possible; within what space of order knowledge [is] constituted; on the basis of what historical *a priori*, and in the element of what positivity, ideas [can] appear, science be established, experiences be reflected in philosophies, rationalities be formed, only, perhaps, to dissolve and vanish soon afterwards.

The chapters included in this volume are multidisciplinary in nature. The authors tackle the challenge of unravelling research from diverse methodological, theoretical and conceptual frameworks including Latinx and Chicana Studies (Sztainbok & Gajardo, Ch. 2), archival research (Macías, Ch. 3), ethnology (Angod, Ch. 4), narrative research (Badwall, Ch. 5; Janzen & Strega, Ch. 8), Mad methodologies (LeFrançois & Voronka, Ch. 6), community-based participatory research (Janes, Ch. 7), and big digital data (O'Connell, Ch. 9). The authors incorporate a diversity of theoretical voices into their research including critical race theory, critical social theory, decoloniality, postcolonialism, Indigenous epistemologies, transnational feminism, post-structuralism, etc. In the process, they probe the ethicality of these methodological and theoretical frameworks and situate them, as well as their research, within the sociopolitical and historical contexts influencing and shaping their work. The authors delve into issues such as the constitution and regulation of research subjects and participants through, for example, practices of collecting big digital data (O'Connell, Ch. 9) and the recruitment of community participants to assist in research work (Janes, Ch. 7). They reveal ethical dilemmas and political implications associated with practices of representation, writing and reporting on, for example, racialized social workers' experiences of white dominance (Badwall, Ch. 5), testimonies by street sex workers (Janzen and Strega, Ch. 8), racialized encounters in international humanitarian work (Angod, Ch. 4), stories of violence collected in archives (Macías, Ch. 3) and practices of research and writing about the Global South within contemporary geopolitical power structures (Sztainbok & Gajardo, Ch. 2).

Despite the diversity of these research endeavours, one central thread links the chapters: questions of research ethics are always and simultaneously questions of methodology and politics. In other words, research ethics cannot be disentangled from issues related to politics, theory and practice, and, as a result, any proposal for ethical practice in research must remain cognizant of the entanglement of methodology and politics. Furthermore, questions of ethics, methodology and politics are themselves also questions of subjectivity. That is, they are questions raised, not by a researcher that exists a priori and independent from the research, but by a subject-researcher that is called into being through the research: through the encounter with an Other whose life, and sometimes death, the research seeks to capture and bring into existence as knowledge, and through the ongoing search for ethical practice. In this way, the chapters unsettle commonly accepted ideas that an impartial, rational and unencumbered researcher exists and can somehow outline an ethical practice in advance of the application of any methodology, independent of the context within which the research exists. Instead, within the chapters, the work of knowledge production emerges as an activity that is ultimately enmeshed in issues of methodology, politics and subjectivity; and it is from within these entanglements that authors propose possible, yet always imperfect, ambiguous and trepidatious ethical directions for scholars, students and researchers seeking possible ways forward.

Research, Power and Politics

Following on the footsteps of critical social theorists, and post-structural and decolonial thinkers, the contributors to this volume stress the importance of situating research and its related ethical negotiations within social power relations such as geopolitical, imperial and colonial power structures and systems of knowledge; white supremacy and processes of racialization; transnational politics of knowledge production and their associated politics of representation; neoliberal governmentality; biomedical and psychiatric systems of regulation of knowledge and research; colonial and imperial civilizational discourses and their manifestation in professional narratives of helping and benevolence; and politics of memory and witnessing.

For instance, Sztainbok and Gajardo (Ch. 2) argue that research is situated within geopolitical, imperial, colonial and transnational contexts that influence the constitution of certain knowledge as science while other knowledge becomes culture, anecdote and experience (see also Mignolo 2007; 2011; Quijano 2007). These geopolitics of knowledge production, as Sztainbok and Gajardo observe, create conditions in which subjects and knowledge emerging from the real and imaginary space called the Global South — including the knowledge produced by subalternized researchers in the Global North — are always already known, always already located within specific parameters of intelligibility, always "heard through the accent." In a similar vein, Janzen and Strega (Ch. 8) argue that these geopolitical, imperial and colonial contexts determine how the stories shared by participants — especially participants who are marginalized by gender, colonialism, racialization, poverty, etc. — are taken up, heard and/or unheard in research.

In her reflection on the difficulties of writing about racialized encounters within international humanitarian work, Angod (Ch. 4) exposes the methodological challenges of producing knowledge about practices of racialization within imperial and global social power relations. This reflection leads her to argue for a politics of accounting for the distinct positionalities of researchers and participants and for the ways in which researchers — including racialized researchers — share historical responsibilities for global and colonial racial and epistemic structures. Similarly, in her discussion of the ethics of reporting on the experiences of racialized social workers within white supremacy, Badwall (Ch. 5) cautions racialized researchers against assuming similarity, or an insider position, in relation to research participants based solely on shared racial identity. Unproblematic assumptions of sameness, she argues, can result in the effacement of the complex histories of racism and the multiple social and political conditions that shape how race is experienced and lived by racialized communities.

LeFrançois and Voronka's (Ch. 6) critique of biomedical and psy research in mental health highlights the way in which these research fields both continue to sustain the subjugation and disciplining of people constituted as mad, and remain rooted in histories of scientific racism, colonial power structures and their historically constituted taxonomies of difference. Biomedical epistemologies and the psy system, they argue, not only ignore the complex experiences of madpeople, but also subjugate mad epistemologies, denying legitimacy to mad ways of knowing and being in the world.

In Chapter 3, I engage in an exploration of the ethical challenges associated with archival research, and I unsettle the notion that archival research — as work done on data that is in the public domain — is somehow free from the ethical challenges that may affect research involving "live" participants. In the process, I delve into the nature of archives as devices with complex historical and social functions, situated within historical and political contexts, and implicated in turning certain experiences, documents, stories, etc. into archival records. I argue that archives are not neutral depositories of records; rather, they produce records through the complex interplay of power and knowledge. As a result, archival research can never be free of the power-knowledge regimes that shape the archive and that regulate knowledge production. In the case of archives containing testimonies of state-sponsored terror practices in Chile, which is the case that concerns me, my work in the archives, as well as the work of representation associated with research, are entwined in the same politics of truth that determine what stories of terror are allowed to exist in the archive. Therefore, archival research on these records must take into consideration the social power relations that shape the archive if we are to conduct ethical, or less unethical, archival research.

In her analysis of the practices of collecting big digital data, O'Connell (Ch. 9) also delves into the political issues associated with the production of digital archives and its related practices of collecting digital information. O'Connell situates the ever-expanding collection of digital data within what she calls "informational capitalism" and its related "digital empire." Digital research and the collection and management of big data, she argues, not only bypass conventional — though arguably limited — academic ethics review processes; they also reconstitute knowledge-producing labour, privatize data and reformulate issues such as consent and privacy to fit within neoliberal, individualistic discourses and systems of governance and surveillance. While digital data is commonly assumed to be "public" and "neutral," O'Connell reveals how this data is in fact the property and product of private corporations with ever-increasing roles in the surveillance and securitization of vulnerable populations and the public in general.

Finally, in her critique of community-based participatory research (CBPR), Janes (Ch. 7) unpacks and politicizes concepts such as collaboration and participation, concepts that CBPR continues to hold dear, but that remain steeped in unequal structures of epistemic governance as well as in neoliberal and capitalist politics of knowledge extraction. Using Foucault's concept of governmentality, Janes reveals how community collaboration is regulated, disciplined and ultimately reconstituted to fit within neoliberal notions of knowledge accumulation, commodification and dissemination. Practices of inclusion and strategies to promote community participation, she shows, can also operate as forms of epistemic governance and dominance grounded on insidious and far-reaching neoliberal politics of extraction. CBPR operates as "a technique of inclusion" that ultimately responsibilizes communities for their social problems while appropriating and managing their labour and knowledge.

The contributors draw on their subject positionality to theorize the ethical and political implications of contemporary research practices. As they grapple with the complex ethical dilemmas that can both under-mine and enrich social science research, they also recognize, acknowl-edge and critically engage with conditions of complicity that implicate us in practices of knowledge extraction and in the production of knowl-edge about "Others." Angod (Ch. 4), for instance, interrogates her role as a racialized researcher extracting data and producing knowledge about racialized encounters in the context of North-South unequal power re-lations. In Chapter 3, I also reflect on my own complicity in practices of reporting and representation of terror stories captured in official ar-chives, at the same time that I trouble any claim to innocence and cer-tainty in the representational work associated with knowledge produc-tion. Janzen and Strega (Ch. 8), on their part, reflect on the challenges they confront when collecting street sex workers' testimonies of violence within the context of colonial histories and their interlocking relation-ship to patriarchy. Colonialism and patriarchy, they argue, continue to make marginalized women, specifically Indigenous women, into easy targets of research. Janzen and Strega identify the challenges of having to adhere to ethical conventions that require that the data be "'scrubbed clean' of identity," severing the subject from her own story in the ex-tractive process of research and knowledge production. Such scrubbing, they propose, constitutes a form of epistemic violence that implicates researchers in critical ways.

The contributors scrutinize conceptions of research that are com-monly unspoken, assumed unquestionable and invisible in their taken-for-granted-ness. Most critically, they stress that power is unescapable because researchers are always situated within practices and traditions that rely on the desire to "know." Yet, as Sztainbok and Gajardo (Ch. 2) observe, for example, power can, at times, be exercised in productive ways. Sometimes categories are needed and borders need to be named and evoked for the purpose of justice. Building on Gloria Anzaldúa's in-fluential work, Sztainbok and Gajardo argue that racialized and Southern scholars exist *entremundos* (between worlds), a positionality that is not always limiting. Rather, existing *entremundos* has its advantages because within it, "normative scripts can be transformed to produce multiple inhabited selves." As I also propose in Chapter 3, practices of representa-tion in research can take the form of political action, an action that is necessary, at the same time that it is situated within political, histori-cal and social contexts. And, as Janzen and Strega (Ch. 8) suggest, it is possible for researchers to become witnesses to the stories of street sex workers, and to the ways in which, through their demand for narrative sovereignty, street sex workers exercise their "will and drive to *live*," in spite of the social, political and historical forces bent on bringing about their death.

By scrutinizing the ethicality of their own research projects, the authors unsettle the very ground on which they stand, and in the process, they destabilize their and other researchers' claims to ethical certainty at the same time that they challenge institutional conceptions of ethics that, as Janzen and Strega (Ch. 8) argue, "are long on legalities, but short on justice." Thus, it is critical to reemphasize that the authors do more than provide important critiques of the methodologies that inform their research and of the practices associated with the contextual and politically significant work of producing knowledge. They also present us with discussions in which ethics becomes a question of methodology and politics. That is, ethics are not prior to methodology and politics are not external to research. Rather, ethics and politics are intrinsic parts of every aspect of research.

The Subject-Researcher

The socio-political and historical contexts of research situate and implicate the researcher as a subject that is constituted and takes on the role of researcher in the minutia associated with research work, as well as in the relationships between researcher and subjects/objects of study. Several of the authors problematize the decision-making practices of researchers, challenging ideas of neutrality and objectivity in decisions regarding methodologies, recruitment, reporting, writing, representation, etc. By so doing, the authors politicize decision-making practices in research regarding, for example, how racialized resistance and experiences of racism, sexual violence, street sex work, and stories of violence are constituted as the data that is then fragmented, interpreted, analyzed, and finally written in and/or out of research reports. These decisions are not made by a self-contained, independent, and unencumbered researcher. Rather, they are constitutive of the researcher and their relationship to their topic and research subjects. In other words, the researcher is not as a pre-existing character, but rather emerges in the very performative work of research (see for instance, Macías Ch. 3). Furthermore, the researcher-subject is always situated and regulated within regimes of truth, geopolitics of knowing, social structures, scholarly practices, politics related to publication and research funding, labour practices within the academe, etc. (Gill 2010; Mignolo 2009; Moore 2010).

As they unpack the self-constituting aspect of research, the authors model a form of reflexivity that departs from what is commonly understood as critical self-reflection. While it has become a common and advisable practice in social science research (see for example Gallagher 2000; Harding 1992; Haraway 1988), critical reflexivity has also come under scrutiny. At best, it is considered a form of self-indulgence (Sanchez Tylor & O'Connell Davidson 2010); at worst, it is seen as another way of re-inscribing, through practices of confession, white dominance and the moral superiority of white western subjects (see for example Badwall 2016).

Instead, the form of critical reflexivity that the authors in this collection model is one that shares a commitment to unsettle any claims for the stability of the subject-researcher, and, as a result, it cannot easily be deemed self-indulgent or confessional. As I suggest in Chapter 3, for instance, an ethical practice of reflection requires that we render the subjectivity of both the researcher and the researched precarious, always-in-progress, yet permanently situated within sociopolitical and historical contexts. This precarity is not meant to imply that the researcher is powerless or vulnerable, but rather that her very constitution as a researcher is always in process, a project in the making and always historical and political. As Badwall (Ch. 4) proposes, conducting research as a racialized researcher with racialized participants requires an attitude of vigilance and a commitment to resist the impulse to find commonality in narratives about experiences of racism. The subject-researcher, in Badwall's reflection, is one that resists the desire to both separate her own experience from that of her participants at the same time that she resists the impulse to unproblematically assume a common ground. This subject-researcher is one that also understands that her subjectivity and multiple subject positions are always present in the research. Badwall's commitment is to practices of intersubjectivity and reflexivity that can lead to more complex and fundamentally anti-essentialist analyses of racism.

On their part, Sztainbok and Gajardo (Ch. 2) as well as Angod (Ch. 4) argue for practices of reflexivity that render the positionality of the researcher "opaque" while renouncing any claim to universal impartiality, rationality and ethical certainty. Janzen and Strega (Ch. 8) engage in a practice of reflexivity that is situated in the intersubjective relationship between the researcher and the participant in which participants issue a demand for "narrative sovereignty," a demand that calls the researcher to become a witness to the participants' mnemonic labour. While they do not call it critical reflexivity, Janzen and Strega model a form of reflection in which they remain aware of the challenges of manoeuvring institutional demands, historical conditions and social power relations as they answer the participants' demands.

It is important to stress that the form of reflexivity performed by the authors is not meant to re-centre the researcher as a subject capable of independent decision making and controlling all aspects of the research, nor as a practitioner capable of determining ethical practice outside socio-political and historical contexts. Rather, the forms of reflexivity that the authors propose is one that is always in dialogue with others. That is, reflexivity is not an individual process but rather a collective one, always taking place within social, historical and political contexts. As a result, reflexivity emerges as a form of social responsibility, a form of political action, and a commitment to give up the search for any form of authenticity and certainty. Reflexivity is ultimately a process of interrogation and questioning the conditions under which research leads to knowledge. Furthermore, reflexivity is a collaborative process, a process that takes place in dialogue with others, both through an engagement with the work of critical thinkers, or, as in the case of Sztainbok and Gajardo (Ch. 2), in the meetings of critical minds willing to challenge one another. Most importantly, reflexivity in the chapters in this book is a form of unapologetic labour and an activity that resists the kind of unproductive confessional practices that characterize self-reflective statements.

Ethics and Methodology

The search for a common conception of ethics was never the purpose of this book and, in fact, the authors put forward a diversity of ethical proposals that include conceptions of ethics as performative, ambiguous, undomesticated, undisciplined and accountable. The authors also conceptualize ethical practice as being fundamentally intersubjective, possible only in the constitutive relationship between the researcher and the subjects of research in which research subjects issue a demand that the researcher must answer (Janzen & Strega, Ch. 8). This intersubjective relationship is also one in which the researcher's desire for common ground needs to be interrogated (Badwall, Ch. 5). Further, in this intersubjective relationship, as Janes (Ch. 7) proposes, the researcher is required to negotiate both the oppressive and liberatory aspects of any methodology and live with both the impossibility and the necessity for equitable practices of knowledge production.

In the same way that decisions about methodology cannot be separated from the political context within which research takes place, ethics appear in the chapters as always negotiated within, and impacted by, the political. The authors propose that ethics are never separate from both methodological decisions and the political context within which their research endeavours are situated. That is, ethical practice is neither possible a priori of decisions of methodology, nor independent from historical, social and political contexts and are, in fact, negotiated — in ways that are always uncertain and messy — in the entanglements of politics, power and practice. As a result, rather than offering satisfactory resolution to the ethical dilemmas they confront, the contributors to this collection offer glimpses of their ongoing and always unresolved processes of ethical reflection and questioning.

For instance, as a I reflect on the ethical challenges associated with researching stories of state-sponsored terror recorded in archives (Ch. 3), I propose that any ethical practice in research must be negotiated in the very narrow and politically relevant space between the records of violence found in archives and the practices of representation in which researchers engage. I propose that this narrow space is significant because in it the subject researcher, and the research itself, is constituted through the quotidian labour associated with transforming records into data. That is, the researcher is called into being through the work of collecting, organizing, fragmenting and reporting on the records. Ethics, I propose, is the performative and always un-realized and perilous action through which researchers come into being through the work they perform within the narrow space between violence and its representation. As performative, this form of ethics renders the subject precarious in ways that opens up multiple opportunities for transformative action. This way of understanding ethics stands in contrast to traditional conceptions of ethics as rules and codes of conduct negotiated by a stable subject that is independent of the research. In fact, this understanding of ethics as both performative and precarious render the subject–researcher and the research work uncertain, always a project in the making in the constantly shifting and political work of knowledge production.

Sztainbok and Gajardo (Ch. 2) propose an ethics of ambiguity when engaging in research within the geopolitical structures that continue to rely on the establishment and perpetuation of global, racial, imperial political orders, systems of inequality and regimes of knowledge. This ethics of ambiguity requires that researchers from the Global South, as well as subalternized researchers in the Global North, commit to inhabit a space Sztainbok and Gajardo define as a borderland: a place in between worlds, as well as a place in which different worlds, cultures and people edge one another. In the borderlands, researchers can both resist the impulse to know at the same time that they recognize that some knowledge is needed for justice. In the borderlands, researchers can engage in the difficult work of revealing and naming racism, imperialism and white supremacy while negotiating their own uncertain roles as knowledge producers with and about the Other. Finally, in the borderlands, racialized and marginalized researchers can adopt an ethics of ambiguity, characterized by a commitment to be undomesticated and undisciplined, to speak against racism while revealing its modus operandi, to remain part of their communities yet resist the impulse to become native informants, and to unsettle and hopefully dismantle commonly accepted notions of impartiality as well as knower-known binaries. Ambiguity, Sztainbok and Gajardo argue, is not the same as ambivalence — understood as the balancing of opposing perspectives — but rather, a commitment to transformational politics, to unsettle, and to revealing power, epistemicide, racism, etc. Ethical practice is, according to Sztainbok and Gajardo, a commitment to continuous questioning, and is fundamentally a political project. Finally, this ethics of ambiguity is characterized by a commitment to both humility and un-domestication: humility required to do away with the desire to ever know everything, and un-domestication understood as a refusal to unproblematically accept any claims to stable subject positions and universal stories or narratives.

Angod (Ch. 4) builds on the work of Sherene Razack, a Canadian critical race scholar, and proposes an ethics of accountability defined as a commitment to recognize not only how racialized researchers are subordinated but also how they contribute to the subordination of others, of the people with whom, on whom and/or about whom their knowledge-producing work is performed. This commitment to accountability requires that researchers recognize that they both shape and are shaped by their encounter with their research subjects. This ethics of account-ability, Angod proposes, imply an obligation to reveal what is invisible to, and unseen by, the colonializing gaze, while avoiding sliding into po-sitions of innocence. Angod illustrates what an ethics of accountability make possible in her own ethnographic work, in which she attempts to denaturalize some of the normative stories told about racialized children by elite white volunteers doing work in South Africa. Readers may find her discussion of how she engaged in practice of observation and analy-sis instructive of the ethical commitment she puts forward.

As teachers of research, we commonly ask students/researchers under our supervision to reflect on why they want to do research, and many times we advise them to choose research topics or issues to which they feel a close connection, or communities with which they share a com-mon experience or history. We assume that having shared experiences can lead to more ethical research practices, or that insider research can help advance social justice. Yet, Badwall (Ch. 5) cautions racialized re-searchers against unquestioned assumptions of insider-researcher posi-tions when doing research on racism. She urges us to resist the impulse to assume sameness because such an assumption creates the illusion of the existence of one authentic universal voice that can tell one story of racism. Yet, she does not adhere to unproblematic assumptions of out-sider-ness either; for racialized researchers do have their own embodied knowledge of racism that inform their work. Instead, Badwall proposes that we situate ourselves in what she calls a "third space": space that is neither inside nor completely outside the communities and experiences of racialized people. In this third space, researchers can resist reading their own experience into the narratives offered by participants and can avoid producing a single essentialized story of racism. From this third space, researchers can tell complex stories of how racism operates in ways that both reveal the connections that exist between diverse narra-tives of racism while honouring the complexity, diversity and contextual character of people's experiences. It is important to mention that Badwall does not claim that in this third space, we may find an all-knowing, ob-jective or impartial subject-researcher, a researcher unburdened by as-sumptions of commonality or difference. Rather, the researcher situated in this third space is a subject that labours with full awareness of how her own experience influences her work while remaining attentive to the complex ways in which racism and racial injustice systematically operates in people's lives. Through this commitment to complexity, Badwall proposes, the researcher can allow for other voices and other stories to emerge and speak through the data.

As they reflect on the politics of knowledge production concerning people historically labelled as mad, LeFrançois and Voronka (Ch. 6) argue for the maddening of both research and of ethics. In the process, they show how ethics, epistemology and methodology are inseparable and must always be considered together. Building on Derrida's work, LeFrançois and Voronka argue that ethics requires a commitment to remain in a suspended moment prior to action, a moment in which justice is perhaps still possible, and in which researchers live with the tensions associated with every research decision without attempting to resolve them. Ethical actions in this moment are fundamentally "recalcitrant, unruly, uncontainable, disorderly, unstable, ungovernable." Yet, researchers need to remain committed to defying and eschewing dominant, colonial, racist and positivist systems of knowledge production. In order to realize this ethics of unruliness, LeFrançois and Voronka argue for the maddening of research. That is, for the development and advancement of mad epistemologies, mad theories and mad methodologies as strategies to decentre and resist dominant biomedical, psy, and sanist systems of knowledge production. A mad epistemology centres the ways of knowing and being of madpeople at the same time that it unsettles and decolonizes scientific knowledge. Most importantly, a mad methodology creates possibilities for transformative processes of mad subjectification while creating knowledge from the standpoint of madpeople, and revealing the political context within which research is situated.

Janzen and Strega (Ch. 8) centre the issue of intersubjective relationality when reflecting on their research work with women transitioning out of street sex work, many of whom were Indigenous and racialized, and who, as part of the research, shared their testimonies of violence and trauma. Decisions about methodology also emerge as closely linked to ethics and politics in this chapter, and this link is reflected, for instance, in the decision to shift methodological approaches — from grounded theory to narrative research — in order to both respond to the ethical demand for narrative sovereignty issued by participants and account for how narratives are embedded in social, political and historical contexts.

Responding to participants' ethical demands, Janzen and Strega suggest, requires recognition of the unequal and uneven labour associated with the work of memory as work that is still carried out by Indigenous, racialized and poor women. Yet, despite this unevenness, memory work can also constitute acts of resistance and insurgence to which researchers must bear witness.

Janzen and Strega and their research team began their research with the assumption that, as researchers who shared lived experiences with their participants, they were better suited to conduct the work than researchers who did not share the same experiences. Yet, they soon recognized that there remains a measure of distance between researchers and participants, a distance that cannot be easily bridged. This distance, Janzen and Strega propose, constitutes a "ethically trepidatious zone," a zone that while troubling notions of commonality, still presents important possibilities for ethical action. This zone is also a place where an intersubjective and dialogic relationship between speaker and listener can be forged and in which researcher and participant negotiate their subjectivities. That is, neither the speaker nor the listener comes into this relationship as fully formed subjects, but rather emerge as subjects within the space that both separates and connects them. While uncertain and "ethically trepidatious," this space between participants and researcher is also a space in which it is possible for researchers to adopt an "ethics of witnessing," understood as a form of witnessing that takes place within an "intersubjective present" where the researcher bears witness to the labour of memory, the "performance of testimony," and the participants' "will and drive to *live.*"

The entanglement of ethics, methodology and politics is also a central theme in Janes' chapter on CBPR (Ch. 7). Although Janes challenges and ultimately demystifies claims that CBPR is a more just, and thus more ethical, approach to research, she does not propose the complete elimination of CBPR. Rather, she remains committed to searching for possible opportunities for ethical practice in CBPR; for ways of "not being governed quite so much," for chances to think differently about community participation and for opportunities to practice more transformative forms of community engagement. Janes is committed to remain in the space between the oppressive and liberatory effects of CBPR in order to recognize both the impossibility and the necessity of equitable knowledge production. In this space, Janes suggests, it is possible for researchers and communities to resist the desire for proximity and to decentre the academe as the sole site for knowledge production. Finally, in this space, it is possible for communities and researchers to imagine transformative practices of knowledge production that can ultimately challenge hegemonic neoliberal conceptions of knowledge.

O'Connell (Ch. 9) turns her attention to the ethical challenges posed by intensifying practices of digital data gathering, management and control. She is particularly concerned with how corporate practices of digital data management intersect with academic research in ways that sidestep ethical institutional safeguards and rules related to confidentiality, risk and informed consent. She warns academics not to assume that digital data is "in the public domain." Rather, she reveals how digital data is, in fact, owned and controlled by transnational corporations that do not have to comply with the same practices that regulate academic research. Furthermore, O'Connell argues that practices of digital data collection are not only contributing to the constitution of a corporate digital empire but are also reconfiguring and reformulating concepts such as privacy, private-public distinctions, consent, confidentiality and, ultimately, knowledge. While accepting the limitations of traditional concepts of informed consent, confidentiality and risk — notions closely linked to institutional ethics review processes and firmly grounded on western, scientific, colonial and racist conceptions of the subject in research — she alerts us to the importance of reconceptualizing and, at times defending, these traditional conceptions of ethics especially in the era of big digital data.

It has been a tremendous honour and privilege for me to read the chapters in their different iterations and to engage the authors in enriching discussions and collaborative processes of thinking and reflection about research, ethics and politics. The multidisciplinary character of the chapters is bound to contribute to politically relevant debates concerning the production of knowledge in the social sciences and to reflections on the challenges of producing ethical knowledge. Thus, I hope this book will enrich the thinking and reflection of those searching for more nuanced, complex and critical engagements with questions related to the ethics and politics of knowledge production in social science research.

References

Agamben, Giorgio. 2009. *The Signature of All Things: On Method*. New York: Zone Books.

Badwall, Harjeet. 2016. "Critical Reflexivity and Moral Regulation." *Journal of Progressive Human Services* 27, 1: 1–20.

Canaan, Joyce, and Wesley Shumar. 2008. "Higher Education in the Era of Globalization and Neoliberalism." In *Structure and Agency in the Neoliberal University*, edited by Joyce Cannan and Wesley Shumar (1–32). New York and London: Routledge.

Foucault, Michel. 2005. *The Order of Things*. New York and London: Routledge

Gallagher, Charles. 2000. "White Like Me?" In *Racing Research, Researching Race: Methodological Dilemmas in Critical Race Studies*, edited by France Winddance Twine and Jonathan W. Warren (67–99). New York and London: New York University Press.

Gill, Rosalind. 2010. "Breaking the Silence: The Hidden Injuries of the Neoliberal University." In *Secrecy and Silence in the Research Process: Feminist Reflections* [Kobo version] edited by Roisin Ryan-Flood and Rosalind Gill (Chapter 7). New York and London: Routledge.

Giroux, Henry. 2002. "Neoliberalism, Corporate Culture, and the Promise of Higher Education: The University as a Democratic Public Sphere." *Harvard Educational Review* 72, 4: 425–463.

Haraway, Donna. 1988. "Situated Knowledges: The Science Question in Feminism and the Privilege of Partial Perspective." *Feminist Studies* 14, 3: 575–599.

Harding, Sandra. 1992. "Rethinking Standpoint Epistemology: What Is 'Strong Objectivity?'" *The Centennial Review* 36, 3: 437–470.

Kuhn, Thomas. 1970. *The Structure of Scientific Revolutions*, second ed. Chicago: The University of Chicago Press.

Mignolo, Walter. 2007. "Delinking: The Rhetoric of Modernity, the Logic of Coloniality and the Grammar of De-coloniality." *Cultural Studies* 21, 2–3: 449–514.

___. 2009. "Epistemic Disobedience, Independent Thought and Decolonial Freedom." *Theory, Culture and Society*, 26, 7–8: 159–181.

___. 2011. *The Darker Side of Western Modernity: Global Futures, Decolonial Options*. Durham and London: Duke University Press.

___. 2015. "Foreword: Yes, We Can." In *Can Non-Europeans Think?* by Hamid Dabashi (viii–xlii). London: Zed Books.

Moore, Henrietta L. 2010. "Forms of Knowing and Un-Knowing." In *Secrecy and Silence in the Research Process: Feminist Reflections* [Kobo version], edited by Roisin Ryan-Flood and Rosalind Gill. London: Routledge.

Quijano, Anibal. 2007. "Coloniality and Modernity/Rationality." *Cultural Studies* 21, 3: 168–178.

Sanchez Taylor, Jacqueline, and Julia O'Connell Davidson. 2010. "Unknowable Secrets and Golden Silence: Reflexivity and Research on Sex Tourism." In *Secrecy and Silence in the Research Process: Feminist Reflections*, edited by Roisin Ryan-Flood and Rosalind Gill (42–53). London & New York: Routledge.

2

Latina Knowledge Production and the Ethics of Ambiguity

Vannina Sztainbok and Lorena M. Gajardo

> We are learning to depend more and more on our own sources
> for survival, learning not to let the weight of this burden, the
> bridge, break our backs. (Anzaldúa & Moraga 1981/1983, iv)

In 2016, the authors and two other colleagues, Teresa Macías and
Magaly San Martín, met to think and talk together about the epistemological and ethical challenges we encounter as researchers and scholars
who are *entremundos/between worlds*,[1] that is, who inhabit the borderlands geographically and in terms of consciousness and cultural production (Sandoval 2006 xiii). Our origins are in the Southern Cone of Latin
America — Chile and Uruguay — but we now inhabit the North. Our
histories, as Latinas[2] in Canada, articulate with the late 20th-century history of forced migration of populations expunged and exiled from the
Southern Cone as a result of authoritarian regimes intent on violently
imposing neoliberalism in Latin America/*Abya Yala*.[3] Our research
and scholarship are in multiple sites, which can be broadly described
as: Latin American women's political activism in Canada (Magaly);
theorizing *Latinidad* in Canada, coloniality, and Latina/Chicana feminisms (Lorena); racism in the Southern Cone (Vannina); and truth and
reconciliation and nation building (Teresa). And although we are not
uniformly positioned as Latinas or as knowledge producers, we share
à desire to understand how the politics of knowledge production creates specific considerations and necessitates particular negotiations for
subjects who have been historically marginalized or excluded from its
practice. Stemming from that conversation in 2016 this chapter focuses
this concern in terms of our *Latinidad* — something that is always present whether it is we who "choose" to foreground it or not. In particular,

we explore the implications of "being heard through the accent" (Lorena 2016 Conversation), a term that describes the process of always being already known: before we speak, before we write, before we create. But we do not regard "being heard through the accent" as a categorical imperative, as something that irrevocably defines our intellectual labour and creativity as Latina knowledge producers. Instead, we acknowledge its power as one of the disciplinary technologies that circumscribes and localizes our academic knowledge production within specific parameters of intelligibility, given our positionality as Latinas.

We begin, in the next section, by turning briefly to Michel Foucault and Gayatri Spivak, who help us to situate knowledge production within already and always operating relations of power that impact the question of producing ethical knowledges. We then turn to the work of Gloria Anzaldúa, whose undisciplined and undomesticated forms of inquiry inform our own. By using the term "undisciplined" we are not implying that Anzaldúa's intellectual labour is not the product of serious engagement and practice; doing so would continue to re-inscribe Chicanas and other Latinx bodies as somehow deficient or incapable of generating transformational knowledge. Rather, "undisciplined" is used to highlight how Anzaldúa's intellectual work bursts the many boundaries — disciplinary, linguistic, stylistic — that cage in our ideas. Inspired by Anzaldúa, who calls for non-hierarchical ways of generating knowledge, we use conversation as a tool to identify some of the ethical challenges we have experienced as Latina scholars. In doing so, we have attempted to resist the extractive processes that we critique below by centring how the ideas presented in this paper were generated through, rather than mined from, the conversation. Translated into what attempts to be a "straightforward" book chapter, we struggled with a way of conveying ideas generated through conversation in a format that presumes a single authorial voice (even when it is co-written). Rather than resolve the tension, we at times identify the speaker, and at times blur who is saying what. We grappled with the necessity of reflecting our specificities, while also troubling the myth that it is individuals who make theory. Lorena Gajardo (2011) refers to this as the I/we, a way of knowing that evokes our distinctiveness as subjects or individuals who create knowledge through embodied, historical and localized practices instead of through disarticulated and abstracted rationality. Our personal stories combine and connect with our histories to generate possibilities for personal/collective transformation. This I/we emerges as an articulated site of enunciation from which we can listen, speak and write in that "undisciplined" way that Anzaldúa proposes as a way towards transformation and solidarity. It is not the case that the four of us think in unison, but that the complexity of the questions we wrestle with can only be communicated through the plurality and collision of our voices. Before we continue, we want to emphasize that if this paper sounds serious, it was conceived through rigorous discussion accompanied by laughter, food and drink. We approached the conversation and its translation with playfulness, which, as described by María Lugones (1987), is an attitude of moving through an activity with intention, but no set rules, and an openness to uncertainty and surprise. It is from this space that we discuss how Anzaldúa's embrace of ambiguity and her recognition that knowledge is always partial, can reframe how to conceive of the ethical in relation to knowledge practices.[4]

Dominant Knowledges and Making Others Intelligible

Knowledge production is always implicated in the myriad of ways in which power is exercised in society. Historically, the hierarchical organization of knowledges also functions as surveillance. For Foucault (1972, 219), this means that what we come to know as truth is always produced within a "grid of intelligibility."

> But this will to truth, like the other systems of exclusion, relies on institutional support: it is both reinforced and accompanied by whole strata of practices such as pedagogy — naturally — the book-system, publishing, libraries, such as the learned societies in the past, and laboratories today. But it is probably even more profoundly accompanied by the manner in which knowledge is employed in a society, the way in which it is exploited, divided and, in some ways, attributed.

There is, therefore, no innocent search for truth. Knowledge and the "need to know" are connected to power and, as such, have consequences. Rather than searching for truth, Foucault is interested in what the search for truth engenders, the chain of practices, events, the inclusions and exclusions, the violence that it unleashes.

Following Foucault's proposition, one of the ethical challenges of doing research that, broadly speaking, seeks to gain insights into power relations linked to the geopolitical region known as Latin America is to recognize that engaging in "making sense" of the South has been part of an imperial project. As Poblete (2003) points out, Latin American Studies as an area of research in the U.S., has an origin story that ties its emergence as an interdisciplinary field where the social sciences predominated to the Cold War. Within this historical context, "new U.S.-centric, area-specific knowledges were generated" where both the U.S. and western Europe become the centre, "from which all the perspectives that constituted a certain sector of the world as a region emanated" (Poblete 2003, xii). And, as Poblete says, this was not just merely a question of area studies knowledge being responsive to perceived national interests, but it had a further consequence, it made U.S. knowledge "claim for itself the space of universality against which all others were localized regional variations/deviations" (Poblete 2003, xiii).

> We always have to be wondering, we always have to remember where Latin America became not only an object of study, but of interest, to be studied, right. The North, the U.S., needed to know "who are these people that we've been possessing?" (Lorena 2016 Conversation).

In the intersection of knowledge production with power, where the aim is to further "national interests" or the hegemony of western thought, claims of neutrality or objectivity are suspect. Because we agree that knowledge about the Other is always tied up with relations of power, we recognize that work that attempts to make the South "intelligible" is subject to ethical considerations, which are themselves connected to both the methodological limitations of producing partial knowledge as well as implicated knowledge. By negotiating dominant paradigms through ruptures, rejections, and/or re-framings, we aim to identify limits and move beyond them. But, is this possible? Can we find ways of producing ethical knowledges by escaping the spectres of power?

Spivak (1988), in her essay "Can the Subaltern Speak?," challenges us to think of the problem otherwise. In this influential work, Spivak launched a critique of the western subject via an exploration of discourses surrounding the Indian practice of *sati*, the willing suicide of widows who follow their husbands into the funeral pyre. Spivak was interested in showing how the intersecting debates over the practice within British colonial discourse and Hindu philosophy make it impossible to imagine an agentic feminine subject position. The subaltern woman's voice cannot emerge between the nexus of patriarchal and imperial discourses. This discussion formed part of a larger argument in the essay, where Spivak was expressing her frustration with two positions taken by western intellectuals: either speaking for the marginalized or insisting that the marginalized can speak for themselves. Neither position, she argues, dislodges imperial relations. The ethical task is to "critique postcolonial discourse with the best tools it can provide" rather than "substituting the lost figure of the colonized" (Spivak 1988, 295). For Spivak, then, refusing to produce knowledge — ethical knowledge — is not an option. It is actually incumbent upon those who question the complicity of western epistemology to use available tools to dislodge hegemonic hermeneutics and ontologies. It is interesting to note that even Spivak, a brilliant and internationally recognized scholar, points to the disciplined translations of her work when she mentions that she may be misread as engaging in a "nostalgic investigation of … lost roots" (1988, 281). Her example (the *sati*) risks overwriting her theoretical contribution. Indeed, many discussions of this piece continue to focus on the female subaltern/ritual suicide, rather than the problematization of the western intellectual.

We find both Foucault and Spivak useful in terms of the questions they ask us to consider — namely, the embeddedness of knowledge production with power and the concomitant western-centric hermeneutics and ontologies, as Spivak would call them, that mirror imperial histories. To help us turn towards useful ruptures that might illuminate different paths and methods of writing about the South, about Latinx bodies, and about difference in general, we turn to the work of Anzaldúa. Though drawing on different intellectual traditions, Anzaldúa was also concerned with the conditions under which speech could be uttered and heard. We revisit her influential 2007 [1987] work *Borderlands/La Frontera* to specifically look at the ways in which she works with her voice to create an unapologetic, undomesticated, and undisciplined "wild tongue" (Anzaldúa 2007 [1987], 76). In so doing, Anzaldúa shows us a possible path toward ethical ways of creating knowledge in its multiple manifestations — artistic, literary, cultural, historic, academic — by utilizing what we refer to as an ethics of ambiguity.

Anzaldúa's Undisciplined Knowledge and the Ethics of Ambiguity

Refusing to be tamed or to be domesticated, Chicana and queer intellectual, activist and scholar, Gloria Anzaldúa produced a form of decolonial knowledge that centred a counter narrative from the margins, one that theoretically and otherwise examined new and different possibilities of being in the world as a lesbian Chicana. If the demand is always to situate oneself within pre-existing parameters of knowledge that manage the intelligibility of Other tongues, then Anzaldúa challenged this by creating what Mignolo (2000) and Saldívar refer to as a new logic that creates a new "epistemological ground upon which versions of the world may be produced" (Saldívar 2007, 348). It is in Anzaldúa's *Borderlands* that this new approach emerges, creating new categories of analysis like borderlands and the new *mestiza*. This mode of theorizing is contextualized and embodied and takes place within the materiality of historical processes; it is a way of writing and communicating this knowledge in a manner that challenges fragmentation or reduction, producing practices of knowing that are at once perilous and potentially transformative.

Two of Anzaldúa's concepts that remain highly influential are her ideas of borderlands and the new *mestiza*. The idea or category of the borderlands grows out of a need to contest exclusionary hegemonic projects — national and otherwise — that regard or position alterity at the very margins of belonging. Creating the borderlands is, for Anzaldúa, a way of providing a space of inhabitation for those whose difference is deemed as unacceptable because they do not conform to imagined, normalized ontologies and are not likely to be claimed as "real" or "genuine" within extant regimes of ruling (Gajardo, forthcoming). As a concept, the idea of borderlands enables the interrogation of all modes of exclusion based on neatly created borders that demand docility, negation and alienation.

> She [Anzaldúa] moved into unexpected territory, daring to risk lines of inquiry and, like Michel Foucault, interrogated existing discursive fields. She moved beyond the Chicano nationalist project and issued a postnationalist feminist project in which la nueva mestiza, the mixed-race woman, is the privileged subject of that in between space, that interstitial space that was formerly a nation and must be without borders, without boundaries. She challenged Chicano nationalist discourse and critiqued the dis-

cursive nation as a space that negates feminists, queers (jotas y jotos), and anyone who is not of "pure" Chicano blood or lineage. (Pérez 2005, 6)

The new *mestiza*, who resides in the borderland, reclaims humanity for those pushed to its edges: the queer, the migrant, the disabled, the Indigenous, the Other. As Alarcón (1999, 66) points out, the new *mestiza* does not recycle *mestizaje* as a technology of whitening the "race," but rather it is a concept that is "always already bursting its boundaries." Anzaldúa's new *mestiza* is, instead, a contingent signifier with alternate meanings that emerges within the context of U.S. history and represents both a recognition and a struggle against the white supremacist parameters that form the basis of melting pot ideology (Alarcón 1999, 66). Its use is not one of erasure of indigeneity, nor is it a way of replicating a hierarchized duality like the term Mexican-American, which María Lugones explains positions the Chicana body as inferior to the "authentic" American (1992, 35). Instead, the new *mestiza*, according to Sonia Saldívar-Hull (1999), represents a "new political stance as a fully racialized feminist Chicana" that is tied to histories of resistance by "subaltern Indian women of the Americas" (1999, 5), or as Anzaldúa says, "My Chicana identity is grounded in the Indian woman's history of resistance" (Anzaldúa, quoted in Saldívar-Hull 1999, 5). It is through this re-centring of histories of Indigenous women's resistance that Gloria Anzaldúa creates non-essentialized, political Chicana subjectivities:

Claiming all parts of her identity, even those that clash, she escapes essentialist categories and envisions one provisional home where she can "stand and claim my space, making a new culture — *una cultura mestiza* — with my own lumber, my own bricks and mortar and my own feminist architecture." (Anzaldúa, quoted in Saldívar-Hull 1999, 5)

The alienating border/margin is transformed by Anzaldúa into a place — the borderlands — where normative scripts can be transformed to produce multiple inhabited selves. Although the borderlands is the place where we can have the possibility to "chisel my own face" and "claim my own space" (Anzaldúa 1999 [1987], 44), the recreating of home is not an easy nor a taken-for-granted process. To create oneself anew, to be multiply inhabited, demands a serious engagement with one's traumas (psychological, historical) and one's context (communities, nation and location within the hierarchies) that interpellate our being. In order to do this work, Anzaldúa's carefully wrought text evokes contradiction and ambiguity as one of the crucial interventions the new *mestiza* must embrace; she points to the need for the dissolution of categories, while also recognizing that at times they must be named.

> She [the new *mestiza*] has discovered that she can't hold concepts or ideas in rigid boundaries. The borders and walls that are supposed to keep the undesirable ideas out are entrenched habits and patterns of behavior; these habits and patterns are the enemy within. Rigidity means death. Only by remaining flexible is she able to stretch the psyche horizontally and vertically. (Anzaldúa 2007 [1987], 79)

For example, we would venture to suggest that Anzaldúa is, in fact, one of the precursors to whiteness studies. It was the naming of whiteness in the critiques brought forth by Black feminist, Chicana, and other women of colour scholars that drew attention to the necessity to theorize whiteness. Yet, Anzaldúa also reminds us that we should not reify these boundaries as given, rigid, or permanent. Anzaldúa was writing of the many interconnected boundaries that are used to hierarchize human beings: gender, sexuality, race, ethnicity, language, nation. As a lesbian, Chicana, Texana, someone who was always falling on the "wrong" side of the borderlands, she was foregrounding the extent to which we are simultaneously subjected to, and interpellated by, hierarchical thinking.

> The borderland as constituted *conceptually* by Anzaldúa is a rejection of dichotomies and of the dichotomizing impulse that constitutes the border, the split. Even the rejection of dichotomizing, that is the limen in its conceptual sense, is historicized since she connects it to the historical conquests of 1492 and 1848. She associates the dichotomizing impulse rather tightly with European modernity. (Lugones 2006, 80)

For instance, Sztainbok's (2008; 2013) investigations into the fetishization of Blackness in Uruguay led her to think about whether it is possible to research, think, and write about Black and white subject positions, bodies, and spaces without reifying the Black/white binary that constitutes racial hierarchy, and without reifying the fetishization of Blackness.

Similarly, Gajardo (forthcoming), is concerned about remaining vigilant when it comes to doing research with racialized Latinx populations so that it does not have the unintended result of reproducing dominant tropes about Latinx bodies (see also Badwall in this volume). For example, continuing to rely on methodologies that reproduce hierarchies where the researcher becomes the one node through which hermeneutical and epistemological work occurs may end up reproducing the very privilege, in this case epistemological, that positions Latinx bodies as being primarily resources. And, in this manner, even if not intended, it may reinscribe familiar racialized tropes about Latinx bodies (Gajardo, forthcoming). Anzaldúa's theorization of the borderlands is a reminder that, although we have not invented these borders, we are often compelled to invoke them in order to make racism visible, in order to be legible, and in order to formulate a political position, while at the same time recognizing their implied limits and exclusions.

Despite the difficulties, Anzaldúa issues an urgent call to think together aspects of existence that are commonly put in silos — the psychological, spiritual, political, cultural, geographic, historic:

> The actual physical borderland that I'm dealing with in this book is the Texas U.S. Southwest/Mexican border. The psychological borderlands, the sexual borderlands and the spiritual borderlands, are not particular to the Southwest. In fact, the Borderlands are physically present wherever two or more cultures edge each other, where people of different races occupy the same territory, where under, lower, middle and upper classes touch, where the space between two individuals shrinks with intimacy. (Anzaldúa quoted in Pérez 2005, 3)

Informed by Anzaldúa, we explore an ethics of knowledge production that accepts ambiguity:

> She puts history through a sieve, winnows out the lies, looks at the forces that we as a race, as women, have been a part of. Luego bota lo que no vale, los desmientos, los desencuentros, el embrutecimiento. Aguarda el juicio, honor y enraízado, de la gente antigua. This step is a conscious rupture with all oppressive traditions of all cultures and religions. She communicates that rupture, documents the struggle. She reinterprets history

and, using new symbols, she shapes new myths. She adopts new perspectives toward the darkskinned, women and queers. She strengthens her tolerance (and intolerance) for ambiguity. She is willing to share, to make herself vulnerable to foreign ways of seeing and thinking. She surrenders all notions of safety, of the familiar. Deconstruct, construct. (Anzaldúa 2007 [1987] 82)

Anzaldúa calls for speaking as embodied subjects, speaking as non-alienated subjects who form part of communities and their histories, speaking from partial perspectives that respect our ways of re-membering and re-visioning. It is imperative to do this speaking while keeping in mind the importance of challenging modes of comprehension and translation produced by epistemic hierarchies where Other bodies are disciplined while simultaneously being consumed. During our conversation, the authors and our colleagues discussed the politics of letting go of "truth" and intelligibility, favouring instead the embrace of an ethics of ambiguity. For Teresa, an ethics of ambiguity entails rendering the researcher "opaque" and knowledge "suspect" (Spivak 1988). For Magaly, this entails "rejecting that position of the all-knowing researcher and admitting you are in the process of becoming, something that Mignolo calls the zero-point"[5] (Magaly 2016 Conversation). For Lorena, it means consciously engaging that which may be useful, even if temporarily, and shedding that which reproduces the domestication of knowledge production. Vannina and Teresa added that an ethics of ambiguity requires a humility that decentres the researcher and doing away with the binaries of knowing/not knowing, intelligible/unintelligible. In effect, an ethics of ambiguity requires questioning attachments to "truth," and instead, aiming for unsettling knowledge and acknowledging that understandings are contingent (2016 Conversation).

To this end, Anzaldúa makes the reader work. She evokes multiple, but not open-ended meanings. By forcing the reader to grapple with the contradictions in the text, she opens up possibilities. She opens up the possibility that it is the grappling, *el luchar*, that is essential, rather than the fixing of meaning. Yet, while she evokes contradiction and ambiguity, for Anzaldúa (2007 [1987]), ambiguity is not ambivalence. It is significant that she calls for a "tolerance (and intolerance) for ambiguity" (79).

This assembly is not one where severed or separated pieces merely come together. Nor is it a balancing of opposing powers. In attempting to work out a synthesis, the self has added a third element which is greater than the sum of its severed parts. That third element is a new consciousness — a *mestiza* consciousness — and though it is a source of intense pain, its energy comes from continual creative motion that keeps breaking down the unitary aspect of each new paradigm. (Anzaldúa 2007 [1987], 79–80)

As Anzaldúa (2007 [1987], 80) says, this is not a matter of "balancing" perspectives; it is a commitment to continual questioning: "breaking down the unitary aspect of each new paradigm." Anzaldúa refuses the idea of arriving at one "truth" that will fit all. Instead, labouring, grappling and questioning are perpetual.

The work of *mestiza* consciousness is to break down the subject-object duality that keeps her a prisoner and to show in the flesh and through the images in her work how duality is transcended…. A massive uprooting of dualistic thinking in the individual and collective consciousness is the beginning of a long struggle, but one that could, in our best hopes, bring us to the end of rape, of violence, of war. (Anzaldúa 2007 [1987], 80)

For Anzaldúa, adopting an ethics that unsettles meaning is a political project, inextricable from social, cultural, and political struggle. It is important to recognize that as a travelling theory in the sense that Said (1983, 226) utilizes the concept, i.e., as emphasizing contingency and dynamic responsiveness, Anzaldúa's work is always situated and encourages hermeneutical practices that are in themselves to be contextualized and questioned. There is a constant questioning of established dogmas to make possible the likelihood of fruitful ruptures. This is a process that enriches the ongoing experience of theorization.

Anzaldúa's embrace of ambiguity provides us with a meaningful way to approach ethics in knowledge production. She points to how experience, both individual and collective, historical and local, disturbs patterns of appropriation that are more or less the property of hegemonic knowledge. For example, the subject is understood as embodied but in a broader sense, one that goes beyond reductive or essentialized identity because subjects are placed among the multiple experiences and histories, individual and collective, that traverse them and that have to be contended with in the process of becoming. In this process, Anzaldúa's theorizing points to the importance of recognizing the borderlands as a continued site of struggle and negotiation. It is a space where all operating constraints on the possibilities of being in the world are to be faced. There are no pure subjects who can claim idealized returns or move forward in unquestioned identifications. In this place, where negotiation and constant questioning are the order of the day, knowledges that have been marginalized are neither "given" voice nor translated. As embodiments of struggle, of individual and collective *lucha* in the borderlands, different ways of knowing are made possible by surviving the violent processes of coloniality and through the hard labour of making decolonial knowledges. This embrace of decolonial knowledge production recognizes the dangers of succumbing to reductive cultural and identity practices, moving instead toward the possibility of generating undisciplined and undomesticated knowledges that value speaking with and from "wild tongues" (Anzaldúa 2007 [1987], 76).

An ethics of ambiguity maintains these ideas in consideration when producing knowledge. It demands that many balls be kept in the air at once; it demands looking not only unidirectionally at those peoples and processes we research, analyze, and explain but also maintaining an uneasy sense of being part of the process ourselves, as individual researchers and as embodied researchers, in the Anzaldúan sense.

The Challenges of Being
"Heard through the Accent"

To engage an ethics of ambiguity during the process of knowledge production is already a difficult task because it is a mode of writing against the grain that requires conscious commitment and constant awareness of potential challenges. One of the powerful ways in which *Latinidad* is contained in terms of its knowledge producing capacity or ability is through a discourse that limits its parameters of intelligibility. What we mean or want to say, what we utter and write, is sieved through a practice of translation that tends to position our work through a lens of difference or of "being heard through the accent" (Lorena 2016 Conversation). This process of differentiation constrains the ways that our research is understood; it functions as a kind of permission to enact a normalizing translation where our bodies and our knowledge are placed within parameters of intelligibility that produces both as in need of being re-placed in a location where they can be made comprehensible. In problematizing "being heard through the accent," we do not want to imply that there is one correct way to be heard or comprehended. Academic work is always in conversation with audiences and open to interpretation. But, being read or heard through the accent points to specific ways of reading, readings that domesticate and localize the speaker. We are referring to identifiable "grids" of "unintelligibility," which tend to reduce our scholarship to the local, to the body, and to identity (Vannina 2016 Conversation).

Teresa, for instance, uses a biopolitical lens to analyze the Chilean Truth and Reconciliation Commission. Even though she frames her work as being about nation making through regimes of truth, her work is often interpreted or translated as being about human rights and torture. Both the site of research and the body that presents it overwhelms the theoretical implications:

> "You're talking about human rights violations." No, I'm talking about the production of nation through discourses of human rights or regimes of human rights. The only experience that can be read onto my body is that I could potentially be a victim of human rights violations, or human rights violations are presumed to be part of my history. So, I am expected to speak from that position. And then, because I don't speak about those things [being violated?], I get attacked. (Teresa 2016 Conversation)

Teresa is required to produce herself as a tortured subject. Her work is not heard as making a theoretical contribution.

In Vannina's experience, the accent is "heard" through her syllabi.

> If I teach a course on race and ethnicity, which focuses on the North American experience, it is universal. If there is a focus on Latin America/Abya Yala, it is now read as local; it is not of interest to a general audience. Knowledge production that focuses on scholarship from and on the South cannot possibly be relevant to understanding the world. As a Latina Latin Americanist, I can only contribute to localized knowledge. (Vannina 2016 Conversation)

Magaly has also experienced "being heard through the accent" in terms of how her research has been taken up.

As a scholar, my research speaks to the erasure of Latin American women's political agency and leadership from the Canadian feminist historiographies. The only research that seems to abound tends to place Latinxs exclusively and perpetually in the role of victims. So, when I introduced my research, the immediate association was to link it to Latinxs as "migrant workers." It almost seems that it was impossible to think about Latinxs as active political leaders. (Magaly 2016 Conversation)

And, like many other women of colour faculty, Magaly is turned into the "expert" on teaching anti-oppression courses. These courses tend to face resistance from students who encounter syllabus material that challenges their privilege and, therefore, dismiss these courses as irrelevant to their programs.

For the longest time, I was the only person teaching all of the "isms" in a particular program at the College. This put me in a position where I was constantly abused by the students because they were really upset that they had to learn the subject. This took a tremendous emotional toll. I was asked to do the same "diversity" course in the gerontology program and, when I presented my course to other faculty, two white professors were really excited and they kept exclaiming, "Oh, my god, this is awesome. This is fantastic. I never knew any anything about this." Brampton (the location of the College) is a racialized place. I would venture to say that 70%–80% of the students are racialized. And, as white professors, you do not know about these issues? It's unconscionable. It's really outrageous. (Magaly 2016 Conversation)

For Lorena, whose area of studies is *Latinidad* in Canada, it is very difficult to be heard as someone who is trying to theorize a position that she is also presumed to embody. Although her work is centred on the way in which dominant national discourses produce Latinx subjectivities and the latter's negotiations with these discourses, it is often conflated with scholarship where the imperative is to look at the settlement practices of immigrants or with testimonial renderings of Latinx experience.

In my work, I'm presumed to be writing in a kind of testimonial manner, and about me; it's supposed to be about my auto-

historia, right. So, it's very difficult to overcome this, and it gets reduced … It is difficult to convey that what I am doing is analyzing how coloniality and other hegemonic discourses produce dominant scripts about *Latinidad* and how these are negotiated by Latinx subjects. (Lorena 2016 Conversation)

Scholars (see Anzaldúa 2002, Mignolo 2009, Richard 2005 and Sandoval 2000, among others) have pointed out that to be entered into the academic process is to engage mechanisms of control or normalization that position knowledge in hierarchical relationships, where the knowing subject does not reside/originate in the South because "… the North has theory; the South has culture" (Magaly 2016 Conversation). This is what Mignolo (2009, 2) refers to as the "geopolitics of knowledge" and the "epistemic privilege of the First World." As a result of imperial relations, the West/Northern academy defines the parameters for knowing: what is considered theory, what is considered folklore. Like other scholars, Mignolo locates Kant as demarcating the boundaries between reason and not reason. For Kant, only the educated are capable of knowledge production and not all humans are equally capable of education (Mignolo 2000; Spivak 1988). The "uneducable" include "women," the poor and the "savage" racial other (Spivak 1999, 13). As such, Southern scholarship is not heard nor read for its theoretical contribution, but for the exotic, violent, or dangerous nature that it supposedly embodies. In the words of Trinh Minh-ha (1989, 149), "The Man can't hear it the way she means it."

It is important to recognize that this complicated positioning is historically specific (the four of us are not positioned uniformly), but not unique. Other academics — including those who are Black, Indigenous, queer, racialized, and those who originate in, or are presumed to be from, the Global South — face tokenization, expectations of authenticity, or the risks of becoming a native informant. As Lorena put it, some of us are at risk of becoming "extractive subjects":

It's actually the construction of an extractive subject … it's a location that you can take things from, but you leave it empty and you have a right to enact that extraction upon that body. So I call [the Latinx subject] an extractive site. (Lorena 2016 Conversation)

According to Gajardo (forthcoming) the production of Latinx bodies as extractive sites occurs through a variety of processes — material, representational, epistemological, historical — that attempt to contain Latinx subjects as sites of exploitation, consumption, and tropicalization.[6] Circumscribed by coloniality and neoliberal discourses, Latinx bodies are re-placed within hierarchies of worth where they no longer matter as thinking, feeling, autonomous subjects. They are removed from the human, as Wynter (2003) would say, in order to convert them into cheap labour and sources of pleasure and danger for the entertainment and use of others. Extraction or producing Latinx bodies as extractive sites, within a neoliberal context, is also about disarticulation — about removing the subject from history and context so in that fragmented state, dominant hails or interpellations may be masked as performances of individual choice to explain away subjects' material and discursive vulnerability and availability (Gajardo forthcoming).

When attempting to make knowledge on our terms and through our own parameters of worth, Anzaldúa's ethics of ambiguity helps us navigate the challenges discussed above by pointing to ways that do not engage the extractive logic that marginalizes, subjects, and circumscribes our multiplicity, our many tongues and bodies. Anzaldúa challenges the normalizing "will to truth" and produces alternative ways of remembering and revisioning, linking her work and knowledge production to personal and collective narratives that populate the borderlands with the bodies and histories of those who are usually not recognized as valid and valuable. By writing in a way that interrupts conventional ways of theorizing, she is able to conceptually open up the expressive terrain of knowledge making or theorizing and although some have criticized her use of diverse modes of writing that fall outside the domain of disciplinary knowledge production (Alcoff 2006, 256), it is this very practice that enables her to connect and embed subjects and knowledges as multiple and articulated. She writes in a way that allows for multiple readings; we do not claim to have *the* reading of Anzaldúa and we recognize *Borderlands/La Frontera* as a complex, multi-layered text with many nuances. For this very reason, we feel it must be approached with our most critical capacities, "*la facultad*" Anzaldúa might say, carefully attuned, a courtesy which she, as a Chicana, queer body, has been seldomly granted (Alcoff 2006, 256) and which has more often than not subjected her and her work to the logic of extraction. In undertaking to create new theory and narratives about Chicanas, while simultaneously expanding ways of understanding, Anzaldúa unapologetically and determinedly positions herself — a Chicana, queer body — as knowledge producer and, in so doing, populates this terrain traditionally reserved for privileged bodies with her "wild tongue" (Anzaldúa 2007 [1987], 76).

> What is considered theory in the dominant academic community is not necessarily what counts as theory for women-of-color. Theory produces effects that changes people and the way they perceive the world. Thus we need teorías that will enable us to interpret what happens in the world, that will explain how and why we relate to certain people in specific ways, that will reflect what goes on between inner, outer and peripheral "I"s within a person and between the personal "I"s and the collective "we" of our ethnic communities. Necesitamos teorías that will rewrite history using race, class, gender, and ethnicity as categories of analysis, theories that cross borders, that blur boundaries — new kinds of theories with new theorizing methods. We need theories that will point out ways to maneuver between our particular experiences and the necessity of forming our own categories and theoretical models for the patterns we uncover. (Anzaldúa 1990, xxv)

As we continue to grapple with the implications of our positionality, we take inspiration from Anzaldúa's methodology and epistemology. As Latina scholars (whether self-named or not), the convergence of our positionality with the desire to engage in ethical knowledge production, even if imperfectly or necessarily incomplete, is always a question we consider important. We turn to Anzaldúa here in order to explain how we see the practice of ethical knowledge production unfolding in order to present some of the components we have, so far, identified as forming part of that process. And, we want to highlight how her work inspires and compels us to think deeply about what it means to conduct research that does not unconsciously reinscribe the dominant narrative, research that keeps the questioning open, research that is also accountable to the communities with whom we are engaged. And as mentioned above, Anzaldúa points to a methodology that is anchored in multiplicity, history, materiality, and non-fragmentation that refuses to be trapped within the normalizing "will to truth," and to engage in the production of alternative ways of re-membering and re-visioning (Anzaldúa 2002, 546).

Concluding Remarks

Importantly, we do not want to claim a space of innocence.

> While violence is done to us, in our efforts to live as Latina academics in a Canadian context, we also become complicit in the violence that is done through the research. (Teresa 2016 Conversation)

Engaging in academic knowledge production entails navigating disciplinary ways of theorizing about ourselves and about others. As Latina scholars, it is not possible for us, nor, we would argue, for anyone in similar circumstances and positionalities, to stand outside the discursive and material practices that rather vigorously privilege certain modes of methodological and epistemological practices that reproduce, whether wittingly or not, epistemological inequalities and hegemonies. These practices have been developed over time and reflect the matrix of power within which all knowledge production occurs (Mignolo & Walsh 2018). As Probyn-Rapsey (2007) explains, complicity is not really a choice; it is one of the conditions of doing knowledge production within structures of hegemony. When complicity is understood not as guilt or shame (although these emotions may be present at the individual level), but rather as a relation that is "horizontal with pervasive breadth as in a network," it becomes not confined to an event but a structural relationship that is difficult to elude because "it exists in multiple, networked, forms" (Probyn-Rapsey 2007, 68). So, it is not in attempting to separate ourselves from it that we can find any kind of ethical direction, but rather acknowledging complicity brings us into community with others, which Probyn-Rapsey (2007) points out is an important way of acting responsibly, i.e., in a manner capable of truly responding to others. Yet, due to hierarchical structures, we do not all have the same relation to complicity. "Complicities are not equivalent; being complicit as a colonizer, as migrant, as Aboriginal, as man, woman, queer, classed, these are all differently negotiated and mobilized" (Probyn-Rapsey 2007, 72).

For us, what remains important for those who want to approximate ethical knowledge production practices is to ask not whether there is complicity but how can our work, our intellectual labour, function to interrupt the dominance of what Mignolo and Walsh refer to as "the idea of dislocated, disembodied, and disengaged abstraction, and to disobey the universal signifier that is the rhetoric of modernity, the logic of coloniality, and the West's global model" (Mignolo & Walsh 2018, 3). And, relatedly how can our work seek to mitigate this situation as much as possible? That is, what remains important is how to supplant the "habits of modernity/coloniality" (4) to engage in less abstracted, fragmented and delocalized modes of knowledge production. The idea is not to reject western thought altogether but, rather, to place or replace it within a space where it becomes a part of much larger constellations of knowledge production that reflect, not in utopian, but in ethical, decolonial ways other approaches to methodological and epistemological inquiry (Mignolo & Walsh 2018). Or, as Anzaldúa would reminds us, we still need to make *teorías*, but as she says, theories that are responsive to ourselves, and to ourselves as part of communities and to us as part of larger histories and worlds to "provide new narratives embodying alternative potentials" (Anzaldúa 2002, 560). And we need to engage the ethics of ambiguity while doing so because it encourages us to remember our multiple selves and conditions as well as the contingent nature of being in the world. An ethics, in other words, that challenges us to always see the wounds — those inflicted upon us and those we may inflict upon others — if we are not vigilantly critical, while acting in the world.

We end with a short excerpt from our 2016 conversation, one that in many ways expresses the complexities involved in practicing the ethics of ambiguity:

Vannina: So sometimes it's better to remain unintelligible.

Teresa: I think so.

Vannina: Or maybe even to refuse that as a goal.

Lorena: That could be a strategy.

Vannina: I don't know, I'm not sure what … is at stake.

Lorena: I'm not sure if unintelligible is the space.

Vannina: … maybe not to pose that binary (intelligibility/unintelligibility). Maybe to propose something else.

Teresa: Well ambiguous. I would argue that rather than producing knowledge that produces something completely intelligible is to remain …

Vannina: … to unsettle it.

Teresa: I wonder. If I think about an ethical practice in the work that I do, I wonder if what I can do is to render knowledge and render research ambiguous.

Vannina: An ethics of ambiguity.

Teresa: It's an ambiguity yes. It states that this can be known right now at this moment, within this context but not all the time. What I am saying right now can only be interpreted within this context. And, also, in that sense …

Vannina: There's also a humility.

Teresa: Yes, there is a humility. There is a decentring of ourselves as knowing subjects. And, also an interrogation of our own role as academics. Of our own capacity to even assume we can know something. And in that sense, going back to what Spivak says that research needs to render the subject or the researcher opaque. The role of the researcher, the place of the researcher or the academic or the scholar, knowable. We need to render our own position in the research visible, not only visible to those for whom we produce, to those who may read or consume our knowledge, but visible to those people about whom we're writing.

Magaly: Then it's also rejecting all of the western ideas of knowledge. To be an epistemic dissident.… That's what… because I also think that because you're rejecting that and becoming — you're not all-knowing … But also, I think it forces us to reject the idea that "I can research anything because I am the transparent all-knowing, neutral objective, so I can go and do anything." And to me, personally, it is important that I engage in research where I am personally invested, and also made vulnerable because of that research. I/We are part of the thing that we are researching and therefore whatever happens to the research happens to me, right. And so, there is no pretense of objectivity; it is not a goal. There is no universal knowledge. I am right here with the thing that I am researching.

Acknowledgements: The authors would like to thank Teresa Macías and Magaly San Martín for their insightful contributions at the October 2016 meeting. The opportunity to discuss, as a group, our specific experiences as Latina scholars was invaluable and very useful in helping us develop further some of the ideas presented in this chapter. We are very fortunate to have had the opportunity to meet and talk about issues important to us in community. Gracias.

Notes

1. As Chela Sandoval explains, for Gloria Anzaldúa "EntreMundos" is another way of naming the borderlands: "It is possible to locate such alter-spaces, these border-lands, geographically, materially, yes. But that space *entremundos*, between worlds, Anzaldúa insisted, also exists in consciousness and culture, in all economies of power. The term *entremundos* situates in language that can be experienced and described even though its nature is change — constituted always in relation-to" (Sandoval 2005, xiii).

2. The term Latinization is connected to westernizing and "civilizing" projects and, as such, it is historically implicated in the erasure of Indigenous and African presences (Hill Collins & Bilge 2016). The term Latina, as Levins Morales (2001, 100) explains, "is one of the inventions of solidarity, an alliance, a political necessity that is not the given name of every female with dark skin and a colonized tongue, but rather a choice about how to resist and with whom." *Latinidad*, for us, includes our African, Indigenous, Jewish, and European roots. As a necessary invention, the term connects us to a specific point in time in the late 20th century when the call to identify as Latin American, rather than nationally, becomes associated with a rejection of the fascist, nationalist ideologies of authoritarian regimes that collaborated with northern hegemony. For us, identifying as Latina/Latin American is an expression of our families' and people's histories — as displaced subjects. Our reference to *Latinidad* is a reference to routes and roots; it is a recognition that there are people, pieces, and places that we have left behind and it is an identification that connects us with Chicana and Latinx populations, whose activism and scholarship in North America continues to expand the boundaries of being within *Latinidad* by questioning exclusions. For us, Latina does not point to a "thing" that anyone of us objectively is, or represents. Rather, we think of it as an historical and political positioning, one that expresses a sentiment of solidarity across, and rejection of, borders and a shared history in relation to imposed boundaries between the North and South.

3. The use of referents such as *Abya Yala* (the American continent), *Anahuac* (Meso-america), and *Tawantinsuyu* (the Andes region) are being reclaimed to refer to the vast region south of the Rio Grande as recognition that the term Latin America is a colonial and imperial invention. As San Martín (2017, 11) notes, via Mato (1997), "The usage of the term *Latin* comes from the assumption that millions of inhabitants in the South, Central, and North American continent (if we place Mexico in its correct location) are connected by 'a pair of romance languages, and certain elements of post-colonial history,'" and as a result, other identities were erased. "The term primarily erases Indigenous and Afro-descendant identities, in addition to other identities that are present on the continent, such as Asian and Middle Eastern."

4. In invoking the term "ethics of ambiguity," we draw explicitly on Anzaldúa to work out an ethical grounding for the making of knowledge. We are not referring to de Beauvoir's *The Ethics of Ambiguity* (1948), with its existential focus on ethics and discerning the possibilities for free subjects to act ethically and the dilemma of violence in the face of oppression.

5. This is what Mignolo (2009, 2) describes when he says that within academic disciplines, the knowing subject is presumed to be "transparent, disincorporated from the known and untouched by the geo-political configuration of the world in which people are racially ranked and regions are racially configured. From a detached and

neutral point of observation (that Colombian philosopher Castro-Gómez (2007) describes as the hubris of the zero point), the knowing subject maps the world and its problems, classifies people and projects into what is good for them."

6.   A concept that Esposito (2012) explains was coined by scholars Frances R. Aparicio and Susana Chavez-Silverman to refer to "the system of ideological fictions with which the dominant (Anglo European) cultures trope Latin American and US Latina/o identities and cultures," whose effect has been to essentialize and homogenize *Latinidad* through the use of stereotypes (Esposito 2012, 330).

References

2016 Conversation with Vannina Sztainbok, Lorena M. Gajardo, Teresa Macías and R. Magaly San Martín.

Alarcón, Norma. 1999. "Chicana Feminism: In the Tracks of 'The' Native Woman." In *Between Woman and Nation: Nationalisms, Transnational Feminisms, and the State*, edited by Caren Kaplan, Norma Alarcón and Minoo Moallem (63–71). Durham: Duke University Press.

Alcoff, Linda Martín. 2006. "The Unassimilated Theorist." *PMLA* 121, 1: 255–259.

Anzaldúa, Gloria. 1990. "Introduction." In *Haciendo Caras/Making Face, Making Soul: Creative and Critical Perspectives by Women of Color*, edited by Gloria Anzaldúa (xv-xxvii). San Francisco: Aunt Lute Press.

___. 1999 [1987]. *Borderlands/La Frontera*, second ed. San Francisco: Aunt Lute Books.

___. 2002. "Now Let Us Shift … The Path of Conocimiento … Inner Work, Public Acts." In *This Bridge We Call Home, Radical Visions for Transformation*, edited by Gloria E. Anzaldúa and AnaLouise Keating (540–578). New York: Routledge.

___. 2007 [1987]. *Borderlands/La Frontera*. San Francisco: Aunt Lute Books.

Anzaldúa, Gloria, and Cherríe Moraga. 1981/1983. *This Bridge Called My Back, Writings by Radical Women of Color*. New York: Kitchen Table: Women of Color Press.

Castro-Gomez, Santiago. 2007. "The Missing Chapter of Empire: Postmodern Reorganization of Coloniality and Post-Fordist Capitalism." *Cultural Studies* 21, 2–3.

de Beauvoir, Simone. 1948. *The Ethics of Ambiguity*, translated by Bernard Frechtman. New York: Open Road Integrated Media.

Esposito, Jennifer. 2012. "Is Ugly Betty a Real Woman? Representations of Chicana Femininity Inscribed as a Site of (Transformative) Difference." In *Performing the US Latina & Latino Borderlands*, edited by Arturo J. Aldama, Chela Sandoval and Peter J. García. Bloomington, Indianapolis: Indiana University Press.

Foucault, Michel. 1972. "The Discourse on Language (Appendix)." In *The Archaeology of Knowledge and the Discourse on Language* (215–237). New York: Pantheon.

Gajardo, Lorena M. 2011. "Bridges of Conocimiento: Una Conversación con Gloria Anzaldúa." In *Bridging: How Gloria Anzaldúa's Life and Work Transformed Our Own*, edited by AnaLouise Keating and Gloria González-López (19–25). Austin, TX: University of Texas Press.

___. forthcoming. "Latina/o Crossings: Latin American (Im)migration to the North and the Construction of Latin American Bodies as Extractive Sites."

Hill Collins, Patricia, and Sirma Bilge. 2016. *Intersectionality*. Cambridge, MA: Polity Press.

Keating, AnaLouise. 2005. *EntreMundos/AmongWorlds, New Perspectives on Gloria E. Anzaldúa*. New York: Palgrave Macmillan.

Levins Morales, Aurora. 2001. "My Name Is This Story." In *Telling to Live: Latina Femi-*

nist Testimonios, edited by Latina Feminist Group, Daisy Cocco de Filippis, Gloria Holguin Cuadraz, et al. (100–103). Durham, NC: Duke University Press.

Lugones, María. 1987. "'World Travelling' and Loving Perception." *Hypatia* 2, 2: 3–19.

___. 1992. "On Borderlands/La Frontera: An Interpretive Essay." *Hypatia* 7, 4: 31–37.

___. 2006. "On Complex Communication." *Hypatia* 21, 3: 75–85.

Mato, Daniel. 1997. "On Global–Local Connections, and the Transnational Making of Identities and Associated Agendas in Latin America." *Identities: Global Studies in Culture and Power* 4, 2: 167–212.

Mignolo, Walter D. 2000. *Local Histories/Global Designs: Coloniality, Subaltern Knowledges, and Border Thinking.* Princeton, NJ: Princeton University Press.

___. 2009. "Epistemic Disobedience, Independent Thought and De-colonial Freedom." *Theory, Culture & Society* 26, 7–8: 1–23. doi.org/10.1177/0263276409349275.

Mignolo, Walter D., and Catherine E. Walsh. 2018. "Introduction." In *On Decoloniality: Concepts, Analytics, Praxis* (1–12). Durham and London: Duke University Press.

Minh-ha, Trinh T. 1989. *Woman, Native, Other: Writing, Postcoloniality and Feminism.* Bloomington: Indiana University Press.

Pérez, Emma. 2005. "Gloria Anzaldúa: La Gran Nueva Mestiza Theorist, Writer, Activist-Scholar." *NWSA Journal* 17, 2: 1–10.

Poblete, Juan. 2003. "Introduction." In *Critical Latin American and Latino Studies*, edited by Juan Poblete (ix–viii). Minneapolis, MN: University of Minnesota Press.

Probyn-Rapsey, Fiona. 2007. "Complicity, Critique and Methodology." *ARIEL* 38, 2–3: 65–82.

Razack, Sherene H. 1998. *Looking White People in the Eye: Gender, Race, and Culture in Courtrooms and Classrooms.* Toronto: University of Toronto Press.

Richard, Nelly. 2005. "Globalización académica, estudios culturales y crítica latinoamericana." In *Cultura, política y sociedad Perspectivas latinoamericanas*, edited by Daniel Mato (455–470). Ciudad Autónoma de Buenos Aires, Argentina: CLACSO, Consejo Latinoamericano de Ciencias Sociales.

Said, Edward W. 1983. "Traveling Theory." In *The World, the Text, and the Critic* (226–247). Cambridge: Harvard University Press.

Saldívar, José David. 2007. "Unsettling Race, Coloniality, and Caste. Anzaldúa's Borderlands/La Frontera, Martinez's Parrot in the Oven, and Roy's The God of Small Things." *Cultural Studies* 21, 2–3: 339–367.

Saldívar-Hull, Sonia. 1999. "Introduction to the Second Edition." In *Borderlands/La Frontera*, second edition, edited by Gloria Anzaldúa (1–15). San Francisco: Aunt Lute Books.

San Martín, R. Magaly. 2017. "Treading the New Avenues: Transnational Latina Feminism in Toronto, Canada, 1970s–2000s." Department of Social Education, University of Toronto.

Sandoval, Chela. 2000. *Methodology of the Oppressed.* Minneapolis: University of Minnesota Press.

___. 2005. "Foreword, Unfinished Words: The Crossing of Gloria Anzaldúa." In *EntreMundos/AmongWorlds, New Perspectives on Gloria Anzaldúa*, edited by AnaLouise Keating (xiii–xvi). New York: Palgrave Macmillan.

Spivak, Gayatri Chakravorty. 1988. "Can the Subaltern Speak?" In *Marxism and the Interpretation of Culture,* edited by Cary Nelson and Lawrence Grossberg (271–313). Basingstoke: Macmillan Education.

___. 1999. "A Critique of Postcolonial Reason. Toward a History of the Vanishing Present." Cambridge: Harvard University Press.

Sztainbok, Vannina. 2008. "National Pleasures: The Fetishization of Blackness and Uruguayan Autobiographical Narratives." *Latin American and Caribbean Ethnic Studies Journal* 3, 1: 61–84. doi.org/10.1080/17442220701865846.

___. 2013. "Exposing Her Body, Revealing the Nation: The Carnival Vedette and the Symbolic Order." *Social Identities: Journal for the Study of Race, Nation and Culture* 19, 5: 592–606.

Wynter, Sylvia. 2003. "Unsettling the Coloniality of Being/Power/Truth/Freedom: Towards the Human, After Man, Its Overrepresentation—An Argument." CR: The New Centennial Review 3, 3: 257–337. doi.org/10.1353/ncr.2004.0015.

3

Dwelling in the Ethical Quicksand of Archival Research

Violence and Representation in the Telling of Terror Stories[1]

Teresa Macías

> What right did I have to go through these documents? Were these materials — and the stories carried within them — mine to comb through, to read, to share? Was it fair to my ancestors to tell my story through their lives? To live through their dying, to speak through their silence? (Boon 2019, 45)

In a scene from the movie *Star Wars: Episode II – Attack of the Clones*, the Jedi Master Obi-Wan Kenobi visits the archives searching for a planetary system that does not appear in the charts.[2] He enlists the help of archivist Madame Jocasta Nu who, upon searching the records, concludes that the planetary system does not exist. When Obi-Wan states that "perhaps the archives are incomplete," the archivist responds: "One thing you may be absolutely sure of: if an item does not appear in our records, it does not exist!" (Lucas 2002). While admittedly science fiction, this scene provides a glimpse into the kind of power archives wield and their ontological effect as sites where not only events, experiences, and histories get recorded, but also where their very existence is negotiated. Those of us who do archival research are often seduced by the promises and possibilities of archival records and by the allure of searching in archival vaults, of sitting in their reading rooms, and of losing ourselves in the promise of finding in files, boxes and — nowadays more often than not — search engines pieces of truth, history, life. In the process, we may forget that archives are deceptive; they contain, as Weld observes, "far less than what [they] exclude" (Weld 2014, 13). Furthermore, they are "register[s] of epistemic arrangements, recording in [their] proliferating avatars the shifting tenor of debates around the production and ethics of knowledge" (Arondekar 2009, 2).

In our impetus to mine archives, to extract from them morsels of history, we may not always stop to think about the ethics of archival research. We may not consider the ethical and political dilemmas or implications of working with archival records that are produced through processes of inclusion and exclusion. We may not stop to think about how archives determine what life gets recognition in the records and is, thus, rendered socially and historically relevant, and what life does not. If archives determine what exists and what doesn't, as Madame Jocasta Nu suggests, what are we, archival researchers, to do with the stories we find in archives? Should we conceive of archival stories as simply there for the taking? And, how does any decision about what we do with what we find in archives implicate us in ongoing processes of inscription and erasure that produce both the archive and the knowledge we generate?

The politics and ethics of archival research are the central focus of this chapter. I use my experience working with archival records related to two Truth and Reconciliation Commissions instituted by the Chilean state to account for the legacies of the authoritarian regime that ruled the country between 1973 and 1990: the 1990 Rettig Truth, Justice and Reconciliation Commission (henceforth the Rettig Commission) and the 2003 Truth and Reconciliation Commission on Political Imprisonment and Torture (henceforth the Torture Commission).[3] The records I studied contained quite explicit and gruesome descriptions and testimonies of death, summary executions, disappearances, imprisonment and torture along with evidence of the work done by the commissions to organize the records into a coherent historical account of the military regime.[4] The records were difficult to work with. They were dark, not only due to their detailed accounts of death and suffering, but also because they revealed the archiving tools deployed by the commissions to collect and organize terror narratives and to subject them to hegemonic nation and subject-making projects (Macías 2013). The archives also contained records of the many instances in which graphic descriptions of torture and death were painstakingly recounted in political speeches, pieces of legislation, parliamentary debates, news reports, documentaries, works of fiction and non-fiction, plays, advertisements, etc. The ongoing use of terror stories and their continuing inscription in the archives reflect not only the instrumentality of terror stories for nation building in post-authoritarian Chile, but also the multilayer, performative and violent character of archival documentation (Caswell 2014; Tortorici 2018).

A central argument of this chapter is that a careful and critical consideration of the ethics and politics of archival research requires that we unpack the violence that is at the very core of the practices of representation that constitute both archives and research. I propose that it is impossible to separate ethics, politics and methodology when encountering archived stories and deciding what, how, why and under what conditions to reproduce or retell them in research reports. In the same way that archives are the "result of specific political, cultural, and socioeconomic pressures," so is archival research shaped and influenced by these pressures (Burton 2005, 6). As a result, we need to render thinkable and problematic the brief moment and narrow space between the encounter with archived stories — particularly stories of state-organized terror — and decisions about what to do with them, the moment/space between violence and its representation in which we negotiate between the need to account for violence, and the violence implicit in processes of accounting. This narrow space is constantly shifting, a quicksand, a place in which we precariously stand and on which it is sometimes possible to commit to performative,[5] self-critical, positional and subversive ethical practices. In this narrow space, we become inevitably bound to the archived stories, to the bodies that the stories represent, to the violence of representation and to the politics of knowledge production informing and shaping research.

To be clear, this chapter is not about death and torture or the individual and/or social effects of state terror. Nor is this chapter intended to recount narratives of state terror or to deny the importance of survivor testimonies for social justice work in global and transnational sites.[6] In fact, I caution readers against the temptation to immediately and unproblematically insert real or imaginary terror stories into the reading of this chapter. Such insertion would defeat the purpose of the chapter by skirting over the relationship between violence and its representation that is so central to the ethical and political reflection I propose.

Setting the Stage:
Archives and the Question of Ethics

My research on how stories of state terror appear in the archives and how they are used to mediate nation building was prompted by a political need to call attention, not just to the violence to which the stories attest, but also to the violence implicit in archiving practices. As I argue elsewhere (Macías 2016), instead of thinking of archives as stable, un-implicated, ahistorical, and apolitical container of records, we need to see them as contested sites for practices of containment, registration, inscription and representation that mediate the recognition of certain events — and by extension the bodies involved in those events — and the inclusion of these events in official history (see for example Hacking 2002; Duff & Harris 2002; Cook & Schwartz 2002; Fritzsche 2005; Ketelaar 2002). Archives have ontological and epistemological effects. Through inscription, containment and recording, they produce the thing of which they speak. They capture bodies in power-knowledge regimes and determine, as Butler (2007, 953) suggests, "whose lives are grievable, and whose are not ... which human lives count as human and as living, and which do not ...; [archives] also determine when and where a life can be said to be lost, and that loss registered as the violent loss of life ... [and] when and where the loss of life remains ungrievable and unrepresentable." As epistemological devices, archives produce fields of perceptible reality within which certain things and events can be known and represented, while others remain obscured, silent and unknowable. As Burton (2005, 7) argues, archives are "full-fledged historical actor[s]" implicated in the imposition of "scales of credibility." They constitute knowledge and place it in hierarchical arrangements through, for example, the civilizational differentiation of written and oral history on which colonial violence is predicated.

Yet, as Stoler (2009, 19) suggests, the work of power in archives is never absolute, complete or secured. Rather, archives are "sites of contestation" where knowledge and power are deployed with "piecemeal partiality" and through "spasmodic and sustained currents of anxious labor." Archives shape memory and construct meaning (Caswell 2014). They also evince failures of representation that leave "fingerprints which are attributes to the archive's infinite meaning" (Caswell 2014, 16; see also Bowker 2005). The contested, spasmodic and anxious character of archives was recorded in the records I researched in the form of discrepant accounts, dissenting voices and subjugated knowledge that, in spite of excluding practices, still left traces in the forms of silences, deceiving/ subversive speech, or contradictory stories/records. These conditions signal not only the continuous work of power in archives, but also the struggles, shifts and fissures that make archives ever-evolving power-knowledge devices. For instance, the Torture Commission and its report became tools that survivors, human rights organizations, and the media used and reused not only to retell torture stories and to gain social recognition and visibility, but also to contest, refute, and shift official national narratives. These appropriations, contestations, refusals, and alternative narratives, in turn, became part of an ever-evolving archive of state terror.

In addition, archives are, as Friedrich (2021, 6) observes, "the sum of activities and actions" that implicate those of us who in our own particular ways interact with, work on and participate in archival practices. For instance, in her work on the role of scribes (*escribanos*) in the Spanish empire, Burns (2010, 13) argues that by setting pen to paper and recording in detail the activities that symbolized the taking of possession, scribes extended the paper trail that sustained the Spanish conquest of what is now known as Latin America. "It was largely through these men's agency," Burns says, "that the colonial Latin American archive was formed." In my own work on the Rettig and Torture Commissions, I have shown how the collection and organization of testimonies of terror by the commissions' workers were highly regulated and bureaucratic processes that relied on the collection of individual terror stories in which "survivors were required to exhibit the[ir] wounds ... to make their bodies visible and the object of observation and evaluation by the commission's staff" (Macías 2014, 317). The exhibition of physical and psychological wounds was a condition for the recognition of terror as an *actual event* and a requirement for the admission of testimonies into the archives. Through these regulated practices, the commissions discursively produced the body that became known as survivor: a social category that granted recognition and mediated the acquisition of compensation and benefits. These practices, in turn, allowed the commissions to organize and construct a narrative about the nation's past, to shape how the nation would know the legacies of authoritarianism. Furthermore, the commissions' archiving practices mediated and sustained any subsequent appropriation and redeployment of terror stories, which having been legitimized as actual events by their recording in the archives, could then be used and reused to constantly reconstruct national narratives (see also Ghosh 2005; Stoler 2002).

Archival practices not only determine what is archivable and thus, rendered knowable, they also, as Tortorici (2018, 3) suggests, "influence, and to some extent determine, how contemporary archivists and researchers engage with" archives. Archives, therefore, link the survivors who speak on the record and attempt to give an account of their experience, those who collect and record the testimonies in writing and the archivists who file and organize the records. They also link us, the researchers who work with, or on, the archives. Through our research, writing and knowledge production, we link the readers and consumers of knowledge to this continuous chain in ways that implicate all of us in the ongoing and violent representation of terror stories. Yet, as I discuss in this chapter's final section, none of these actions are secured or uncontested and it is their insecure and contested character that opens up opportunities for politically transformative and ethical archival research practices.

In the course of my research, I lived and worked with the archived accounts of state terror and they became part of the evidence that supported my research findings. I say lived because for years, these records lived in my home in the form of official reports as well as countless printed copies of parliamentary debates, news media, political speeches, testimonies, works of fiction and non-fiction and pictures. The records covered my tables and counter tops; they were there when I awoke in the morning and when I went to sleep at night. They were there when I left for work and when I returned. I took them with me to bed and often they inhabited my dreams. Sometimes, I temporarily set them aside to lay out breakfast or to help my son with his homework, but they always managed to reclaim the space.

While I became keenly aware of how archival practices determined what and how terror stories were made available to me, my own work with the archives required that I perform other forms of operations of inclusion and exclusion that, themselves, imply violence. I enacted this violence in practices of "containment and ordering" in "the labeling of representation" (Grosz 2003, 137), and in moments in which, for example, I made decisions about how to collect, organize and code archived stories to transform them into data; how to de/re/contextualize the records and use them to frame and/or substantiate arguments; which stories to quote or cross/reference (the more or less graphic, violent, dehumanizing, uplifting, etc.) and which records to write and which to leave out of writing. These practices and decisions constitute the "less obvious, and rarely called by this name" forms of violence that are at the core of any research. They are part of the "the domain of knowledge, reflection, thinking, and writing" and of the violence — the "cutting" (Foucault 1981, 134) — that discourse does to things and which Foucault associates with knowledge production and with the constitution of the knowing subject.

The archives constituted a mediating device between the people whose stories they contained and me; the stories had already been captured in the archives and produced by the discursive and material practices that make up the work of archiving (see for example Brothman 2002; Frohmann 2008; Hardiman 2009). In the case of the Torture Commission, for instance, testimonies could not even be traced back to an actual survivor; they were either presented anonymously or fused together into a generalized and un-individualized narrative. In other cases, testimonies had been fragmented, broken up, decontextualized, and recontextualized to fit within dominant and normative national narratives or human rights discourses. I could not assume, therefore, that my encounter with the testimonies was unmediated or similar to an encounter with the face or bodies of victims or survivors. Nor could I assume that these mediating roles and representational practices caused the torture stories to be less true, less embodied, or less authentic than if the stories had been conveyed to me by the survivors themselves. Yet, despite, or perhaps because of, these conditions, I felt the archives and the stories contained in them issued an ethical demand on me and posed ethical questions that I could not easily answer through available conceptions of ethics. I wondered, for instance, whether I should avoid including archived terror stories in my own research writing. If such inclusion was unavoidable, I questioned the purpose and the conditions under which I should recount the stories.

These ethical questions materialized most specifically in the process of writing and publishing the results of my research. My argument that stories of violence mediate nation and subject making required that I use some of the stories in my own writing, making me complicit in their representation, appropriation and circulation. Without using some examples as illustrations, my arguments about the violent inscription of terror stories in archives and in national truth and their problematic appropriation by national subjects did not make sense. If I was going to unpack not only the function of authoritarian terror, but also the use of the stories by post-authoritarian nation and subjects, I needed to engage in the retelling, discursive appropriation and representation of the stories.

My decisions to include or not to include narratives of death and torture in my writing have varied depending on the context within which I am presenting my work, but they have always been met with mixed and passionate reactions. For instance, an anonymous reviewer for one of my publications in which I used torture narratives to illustrate their appropriation and deployment for nation and subject making (Macías 2013) commented that torture stories "*should not* be repeated ... as they accomplish the same thing you seem to condemn, that is, misuse of torture stories and re-victimization by retelling details" (italics in original). By contrast, in the review process for an earlier version of this chapter, published as a journal article (Macías 2016), another reviewer protested with great passion against my decision *not to* include torture narratives in my discussion of the ethics of archival research. In an attempt to either educate me about torture, or to insert some form of authorial voice into my own work, this reviewer proceeded to insert in their review and on the margins of my manuscript a graphic description of the torture suffered by someone they knew. These reactions demonstrate that there is something about terror that demands some form of representation; terror wants to inscribe itself in texts and in archives either in the form of explicit description or well-intentioned refusals to write or tell, which also constitute a form of inscription, a way of speaking terror through silence. Either through explicit description or well-intentioned erasure, terror leaves its trace in the text and, by extension, in the archive.

I argue elsewhere (Macías 2013) that the issue of what to do with archived stories of state terror is not easily resolved through a decision about whether to reproduce the stories in research reports. State-organized terror relies on the deprivation of voice, the imposition of silence on victims, the use of euphemisms (such as abusive or enhanced interrogation) and the rendering of state terror socially unspeakable and thus un-recordable on official state records and social memory (Fietlowitz 1998). For survivors, therefore, speaking about the violence they endured and having their stories recorded and archived constitutes a necessary condition for social recognition and for the reassertion of their subjectivity and citizenship (see for example Avelar 2001; Fuentes 2004; Simpson 2007; Stanley 2004). As Arteaga (2003, vii) argues, language and testimony "conjure up the violence after the fact." He adds,

> for the survivors of bloodletting, words can evoke the memories, almost like echoes, reverberating still in the tremble of the flesh. For others who are not the victim, language can call images of blood to the mind. Whether by analog memory or metaphor image, the linguistic act and event brings red to the fore.

A conscientious discussion of the extensive literature on testimonies and testimonial writing is well beyond the scope of this chapter. Suffice it to say that testimonies are also contested forms of representation that themselves embody failures. Levi (1989) associates this failure of representation with the compulsion to reduce and simplify complex stories in order to render knowable experiences that, by their very nature, are complex and messy (see also Mathews & Goodman 2013). The contestability of testimonies is the result of the limitations and failures associated with the practices of signification and symbolization that is characteristic of processes of giving voice and assigning meaning to unspeakable experiences (Agamben 1999; Levi 1989; Sumic-Riha 2004). Bearing witness "to some traumatic experiences," Sumic-Riha (2004, 18–19) argues, "is doomed to failure not only because one cannot find words to convey to others what is unbearable for him or her. Rather, it is condemned to fail because that to which one is summoned to bear witness resists all attempts at symbolization."

The issue of whether to reproduce terror stories from Chile in my research is further complicated by my social positioning. In conjuring up the violence as a racialized woman from, and writing about, the Global South, I also risk becoming complicit in the circulation of, and trafficking with, stories from the South. Within geopolitical and racial structures of knowledge production and circulation, these stories can get consumed, as Razack (2007; 2009) argues, by national/imperial subjects in the North. Therefore, instead of focussing on the question of whether to re/tell terror stories in research — a question to which, as the conflicting reviews mentioned above suggests there is no easy answer, or at least no answer that would satisfy everyone — I propose that we remain in the narrow, uncomfortable and ever-shifting space and time

— the quicksand — that separates the archived stories of terror and our decision of what to do with them. In this space, we can render critically thinkable and ethically problematic, not only archival practices, but also the very work we do in and with the archives.

Research, Representation and Writing

> Can one truly know the Other without doing violence to [them]…? (Gonzales Echeberría 1998, 145)

If archives are contested devices with historical and social functions that, through inclusion and exclusion, simultaneously constitute and fail to constitute that of which they speak, revealing the violence of representation embedded in the representation of violence, can we not say something similar about research, its relationship to violence and its function as a knowledge production device? Is not all research another archiving practice that inherits not only failures, but also the violence of representation? There are three interrelated and mutually constitutive conditions of research I want to discuss here. First, research is a specific activity and a practice that embodies violence. This violence, Grosz (2003, 134) argues, is inherent to the work of knowledge production and materializes in the specific activities of data collection or analysis associated with methodology, and in the "violence of writing, of thought, and of knowing." Second, through research work, research constitutes researchers as subjects with claims to disciplinary belonging. And third, research is shaped by politics of knowledge production and by the historical geopolitical, racial and institutional apparatus of enunciation that determine the production and reception of knowledge.

In the case of my work, my research took me to the physical space of the archives, where I encountered the many ways in which terror stories were described, organized, recounted and recorded. I also found in the archives the multiple relationships between records, the technical process of inscription, citation, recalling and contextualization that form part of the records' provenance and continuous social life (Caswell 2014; Ketelaar 2002; Stoler 2009). Yet, these records and their relationships, while having been produced through the archival practices already discussed, did not a priori constitute data. They became data through my actual intervention in them, through the many operations of collection, classification, coding, summarizing, cross-referencing, noting, etc., and through the cacophony of theoretical voices that informed, interrupted, interrogated and deciphered the performative work of knowledge production in which I was involved.

The archival data in my research came into being in the "particular ontological, epistemological, and methodological structure" of my research (St. Pierre 2013, 223; see also Bruce 2013; Bridges & van Cleave 2013). Foucaultian discourse analysis determined what and how I considered data. In fact, this framework allowed me to see that the actual pieces of papers and the words on them, which together make up the archival records, did not in themselves constitute data. Rather, something else came into being as data: the discursive practices, rhetorical moves and semantic gestures captured in the records, as well as the historically specific processes of explicit denial, disavowal, and exclusion, or acceptance, avowal, and inclusion that in tandem produced and shifted a truth about terror (Macías 2015). Further, a Foucaultian ontological framework allowed me to see the data not as expression of true or authentic experiences that needed to be recounted, but rather as sites where larger discourses, theories, values, histories, cultures, politics and power manifested so as to produce reality, truth and subjectivity (St. Pierre 2013).

When I encountered terror stories in the archives, I did not see them as expressions of an authentic experience, though at times, that was difficult not to do. Instead, I looked at how terror stories were being allowed to come into existence in the records and how they were being deployed, organized and recounted so as to produce national narratives and subjectivities. To be sure, while I remained aware that terror is felt and lived on the bodies of victims who, through testimonies, attempt to bring to light experiences previously ignored, my attention was on how archives capture, represent and construct national truth out of those testimonies. In the process, other forms of violence, such as the violence of representation, began to reveal themselves as data in the ways in which terror stories were discursively produced and deployed.

Part of my research looked at parliamentary debates concerning compensation policies and benefits for survivors. In the records of these debates, I found many examples of politicians engaging in practices of terror-telling in which stories of torture, rape, disappearances, executions, deaths, etc., were recounted in great detail in order to justify monetary compensation and secure national reconciliation (Macías 2013).

Gendered narrative of rape, torture-induced abortions and pregnancies, as well as poverty and dispossession were particularly prevalent in these practices of terror-telling. In my research, themes such as "torture-telling," "gendered terror stories," "pricing of violence" and "pornographic appropriation" became coding categories that simultaneously turned the records into data and allowed me to theorize and transform data into writable evidence of the discursive materialization of tortured and dead bodies in the archive and in the national imagination.

Through the labour of research, every time my eyes rested on sections of the records in which terror stories were re/told, my mind classified and my fingers and hands highlighted, annotated, cross-referenced, cut and pasted the records into the coding structures and documents of my research. Through this process, the terror stories continued their journey and made their way from archived testimonies, to the terror-telling practices captured in archives, to my own coding and analysis and later into my writing of the research. Their journey does not end there, but in fact continues past my writing to reach readers who, as the reviewers' comments mentioned above suggest, then engage with the terror narratives, those written as well as those unwritten. The journey has concrete effects on the records; they do not remain unscathed as they traverse from testimony, to archive, to research, to writing and to reading. At different stages, things are done to the stories through the many operations involved in discursive representation. For instance, while in the archives, the stories were systematically removed from the systemic practice of violence during the authoritarian regime; in my research, the stories were re-tied to violence, this time, to the violence enacted through processes of accounting. Yet, in binding terror stories to the violence of accounting, I engaged in other forms of retelling that retained violence now in the representational practices of my own research. To be clear, the representational violence displayed in the archives was not an immobile condition of a past from which the records had been created, and it was not separate from my own collection, reading and writing of and about the records. The violence was, in fact, being produced as data through my own intervention in the archives. That is, the violence is ongoing, it was constantly being enacted and re-inscribed through my research work. My own representation of violence is representation piled on top of other representations, and my own writing of the representation of violence is in itself a violence of representation.

In her reading of Derrida, Grosz (2003) argues that it is not just that representation and writing, as fundamental conditions of research, resemble violence, but that they are themselves forms of violence. Representation misses something in violence, as I discussed above in relation to archives, something that leaves a lacuna or constitutes a failure of representation. Representation also requires processes of abstraction and symbolization that simultaneously "open and occlude certain abstract forms of violence that form our reality" (Noys 2013, 13). In determining, for example, which terror stories to reproduce in my writing in order to make evident the violent representation of terror in the archives, I engaged in what Grosz (2003, 136) proposes are the "modes of divergence, ambiguity, impossibility, [and] the 'aporetic' status" of inscription and difference, which are deep-rooted in the constitution of truth. In other words, my attempts to reveal the framing practices present in archives and expand them in order to include in the field of perceptible reality the hegemonic nation building and subjectification processes at work in the accounting for terror, I had to engage in other forms of framing and representation. These framing practices are associated not only with the decision of what stories to include. They are also implicit in the very act of writing that, by following rules of proper order, well-punctuated rhythms, and meaning making, bring the world into existence and us within it (Whitehall 2013). Thus, my own condemnation of terror is, as Grosz (2003, 138) continues, "implicated in the very thing it aims to condemn."

The realization of the violence inherent in representation leads us to the role that research has in the constitution of subject-researcher. As St. Pierre (2015, 110) argues, conventional conceptions of qualitative research, whether positivist, interpretative or critical, are sustained on the idea that "there is a researcher who exists ahead of the research — which is out there somewhere — a self-contained individual who moves right through the process from beginning to end, whole, intact, and unencumbered, already identified and secured in the subjectivity statement." This conception of the researcher, continues St. Pierre, simultaneously reinforces concepts of the immobile human at the centre of any research activity and enables conceptions of truth, reality and experience that continue to organize our way of understanding the world (108). However, this notion of the researcher ignores that research is a performative activity, an activity that, as Foucault (1982; 1994b) argues, allows for continuous and never completed operations of subjectification through which we not only constitute the object of study — the data or even the bodies about which we write — but also ourselves as subjects. Research is a "constitutive action" and a "productive mechanism," with the power to reify and dismantle representational practices and power-knowledge regimes (Pelias 2015, 274), and to call us, researchers, into existence mediating, though admittedly with different levels of certainty, our entrance into disciplinary fields (Denzin 2013; Koro-Ljungberg & MacLure 2013).

Performativity was and continues to be evident at all levels of my research. For instance, it was evident in the deployment of ambiguous and at times contradictory subjectivity discourses I used to name myself, or were used to name me, in order to justify the research, obtain credentials or gain access to the archives. Citizenship and scholarly discourses were some of these discourses. They required or allowed me to call on my Canadian or Chilean citizenship, to claim institutional/disciplinary belonging or to speak in voices attuned with those national and scholarly narratives, in order to gain access or credibility. Performativity was also in the aesthetical practices in which I engaged in order to develop and secure the relationships with archivists and librarians needed for data collection. It was, and continues to be, in my own internal chatter through which I convince myself that the research was worthwhile to do. It was and is in the writing and presentational practices in which sometimes I purposefully made, and continue to make, myself in/visible in the text while rendering intelligible the violent constitution of national truth about terror. Performativity is in the minutia associated with research, in routine and quotidian activities and in the professional discourses that constitute the "cultural locus" of meaning on which, even if at times in conditions of precarity, I can claim belonging in certain disciplinary fields (Butler & Salih 2004, 23). Finally, the very act of writing this chapter, speaking with and along specific theories in order to render bare the ethical challenges associated with archival research, is itself a performative and self-constituting action through which the researcher in me is called into being. To be sure, none of these performative acts constitute a choice made by a pre-existing stable and conscious identity that exists before the research, an identity that conventional researchers assume can be made visible and known through self-positioning or self-reflection (St. Pierre 2015, 110). Rather, the subject-researcher, the "I" in my research, was and continues to be constituted within power-knowledge regimes and through my own speaking in the scholarly discourses that allow me to continuously come into being as a researcher.

Finally, as researchers we continue to carry out our work within highly regulated apparatuses of enunciation that determine the position of research and researcher within regimes of truth and within global and historical geopolitical, colonial, patriarchal and racial structures (Mignolo 2009). Research is shaped and regulated by politics of knowledge production that, through funding structures, publishing politics, institutionalized disciplinary hierarchies, politics of evidence, regulated and precarious academic labour structures and geopolitical relations, determine not only what knowledge counts and what counts as knowledge, but also who can claim to be the knower (see for example Canaan & Shumar 2008; Church 2008; van Heugten 2011). By engaging in this research as a woman from the Global South living and working in the North, my attempts to render decipherable and comprehensible Chilean processes of accounting for terror are always situated within "geopolitics of knowing" (Mignolo 2009, 160). That is, my research exists within the global social and political conditions that regulate the circulation of knowledge and bodies between North and South, and that shape how research from and about the South is taken up in the North. Therefore, by doing this research I participate and become implicated in the global politics of knowledge production that constitute the Global South as knowable object within "a racial system of social classification that invented Occidentalism ... that created the conditions for Orientalism ... [and that] remapped the world into first, second and third during the Cold War" (Mignolo 2009, 161).

Although research, as an activity, is contested and my subjectivity as researcher performative, these racial and geopolitical conditions strive to fix, crystalize and contain the research within social power relations and racial systems of classification that consistently shape and restrain what we can know about the Global South and what happens there. For instance, while my research seeks to reveal the politics of representation regarding state terror within larger governmental regimes and apparatuses of ruling, I always run the risk of being taken up as a native informant, as someone expected to speak in the restrictive language of testimony and humanitarianism or within well-established dichotomies of Global North development/civilization and Global South underdevelopment/savagery. Moreover, while my research on the archives had as its goal to render visible hegemonic nation-building projects and their reliance on the careful appropriation and containment of terror stories, within the geopolitics of knowledge production already in place, I am more likely to be taken up as a voice that speaks of, or for, the suffering: an "authentic" voice that can allow readers and listeners in the North to feel they have had a "true" encounter with terror (Razack 2007). In this story, the North always emerges as a place of humanitarianism and modernity. As Sztainbok and Gajardo suggest in this volume, the body that researches, writes and speaks matters; the political context within which research is done matters; and the audience that listens to and reads research matters.

The Ethical Quicksand of Archival Research

> One must grasp, precisely to not fix. To read without a trace ... is not a mandate against archival work, but rather a call to interrogate, without paralysis, to challenge, without ending the promise of a future. (Arondekar 2009, 4)

In his search for the planet that does not appear in the archives, Obi-Wan visits Master Yoda and his class of young initiates and asks them to once again search the records. When Yoda asks the class how it can be that, while a "gravity's silhouette remains ... the star and all its planets have disappeared," one of his students replies that "someone [must have] erased [the planet] from the archive's memory." After praising the young pupil for having such an "uncluttered mind," Yoda turns to Obi-Wan and instructs him to go to the centre of the gravitational pull to find the missing planet. Confronted with the dilemma that concerns me in this chapter — the dilemma concerning not just the question of what to do with archived stories of violence, but what to do with the issue of representation *as violence* — should we answer Master Yoda's hail and search for what is erased from archives? Should we assume that ethical archival research requires that we search for that which, while being erased, leaves a trace, a gravitational silhouette, or a silence that loudly speaks through its absence? Is ethical archival research one that searches for more authentic "images ... more images, [or] images that convey the full horror and reality of the suffering?" (Butler 2004, 146). Should we, researchers, strive to commit these more authentic images to the record? Or, should we refuse to write them into our work, relegating them instead to silence? Would representation or the failure to represent free us from any complicity in the exclusionary practices that make up archives?

As I have argued in this chapter, the search for a practice of archival research that is outside the violence of representation is a futile endeavour, not only because archival practices and practices of representation always convey violence, but also because the work of research and writing always implies a violence of representation. This argument does not mean that archival research is unethical and, thus, should not be done, or that the violence of which I speak cannot ever be productive. Rather, it means that conceptions of ethics grounded on the search for nonviolent ways of doing research, more authentic encounters with the Other, or better ways to represent terror stories fail us when it comes to archival research. Furthermore, as the reviewer comments to which I have pointed in this chapter show, there is no answer to the question of whether to represent terror stories in research that will leave us unscathed.

An ethics of archival research require us to cast our gaze on the very work of representation as violence implicit in research practices, on the subject-researcher engaged in the performative work of representation and on the context within which research is conducted and received. In other words, rather than searching for innocent places outside representation, we must tackle the very issue of representation, what it accomplishes, what it makes possible and when it fails. We need to turn what is at work in representation into an ethics, and commit to dwelling in the uncertain, unstable and ever-shifting ethical quicksand between violence and its representation, that space between the moment we encounter archived stories of terror and we decide what to do with them. In this space, we are always at risk of falling through, of failing because, as Spivak (1999, 242) observes, archival research constitutes both "a reaching and an un-grasping." But also, this quicksand is the site where methodology, theory, politics and ethics meet and where not only knowledge is produced, but also where we, researchers, come into being. This process of becoming is inseparable from the work we do with the records, the many times precarious and faulty minutia of activities, actions and calculations that turn records into data and data into results.

By dwelling in the quicksand between violence and its representation, we can ask why and under what paradoxical conditions archives make terror simultaneously visible and invisible, knowable and unknowable. Such interrogation orients us towards deconstructive practices of archival research that disclose the lines of construction of the archive and lay bare its inner contradictions (Derrida 1976). This commitment to deconstruction extends to our own practices of reading the archive in ways that require us to both acknowledge and renounce our own desire to find in the archive an authentic voice, a subject whose silence we can redeem through our representational practices. As Arondekar (2009, 3) proposes, a deconstructive practice of reading the archive requires us to "[move] away not from the nature of the object [terror], but from the notion of an object that would somehow lead to a formulation of subjectivity: the presumption that if a [terrorized] body is found, then a subject can be recovered." In other words, to read archives in this way means to recognize that archived stories of terror both demand and eschew representation, and that, by extension, our work with the archives remains entangled in practices of revelation and concealment.

Spivak (2010, 263) argues that within the context of western knowledge and the western archive, the researcher is always imagined as an "absent nonrepresenter who lets the oppressed [and the records] speak for themselves." In contrast, by dwelling in the ethical quicksand of archival research we can render bare and resist the seduction of discovery and recovery, the desire for the security that comes from searching, finding and ultimately knowing, and the temptation to seek innocence in the belief that we can give voice to the voices already silenced by the archive. In this quicksand, we can perhaps make thinkable, as both ethics and politics, the very work of representation as violence, not to free representation from violence, but rather to deploy representation in ways that, even if temporarily and precariously, disrupt the power-knowledge relations that affect how the archived story comes into being and becomes un/known and how we come into being and render ourselves known.

We should not assume that by representing or refusing to represent terror stories in our research, we can re-establish and secure the existence of an authentic Other that precedes, overflows and resists representation. Further, we should not presume the existence of an essential transparent subject-researcher who, through her research practices, remains secured in her innocence, unimplicated in the violence of representation and ultimately untouched by history (Hofmeyr 2006). The pursuit for an authentic Other would take us out of the archive, to an imaginary space of unquestionable truth outside representation, a space that not even the testimonies of victims can reach. Such a pursuit would also reinforce the idea that, to paraphrase Spivak's (2010) famous phrase, the survivor of terror *can* speak and do so through us, that if we fall silent and unclutter our minds, we can let the unheard voice of the Other through. We can mine, search, find and retrieve archived terror stories, we can write them or refuse to write them into our research, but we should do so in full view of the archiving and research technologies that undermine and regulate any possibility of recovery. We also need to make visible the ways in which any decision we make concerning the representation of terror stories contributes to our own constitution as researchers.

Finally, as I have argued throughout this chapter, any negotiations we make in the ethical quicksand of archival research, and particularly in regards to whether we represent stories of terror in our writing, are not only ethical but also political and always taking place within the social power relations and the apparatuses of enunciation that Mignolo (2009) identifies. In the context of my work on how the archiving of terror stories secures nation building, and as Razack (2009) astutely observes, "discussions [of terror] create community as much as [terror] itself does." As the reviewer comments I have pointed to in this chapter suggest, terror also has the capacity to build community through the reception and reading of research. Terror demands representation; it calls on the imagination; it invites us to superimpose it and to write it on the margins of texts, even as the text itself refuses to reveal it. Terror also builds community through well-intentioned decisions not to represent, not to write and not to read. Either through well-intentioned erasure, or explicit description, terror mediates and secures our belonging in a community that, particularly in the context of the Global North, knows itself as good and innocent through terror. Either through inscription or refusal to inscribe, terror assert its presence.

Thus, the question is not whether to represent terror stories in research, but rather what such representation accomplishes and how it interrupts any attempts to secure positions of innocence for researchers, for readers and for institutions. As Sztainbok and I (2018) have argued in the context of fictional depictions of torture, the question is not whether to narrate terror, but rather what such narration accomplishes and whether it unmakes the community, nation and subject that terror facilitates in the first place. In the context of the Global North, research that deals with practices of state terror in the Global South are always read as the predictable result of the backwardness of the South. And we researchers from and working on the Global South are always heard through the imperial and colonial scripts that secure the Global South's backwardness and the Global North's development. The southern intellectual, as Sztainbok and Gajardo remind us in this volume, is commonly only heard when she speaks in a tongue, with an accent, or with words already recognized as foreign. Yet, the ethical quicksand of archival research offers possibilities for interrupting both the effects of terror stories in community building and their role in sustaining global power relations. But in order to interrupt, research on the archives of state terror must reveal the fissures and weaknesses of both archival and research practices and make explicit the many ways in which researching, writing and reading about terror can secure and disrupt us.

As Rossiter (2011) proposes, the violence and the cutting of representation are sometimes necessary for justice. At times, we must fix the Other and ourselves in some form of representation and in our writing if we are going to call attention to violence and to conditions of injustice. Such fixing needs to remain a political calculation, a calculation that relies on our capacity to strategically perform the work of research while keeping our commitment to rendering evident, and thus questionable and ultimately precarious, our own constitution and the constitution of the stories of others in the narrow space between violence and its representation. In the quicksand, we can allow the records and the work we do with them to constantly re/constitute us, make and unmake us, at the same time that we seek opportunities for the records and our work with them to disrupt and perhaps unmake the world. Yet, we also need to come to terms with the fact that the archive, like research, promises at the same time that it fails to deliver. It is our job as researchers to expose both the promise and the failure, and to do so while recognizing and unsettling our own and our readers' desire for discovery and for knowing.

Notes

1. Sections of this chapter were originally published in *Intersectionalities: A Global Journal of Social Work Analysis, Research, Polity and Practice*, 2016, 5, no. 1.
2. This example is also cited in Burton (2005) and Ketelaar (2002).
3. The mandate of the Rettig Commission was to account for cases of disappearance and death, while the Torture Commission dealt with cases of political imprisonment and torture. The commissions constituted essential tools for the construction

of a national truth about the atrocities committed by the authoritarian regime. The state then used this truth to declare that the nation had achieved true national reconciliation and could close an obscure chapter in its history. The commissions also provided venues for survivors to speak on the record about their experiences of state sanctioned terror, to gain recognition, and to qualify for monetary compensations (Macías 2010).

4. For further discussion of the Torture Commission and the manner in which testimonies of torture get organized in the official archive of torture in Chile, see Macías 2014.

5. I use the concept of performativity here in a Foucaultian sense, understood as an uncertain and never completed "'self-forming activity,' a concrete and active process of becoming, a technology, and an ascetics of self" (Foucault 1994a, 265 cited in Macías 2012, 6).

6. There is a wealth of multidisciplinary scholarly work that attends to experiences and effects of torture including critical literature on the function of torture as a tool of power. For recent research on the impact of torture on survivors in a global context, see for example Hárdi & Kroó (2015) and Thapa et al. (2003), and for specific work on torture in Chile, see Corral (2011). For research on the experiences of torture survivors see, for example, Stirr (2014). And, for an example of critical work on the function of torture as a tool of power see Razack (2009).

References

Agamben, Giorgo. 1999. *Remnants of Auschwitz: The Witness and the Archive*, translated by Daniel Heller-Roazen. New York: Zone Books.

Arondekar, Anjali. 2009. *For the Record: On Sexuality and the Colonial Archive in India.* Duke University Press.

Arteaga, Alfred. 2003. "Foreword: The Red and the Black." In *Violence and the Body: Race, Gender, and the State*, edited by Arturo J. Aldama (i–viii). Bloomington and Indianapolis: Indiana University Press.

Avelar, Idelber. 2001. "La Práctica de la Tortura y la Historia de la Verdad." In *Pensar en/ la Postdictadura*, edited by Nelly Richard and Alberto Moreira (175–195). Santiago, Chile: Cuarto Propio.

Boon, Sonja. 2019. *What the Oceans Remember: Searching for Belonging and Home.* Wilfrid Laurier University Press.

Bowker, Geoffrey. 2005. *Memory Practices in the Sciences.* Cambridge, MA: MIT Press.

Bridges-Rhoads, Sarah, and Jessica van Cleave. 2013. "Writing the Torment: Aporetic Data and the Possibility of Justice." *Cultural Studies; Critical Methodologies* 13, 4: 267–273. doi.org/10.1177/1532708613487872.

Brothman, Brien. 2002. "Afterglow: Conceptions of Records and Evidence in Archival Discourse." *Archival Science* 2: 311–342.

Bruce, Kristi A. 2013. "Here's Data Now, Happening." *Cultural Studies; Critical Methodologies* 13, 4: 342–346.

Burns, Kathryn. 2010. *Into the Archive: Writing and Power in Colonial Peru.* Duke University Press.

Burton, Antoinette. 2005. "Introduction: Archive Fever, Archive Stories." In *Archive Stories: Facts, Fictions, and the Writing of History*, edited by Antoinette Burton (1–24). Durham & London: Duke University Press.

Butler, Judith. 2004. "Precarious Life: The Power of Mourning and Violence." London and New York: Verso.

____. 2007. "Torture and the Ethics of Photography." *Environment and Planning D: Society and Space* 25, 6: 951–966. doi.org/10.1068/d2506jb.

Butler, Judith, and Sara Salih. 2004. *The Judith Butler Reader*, edited by Sara Salih and Judith Butler. Oxford: Blackwell Publishing.

Canaan, Joyce, and Wesley Shumar. 2008. "Higher Education in the Era of Globalization and Neoliberalism." In *Structure and Agency in the Neoliberal University*, edited by Joyce Cannan and Wesley Shumar (1–32). New York and London: Routledge.

Caswell, Michelle. 2014. *Archiving the Unspeakable: Silence, Memory, and the Photographic Record in Cambodia*. Madison, WI: University of Wisconsin Press.

Church, Jonathan. 2008. "Managing Knowledge: Intellectual Property, Instructional Design and the Manufacturing of Higher Education." In *Structure and Agency in the Neoliberal University*, edited by Joyce Canaan and Wesley Shumar (33–44). New York and London: Routledge.

Cook, Terry, and Joan M. Schwartz. 2002. "Archives, Records, and Power: From (Postmodern) Theory to (Archival) Performance." *Archival Science* 2, 171–185.

Corral, Hugo Rojas. 2011. "Torture in Chile (1973–1990): Analysis of One Hundred Survivors' Testimonies." *California Western International Law Journal* 42: 353.

Denzin, Norman K. 2013. "The Death of Data?" *Cultural Studies; Critical Methodologies* 13, 4: 353–356. doi.org/10.1177/1532708613487882.

Derrida, Jacques. 1976. *Of Grammatology*, translated by Gayatri Chakravorty Spivak. Baltimore and London: Johns Hopkins University Press.

Duff, Wendy, and Verne Harris. 2002. "Stories and Names: Archival Description as Narrating Records and Constructing Meaning." *Archival Science* 2, 2: 263–285.

Fietlowitz, Marguerite. 1998. *A Lexicon of Terror: Argentina and the Legacies of Torture*. Oxford: Oxford University Press.

Foucault, Michel. 1981. "The Order of Discourse." In *Untying the Text: A Post-Structural Anthology*, edited by R. Young (3–14). Boston: Routledge & Kegan Paul.

____. 1982. "The Subject and Power." In *Michel Foucault: Beyond Structuralism and Hermeneutics*, edited by Hubert Dryefus and Paul Rabinow (208–226). Chicago: University of Chicago Press.

____. 1994a. "On the Genealogy of Ethics: An Overview of Work in Progress." In *Michel Foucault: Ethics, Subjectivity and Truth*, edited by P. Rabinow (253–280). New York: New Press.

____. 1994b. "The Ethics of the Concern of the Self as a Practice of Freedom." In *Michel Foucault: Ethics, Subjectivity and Truth*, edited by Paul Rabinow (281–302). New York: New Press.

Friedrich, Markus. 2021. *The Birth of the Archive: A History of Knowledge*. University of Michigan Press.

Fritzsche, Peter. 2005. "The Archive and the Case of the German Nation." In *Archive Stories: Facts, Fictions, and the Writing of History*, edited by Antoinette Burton (184–208). Durham & London: Duke University Press.

Frohmann, Bernd. 2008. "Documentary Ethics, Ontology, and Politics." *Archival Science* 8, 3:165–180. doi.org/10.1007/s10502-008-9073-y.

Fuentes, Claudio. 2004. "Golpe a la Cátedra." In *De la Tortura no se Habla: Aguero versus Meneces*, edited by Patricia Verdugo. Santiago, Chile: Catalonia.

Ghosh, Durba. 2005. "National Narratives and the Politics of Miscegenation: Britain and India." In *Archive Stories: Facts, Fictions, and the Writing of History*, edited by Antoinette Burton (27–44). Durham & London: Duke University Press.

González Echevarría, Roberto. 1998. *Myth and Archive: A Theory of Latin American Narrative*. Duke University Press.

Grosz, Elizabeth. 2003. "The Time of Violence: Deconstruction and Value." In *Violence and the Body: Race, Gender, and the State*, edited by Arturo J. Aldama (134–147). Bloomington and Indianapolis: Indiana University Press.

Hacking, Ian. 2002. *Historical Ontology*. Cambridge, MA: Harvard University Press.

Hárdi, Lilla, and Adrienn Kroó. 2015. "The Trauma of Torture and the Rehabilitation of Torture Survivors." *Zeitschrift für Psychologie*.

Hardiman, Rachel. 2009. "En Mal d'Archive: Postmodernist Theory and Recordkeeping." *Journal of the Society of Archivists* 30, 1: 27–44. doi.org/10.1080/00379810903264591.

Hofmeyr, A.B. 2006. "The Meta-Physics of Foucault's Ethics: Succeeding Where Levinas Fails." *South African Journal of Philosophy* 25, 2. doi.org/10.4314/sajpem. v25i2.31438.

Ketelaar, Eric. 2002. "Archival Temples, Archival Prisons: Modes of Power and Protection." *Archival Science* 2, 3–4: 221–238.

Koro-Ljungberg, Mirka, and Maggie MacLure. 2013. "Provocations, Re-un-Visions, Death, and Other Possibilities of 'Data.'" *Cultural Studies, Critical Methodologies* 13, 4: 219–222.

Levi, Primo. 1989. *The Drowned and the Saved*. New York: Vintage Edition.

Lucas, George. 2002. *Star Wars: Episode II – Attack of the Clones*. 20th Century Fox.

Macías, Teresa. 2010. "'On the Pawprints of Terror:' The Human Rights Regime and the Production of Truth and Subjectivity in Post-authoritarian Chile." PhD dissertation, OISE, University of Toronto.

___. 2012. "'In the World': Towards a Foucaultian Ethics of Reading in Social Work." *Intersectionalities: A Global Journal of Social Work Analysis, Research, Polity, and Practice* 1, 1: 1–19.

___. 2013. "'Tortured Women and Hungry Widows': Patriarchal Neoliberalism and the Logic of Compensational Justice in Chile." *Affilia Journal of Women and Social Work* 28, 2: 126–139.

___. 2014. "'Tortured Bodies': The Biopolitics of Torture and Truth in Chile." In *At the Limits of Justice: Women of Colour Theorize Terror*, edited by Suvendrini Perera and Sherene Razack (309–330). Toronto: University of Toronto Press.

___. 2015. "'On the Footsteps of Foucault': Doing Foucaultian Discourse Analysis in Social Justice Research." In *Research as Resistance: Revisiting Critical, Indigenous and Anti-Oppressive Approaches*, second edition, edited by Susan Strega and Leslie Brown (221–242). Toronto: Canadian Scholars' Press.

___. 2016. "Between Violence and Its Representation: Ethics, Archival Research, and the Politics of Knowledge Production in the Telling of Torture Stories." *Intersectionalities: A Global Journal of Social Work Analysis, Research, Polity, and Practice* 5, 1: 20–45.

Matthews, Graham, and Sam Goodman. 2013. "Introduction: Violence and the Limits of Representation." In *Violence and the Limits of Representation*, edited by Matthews Graham and Sam Goodman (1–11). Hampshire: Palgrave Macmillan.

Mignolo, Walter. 2009. "Epistemic Disobedience, Independent Thought and Decolonial Freedom." *Theory, Culture & Society* 26, 7–8: 159–181.

Noys, Benjamin. 2013. "The Violence of Representation and the Representation of Violence." In *Violence and the Limits of Representation*, edited by Graham Matthews and Sam Goodman (12–27). Hampshire: Palgrave Macmillan.

Pelias, Ronald. 2015. "Performative Writing: The Ethics of Representation in Form and

Body." In *Qualitative Inquiry: Past, Present and Future: A Critical Reader*, edited by N.K. Denzin and M.D. Giardina (272–287). Walnut Creek, CA: Left Coast Press.

Razack, Sherene. 2007. "Stealing the Pain of Others: Reflections on Canadian Humanitarian Responses." *Review of Education, Pedagogy, and Cultural Studies* 29, 4: 375–394.

———. 2009. "Racism, Empire and Torture." *Racism Review: Thoughts on Racism, Culture, Society, Politics*, May 22, 2008. racismreview.com/blog/2009/05/22/racism-and-torture/.

Rossiter, Amy. 2011. "Unsettled Social Work: The Challenges of Levinas's Ethics." *British Journal of Social Work* 41, 5: 980–995.

Simpson, Kirk. 2007. "Voices Silenced, Voices Rediscovered: Victims of Violence and the Reclamation of Language in Transitional Societies." *International Journal of Law in Context* 3, 2: 89–103.

Spivak, Gayatri Chakravorty. 1999. *A Critique of Postcolonial Reason: Toward a History of the Vanishing Present*. Harvard University Press.

———. 2010. "Can the Subaltern Speak? revised edition, from 'History' Chapter of *Critique of Postcolonial Reason*." In *Can the Subaltern Speak? Reflections on the History of an Idea*, edited by R. Morris (21–78). Columbia University Press.

St. Pierre, Elizabeth A. 2013. "The Appearance of Data." *Cultural Studies; Critical Methodologies* 13, 4: 223–227. doi.org/10.1177/1532708613487862.

———. 2015. "Refusing Human Being Humanist: Qualitative Inquiry." In *Qualitative Inquiry—Past, Present, and Future: A Critical Reader*, edited by N.K. Denzin and M.D. Giardina (103–120). Walnut Creek, CA: Left Coast Press.

Stanley, Elizabeth. 2004. "Torture, Silence and Recognition." *Current Issues in Criminal Justice* 16, 1: 1–25.

Stirr, Anna. 2014. "Violence, Torture, and Memory in Sri Lanka: Life after Terror." *Journal of Contemporary Asia* 44, 3: 565–567.

Stoler, Ann Laura. 2002. *Carnal Knowledge and Imperial Power: Race and the Intimate in Colonial Rule*. Berkeley and Los Angeles: University of California Press.

———. 2009. *Along the Archival Grain: Epistemic Anxieties and Colonial Common Sense*. Princeton and Oxford: Princeton University Press.

Sumic-Riha, Jelica. 2004. "Testimony and the Real: Testimony Between the Impossibility and Obligation." *Parallax* 10, 1: 17–29. doi.org/10.1080/1353464032000171055.

Sztainbok, Vannina, and Teresa Macías. 2018. "Making Terror Intelligible: Narrating the Scene of Torture in the Southern Cone." *Canadian Journal of Women and the Law* 30, 3: 423–446.

Thapa, Suraj Bahadur, Mark Van Ommeren, Bhogendra Sharma, et al. 2003. "Psychiatric Disability Among Tortured Bhutanese Refugees in Nepal." *American Journal of Psychiatry* 160, 11: 2032–2037.

Tortorici, Zeb. 2018. *Sins Against Nature: Sex and Archives in Colonial New Spain*. Duke University Press.

van Heugten, Kate. 2011. "Registration and Social Work Education: A Golden Opportunity or a Trojan Horse?" *Journal of Social Work* 11, 2: 174–190. doi. org/10.1177/1468017310386695.

Weld, Kirsten. 2014. *Paper Cadavers*. Duke University Press.

Whitehall, Geoffrey. 2013. "The Biopolitical Aesthetic: Toward a Post-Biopolitical Subject." *Critical Studies on Security* 1, 2: 189–203. doi.org/10.1080/21624887.2013.824656.

4

Accountability in Ethnographic Research

Researching the Making of White/Northern Subjects through Anti-Black Racism while Brown

Leila Angod

> Accountability begins with tracing relations of privilege and penalty. It cannot proceed unless we examine our complicity. Only then can we ask questions about how we are understanding differences and for what purpose. (Razack 1998, 161)

As researchers, we negotiate *accountability* in each phase of our work. We may understand *accountability* very broadly as how we address our complicity with relations of privilege and penalty (Razack 1998). When it comes to our methodological decisions in ethnographic research on race, how might racialized researchers enact accountability in research design and data collection? In this chapter I reflect on my research on elite schools to inquire into the methodological dimensions of accountability by way of two ethical dilemmas that make my research and writing possible. These ethical dilemmas emerge at the intersection of the whiteness I am researching, my body as a Brown woman, and the Black South African context of the study. Striving not to resolve these dilemmas, but rather to articulate for myself an ethical pathway through this work by engaging with these tensions, my work has unfolded in the new directions that I share here with you. I will tell you a bit about the context of my study before elaborating on these dilemmas and how my approach to navigating them offers steppingstones for navigating the structural, methodological dilemmas of conducting ethnographic research on race while racialized.

I research elite schools in Ontario in the context of Canadian settler colonialism, imperialism, racial capitalism and white supremacy. I position political and corporate elites as especially implicated in the colonial and capitalist accumulation of capital, leveraged through their direction and management of the seizure of land and exploitation of humans as labour. Elite schools, as training grounds for young elites to occupy these positions of power, are similarly implicated in these processes. Elite schools as fee-based schools with soaring endowments. These schools' elite status resides in the combination of several additional attributes including their status as independent schools, an exclusive admissions process, unique learning experiences, established histories, a predominantly white student body, and curated landscapes (Angod & Gaztambide-Fernández 2019; Gaztambide-Fernández 2009; Gaztambide-Fernández & Angod 2019). Elite schools are important sites for the study of inequality because they are extreme examples of schooling that are directly implicated in the over-resourcing of white settler populations.

My research on this topic has grown from my five years of experience as a social sciences teacher and director of equity and diversity at a southwestern Ontario elite school. Being one of very few women of colour on a predominantly white faculty with a white faculty culture, I never came to feel at home there. Seeking a place where I might put my anti-racism expertise to good use, I became involved with the school's volunteer abroad program, both as a teacher travelling with students, and a designer and facilitator of pre- and post-trip workshops. My five years of experiences provide the impetus for this research. These experiences are a source of insight into the ways in which race is lived and contested in these spaces.

For my study, I established a relationship with a southwestern Ontario elite girls' school to research their volunteer trip to South Africa. For this part of my project, I aimed to uncover what young elites learn through volunteering with Black South African young people. I sought to uncover if and how the volunteers (white and non-Black, racialized students) learned to become racially dominant subjects, and how the school created the conditions for this learning. In researching the making of dominant racial subjectivities, my study turns away from the colonial impetus of research to analyze marginalized communities, instead focusing on how young people engage with the production of racial dominance.

Elite school scholars call this approach to research power "studying up" (Gaztambide-Fernández 2009, 1). Critical whiteness scholars similarly interrogate racial hierarchies by focusing on the workings of white supremacy.[1] My work does both. To turn my attention to Black children in this encounter would have re-inscribed the colonial relations of extraction I was researching. For example, I was unable to communicate with the South African young people in Zulu; I was not part of their community, nor did they invite me to their community.

In this research, two ethical dilemmas emerge. First, in telling a story about the race-making practices of white and racialized, non-Black elite school students, what happens to Black life and presence? Is it enough to tell the story of how young people enact whiteness? Can I do more than story the objectification of Black young people in this encounter? The second ethical dilemma is that documenting anti-Black racism might work best if I don't intervene when it is happening during data collection. This structural dilemma of ethnographic research puts me in a place of complicity as a non-Black woman of colour, not just with white supremacy, but with anti-Black racism. As non-Black women of colour researching race, how might we make sense of an ethical position in the field as we experience the harm of white supremacy while being called to testify for its specific, anti-Black iteration, all while the enactment of racial hierarchies is the very condition of possibility of our research? Thinking with Macías (this volume), what does it mean to be accountable when we are subject to and implicated in the violence of racialization as we research and write about it?

In navigating these dilemmas, I anchor myself in a classic text: after more than twenty years, Razack's (1998) classic book *Looking White People in the Eye* continues to provide us with a critical race feminist framework for enacting a politics of accountability in research, teaching and activism. In inviting us to be guided by a "search for the ways in which we are complicitous in the subordination of others" (159) through sustained attention to co-constitutive, interlocking axes of domination and oppression, *Looking White People in the Eye* is a call to confront a tendency to slide into subordinated positions without addressing how, at the same time, we contribute to the subordination of others. I explore this tendency in the context of being a Brown woman researching racially dominant subjectivities in an imperial encounter that coheres through an anti-Black and settler colonial orientation to South African young people.

To read for and enact a politics of accountability in research and writing, which I strive to do in the following sections, I am guided by three dimensions that are inherent in and/or emerging from Razack's (1998) work. I propose these as methodological underpinnings of a politics of accountability. The first is, drawing on Lowe (2015), sustained attention to the *conjunctions* between categories and geographies. This approach confronts the colonial logics of separation to inquire into the simultaneity of settler colonialism, western European dominance, and exploited African and Asian labour. For me, as a mixed-race, ambiguously Asian (what I call "Brown") woman from the Global North researching a colonial encounter, this has meant attention to how I am invited to participate in the extraction of capitals (material and symbolic) from Black and Indigenous communities in particular through research, at the same time as I am subject to these extractions as a racialized woman. In order to situate the coloniality of these moments of invitation, they must be understood in the context of colonial racial divisions between Black, Indigenous and Asian populations (categories that frequently overlap given the intimacies between these populations), in which the racial tensions between these groups sustain intervention and rule. Drawing from my own context as a Caribbean diaspora person, I am guided in this thinking by Walter Rodney's (1981) analysis of the racial tensions between Black and South Asian communities in Guyana. As an ethical, political and methodological imperative, attention to conjunctions attunes us to how non-Black racialization is constituted in relation to Black, Indigenous and Black Indigenous communities.

The second methodological dimension of a politics of accountability is *vulnerability*. The refusal to slide into positions of innocence, a refusal that Razack urges us to embrace, demands the openness of being vulnerable. In this issue, Sztainbok and Gajardo refer to such a refusal as the *humility* of decentring ourselves as the universal, knowing subject. I trace the tensions of different kinds of vulnerability in this chapter: the vulnerability of being open to learning, of not being the expert, and of reading moments of vulnerability in dominant subjects, for example, when we may observe the fissures in the making of these subjects. Like Sztainbok and Gajardo, I address the tensions of vulnerability as a woman of colour who is continuously evicted from the position of Expert; simultaneously, I refuse this position of dominance as part of a commitment to a decolonial politics of knowledge production, and, as I later address, even leverage this eviction to further my relationships with participants. Vulnerability not only assists us to address the conjunctions of our research; it may also help to create new possibilities, such as *the new human*, which is the third dimension of Razack's (1998) politics of accountability that I explore.

Engaging in a politics of accountability is a continuous reaching towards what Razack (1998) calls *a new subject* rather than an arrival. We might understand this new subject as Fanon's *new human* (I use *new subject* and *new human* interchangeably) who is a different figure from liberal humanism's universal, dominant subject. In Fanon's closing words of *Wretched of the Earth* (2004 [1963]), he directs us towards new figurings of humanity and new futures: "For Europe, for ourselves and for humanity, comrades, we must make a new start, develop a new way of thinking, and endeavor to create a new man" (239). I consider this new subject in her plurality and in contradistinction to subjects, whether white or of colour, who know themselves as racially dominant. How might we methodologically enact a politics of accountability so as to create the conditions for these new subjects to show up on the page?

Following this introduction, I provide an overview of the scholarship that addresses the risks of researching and writing race. Next, I will briefly present the study that I reflect on in this chapter. Following this, I present two critical incidents from my research data to explore the dilemmas that emerge when we attempt to engage in a politics of accountability. I frame these critical incidents in terms of absence/presence and visibility/opacity. My emphasis on seeing is a nod to Razack's (1998) attention to visibility, gaze and looking back in *Looking White People in the Eye*. I close with questions and provocations on the violence of researching and writing race, specifically, in relation to anti-Black racism and white/Northern subjects as a Brown woman in the Global North.

Race, Research and Innocence: A Starting Point

The tensions that I explore in this chapter emerged while carrying out and writing up ethnographic field research. At the heart of these tensions is the representational violence of researching processes of racialization as a racialized woman. In engaging with these tensions, I join a well-established conversation. In particular, scholars of race and colonialism offer sophisticated analyses of these dilemmas. In the introduction to *Scenes of Subjection*, Hartman (1997) discusses the risks of circulating stories of racial violence. In their familiarity and casual proliferation, these narratives effect a distancing from suffering and may yield nothing more than the pleasures of voyeurism and self-reflection, failing to bring Black subjectivity to life. Hartman (1997) asks: how do we not make the violence we narrate "ordinary so that the pleasures of looking, again and again, incite a second order of violence" (16)? At the same time, Hartman and Wilderson (2003) note the risks of narratives that use celebratory counter-narratives to emphasize the agency of dominated groups. These celebratory narratives risk normalizing, and in fact risk helping, the perpetuation of violence against subjugated populations. Alerting us to these risks of narrating race, McKittrick (2014) asks: "How then do we think and write and share as decolonial scholars and foster a commitment to acknowledging violence and undoing its persistent frame, rather than simply analytically reprising violence?" (18). McKittrick points us toward analyses of race that transcend the mere repetition of violence through narration. Simpson (2007) and Tuck (2009) similarly ask what we hope to gain from retelling stories of violence that Indigenous and racialized communities know all too well. Tuck (2009) questions the implicit theory of change of studies that document the violence experienced by marginalized communities, noting that these stories often fall short of effecting the change that we desire. Rather, these narratives often fail to read the violence of colonization as social and historical, instead telling (yet another) story of damaged people.

In the context of today's crises of what language means, what is true, and what is real, with increasing attempts by right-wing students, professors, policymakers, and politicians to both shut down and leverage critical language, this insistence on naming and defining domination may matter more than ever. At the same time, representational violence makes this naming possible, so that research and writing on race is never free from violence (Macías, this volume). Thinking with Razack's *politics of accountability*, I seek to engage with this precondition rather than seek refuge from it through claims to innocence. In order to research and write about race and racialization, then, we are always already implicated in the violence of representation. As I explore throughout this chapter, the entanglement of our bodies in our research shapes the form that this implication takes. How might we make sense of being with these tensions?

The Ethnographic Study

In this chapter, I draw from my doctoral thesis, *Behind and Beyond the Ivy: How Schools Produce Elites through the Bodies of Racial Others* (2015), to explore methodological dilemmas that emerged when conducting the ethnographic component of my study.[2] I studied a Canadian elite girls' school's volunteer trip to South African. The students were between the ages of fifteen and eighteen and in grades 9 to 12. Four identified as non-Black youth of colour (two East Asian-Canadians, one East-Asian international student, and one other mixed-race Canadian student of colour) and four identified as white. The objective of the trip was for the Canadian group to teach basic computer skills to students at a South African township school; I debunk the volunteers' claims to "teaching" in my study (Angod 2015). I theorize the volunteer abroad trip as a colonial encounter in which the Canadian elite school students imagine themselves as doing the work of uplifting Black children. I demonstrate how the students, both Canadian and international, white and of colour, became white/Northern subjects through an extractive, humanitarian relationship with younger, Black children. This is a relationship of extraction in which Black, Indigenous, and people of colour are mobilized for the accumulation of capitals (Fanon 1986 [1967]; Hartman 1997; Said 1979). I travelled with the group, attended pre-trip meetings, and participated in several school activities throughout the academic year, conducting more than 240 hours of participant observation in Canada and South Africa.

My use of the encounter as methodology is indebted to Pratt (1992), Grewal (1996), Ahmed (2000), Razack (2004), and especially Mahrouse (2014), all of whom conceptualize how dominant subjects are constituted through colonial power relations, a process that is raced, gendered, and intensely affective. This methodological approach emphasizes and captures the moves through which colonialisms are lived through the body, with particular attention to race, gender, and class as interlocking axes of power (Hill Collins 1990; Razack 1998), and specifically, the regulatory function of this relationship in terms of managing colonized populations. The colonial encounter is neither plural nor static; as a researcher, I am shaping the encounter as I am being shaped by it, a shaping that takes form, as I explain below, through my embodiment as an ambiguously Brown woman of colour.

I drew from Mahrouse's (2014) study of processes of racialization in transnational solidarity activism and her uses of the term *white/western* to capture the complexities of who is a dominant subject in the context of the Global North. Mahrouse (2014) writes, and I could not agree more:

> [participants'] First World citizenship and the positioning that it affords them nevertheless racialize[s] them as members of the dominant group, though of course, to varying degrees. Moreover, who gets to be defined as or define themselves as white depends on a number of complex and context specific geographic and social histories whereby groups and individuals marked as white in one context may be differently racialized in another. These definitions depend on multiple factors including diaspora and mixed-race identities and experiences, religion, access to mobility, and language facility, to name a few (18).

For BIPOC folks, being read as globally Northern has some whitening effects. Instead of *western,* I changed Mahrouse's formulation slightly to use the term *white/Northern.* I did this to position Canada within the imaginary of the Global North; my choice of the term *Northern* is intended to emphasize how Canada is imagined through northern climates and geographies, whiteness, and civility, linking it with what Razack (2004, 55) calls the "family of civilized nations." While white/Northern also aptly describes other nations that understand themselves as predominantly white and Northern, in this chapter I use this term to describe the racial and civilizational framing of Canada that takes shape in relation to the Canada–United States border, northern European nation-states, Commonwealth nation-states, and Canadian settler colonialism. The category of white/Northern is important for theorizing relationships of power within my study; white and non-white participants were read in various degrees as white/Northern, as was I, as a simultaneously mixed-race (Brown) woman of colour.

In my subsequent work with this data (Angod forthcoming), I further unpack the Canadian national narratives that underpin the North/South encounter, emphasizing the salience of Canadian settler colonialism and anti-Blackness in the volunteer abroad encounter. The North/South hierarchy in my study operates through Canadian and global anti-Black racism, which delineates the category of the human against Black people and Blackness (Dei 2021; Benjamin 2003; Dumas 2016; Walcott 2014,

Warren & Coles 2020). The North/South hierarchy I trace articulates through anti-Blackness. Let's turn to these conjunctions by way of the first critical incident.

Critical Incident #1: Absence/Presence

The situation that I describe here took place during a computer lesson when a white, Canadian elite school student was trying to coax a Zulu girl into using a paint software program in the way that the elite school student felt was appropriate, in other words, in a way that demonstrated learning by way of compliance with instructions. I reconstruct my field notes at some length here to depict the scene:

> Rachel (a white, elite school student) is showing Nandi, a Zulu girl who is perhaps six years old, how to use a paint program with a keyboard and a mouse. Nandi is excitedly talking in Zulu. Rachel writes some words on the screen while Nandi laughs and points to the screen, tracing what's written on the screen with her finger while Rachel continues to draw. Nandi looks at the screen of her friend Lindiwe who sits beside her, also working with an elite school student one-on-one. Nandi clicks the mouse several times. "Okay, stop pressing that button," Rachel laughs nervously while Nandi clicks all over the screen. Rachel holds Nandi by the waist and under her arm. Rachel tries to coax Nandi to look at their screen rather than Linidwe's monitor. Rachel makes a star and tries to show Nandi, "Look! You can make one, too." Nandi is looking at Lindiwe's screen, as well as that of the girl on her other side. Nandi is trying to press all the buttons while Rachel is trying to hold her hands saying, "No! No touching." Rachel places Nandi's hand on the mouse and guides her to draw. This lasts about three seconds. Nandi looks at Lindiwe's screen and points to images of a star and a heart, and then resumes tapping on all the keys. Rachel laughs in an annoyed way telling Nandi, "Okay. Don't press that anymore. Don't press that button anymore. You're not allowed to. Watch me. Look. Don't press that button anymore." Nandi looks at Rachel and smiles. Nandi points at Lindiwe's screen and the two of them have a conversation in Zulu. Rachel draws a star saying, "Whoa, look at that," trying to get the girl on the other

side of her to look at the drawing. Rachel continues trying to put Nandi's hand on the mouse but Nandi pulls it off each time, talking and singing in Zulu, showing little to no interest in the shapes on Rachel's monitor, and then tracing them again with her finger, calling excitedly to her friend, "Lindiwe! Lindiwe!," showing Lindiwe the images on the monitor that she is tracing. The girls laugh in what feels to me to be a mischievous manner, talking and pointing. Rachel is trying to get Nandi to sit on her stool, and then to sit on her lap, telling her to sit up straight. Rachel is clearly frustrated and trying to mask it with a saccharine tone as Nandi resumes pressing all the buttons. "You're clicking them again!" Rachel says in a cutesy voice. "You're so sneaky!"

In the conversations that ensued, the elite school students and teachers interpreted this child's behaviour and similar actions by other children as evidence of "low attention spans." This kind of deficit thinking characterizes understandings of Black, Indigenous and children of colour in classrooms, an understanding that has life-and-death consequences, including school pushout and the school-to-prison pipeline (Ladson-Billings 2006; Patel 2015; Dei, Mazzuca, McIsaac & Zine 1997), and the grossly disproportionate rates at which these communities are brutally killed in police detention. We can read this scenario in terms of Rachel's sustained resolve and kind persistence in a difficult teaching and learning situation with a mischievous child. This is certainly how the elite school group seemed to read this scenario. Rachel becomes the hero of this story. When Nandi's response renders Rachel's move to dominance largely unsuccessful, Rachel reroutes her move to power by reading Nandi's actions as a social, intellectual and psychological deficit. This narrative nourishes the making of white/Northern femininity through helping and uplifting not-yet-civilized children. And, as researchers, we can (and must) engage in the long-standing work to denaturalize this kind of story by making it visible.

One technique for doing this work is to read absent presences in the data. In *Ghostly Matters* (1997), Gordon writes, "understanding [haunting] is essential to grasping the nature of our society and for changing it" (27). Haunting describes what Gordon names *absent presences*, "how that which appears to be not there is often a seething presence" (8). In a resonant fashion, McKittrick (2014) proposes that we read the archives of anti-Black violence "not as a measure of what happened, but as indicators of what else happened" for the purpose of "thinking about and articulating Black absented presences" (22). Gordon and McKittrick teach us this practice of reading for absented presences, for what is not said and what lies behind the text, that which stories of racialized, anti-Black violence cannot tell us. That which the colonial gaze cannot (and must not) capture helps to consolidate this mode of seeing.

To read for absent presences in the interaction between Rachel and Nandi is to read for that which is not intelligible through the colonizing gaze: the clicks, smiles, pointing fingers and Zulu conversation are resistance to being configured as an object for the extractive making of white/Northern subjects. In this reading, we gesture towards Black subjectivity as the refusal to be subjected under the terms of the white/Northern colonizing gaze and guiding hand. Rather than the one-on-one learning structure that is at the heart of initiatives such as One Laptop Per Child, a non-profit organization that aims to provide marginalized children in the Global South with their own laptop, through Nandi and Lindiwe's side-chat (as a form of backchat) they insist on making meaning and theorizing their experiences together. This is one way in which to read the absent presence of Black life in a story of the extraction of social capital for the production of white/Northern dominance. By narrating what the colonizing gaze must not capture in order to cohere, that is, what must remain unseen to the gaze, we uncover the conditions of possibility for white/Northern power through helping. This approach reveals how the old, colonial practice of constituting empowered, feminine subjects has subtly shifted in the context of today's voluntourism. As I show elsewhere, these practices of *assisting Others into modernity* (Razack 2004) are enacted (and obscured) through the language of *love, partnership,* and *social justice* (Angod forthcoming).[3]

I have learned through my ongoing work with this data that this reading practice is insightful in conceptualizing various kinds of subjects. That which fails to bring the dominant subject into being and is not legible under her gaze tells us something important about who this subject thinks she is. At the same time, in order to read the dominant subject and denaturalize her practices of ordering and mastering Others, we must read that which remains invisible in the encounter, namely, in the context of my study, Black subjects. This is a braided reading practice that reads for dominant subjects through how they mobilize marginalized people as objects while remaining attentive to moments when we may bring marginalized subjectivity to the page. This approach both describes and denaturalizes epistemic violence (while enmeshed in the violence of representation), and creates the conditions for two new subjects to come into relief: the South African child[4] and the non-dominant Canadian teen. In the context of my work on white/Northern subject-making processes, part of being mired in the logics of the racial hierarchies that I am researching means that I can only gesture to new subjectivities, both in terms of who else these elite school students might be and who the South African children are as subjects. However, this gesturing, as the dimension of Razack's (1998) politics of accountability that *reaches beyond* current subjectivities, is crucial to the methodological pursuit of accountability.

Nandi emerges as a young person who pushes against Rachel's casting of her as an object of obedience and control. In reading how Nandi engages with this encounter through resistance and refusal, I leverage my double-edged representational tools to bring her subjectivity into relief; at the same time, however, I cannot come close to capturing the wholeness and fullness of Nandi as a subject. However, what I can offer is a trace of Nandi's presence on the page; without psychologizing or closing my reading of Nandi as a subject, in McKittrick's (2014) words, this offering of a trace is one way for me to do more than *reprise the violence* of this encounter.

Politically, ethically and pedagogically for the reader, I strive to create these traces and pathways so that, while I am describing the violence of race, whiteness does not take up all the space as the whole the story. It is important to me as a race scholar to do more than tell the story of whiteness in my work and how Nandi's subjectivity is elided through a humanitarian encounter of extraction, even when I am researching and writing about white supremacy. I strive to do this work by attempting to bring Nandi into relief and by gesturing to an alternate subject position for the elite school group (what it would mean to not be racially dominant in this encounter, although this would require the group not to be in South Africa in the first place). This reading demands accountability both of the elite school group and me.

I wish to illuminate the contours of this racially dominant subject to help create space around her in which new ways of being and becoming may breathe and take form. Part of this work is accounting for the vulnerability of those moments in which elite school students waver in their enactment of racial dominance. While the group tended to be confident in their readings of the South African children and adults they encountered, there were moments when their subject-constituting process wavered. While my data suggest that elite school students of colour went through nearly the same process of becoming dominant as the white elite school students, it is important to note that the sole questioning of race and class that was expressed to me was from students of colour (Angod 2015). Additionally, it was students of colour who voiced the comments that approached critique, such as the awkwardness of "ten foreigners standing behind you" in the computer lab, and the "ego boost[ing]" nature of the encounter.

I must also acknowledge the limits of my data about the elite school students; I cannot depict this racially dominant subject in her entirety. It is possible that the young people in my study were simply unwilling to share their hesitations and questions with me, perhaps because they had concerns about their teachers and school administrators finding out that the students had questions about what they were doing. It might also have been too unsettling to seriously consider these questions by saying them out loud. Or, these students may simply not have given the issue much thought. What I can do with the data I have, however, is to presume that some doubt existed for these students.

Perhaps, then, there is an opportunity for the elite school students to slip through the cracks of this white/Northern subject-making process, to dwell in these fissures, and to access portals to other ways of being with racialized Others that do not involve an extractive encounter such as this one. This slipping through the cracks would require the elite school students to have some awareness of Canadian anti-Black racism at home and abroad for the accumulation of white/Northern social, emotional and economic capitals. It would also require a vulnerability and humility of being in relationship with Others in ways where Others are valued as equally human, rather than for mastering Others and our/ their differences. All of this awareness requires some vulnerability on my part, in that I am not claiming to have all the ends neatly tied, of being the all-knowing Expert. This awareness brings me to the other subject position that takes shape through my research and writing and which I touched on above: me as a woman of colour researcher.

Critical Incident #2: Visibility/Opacity

Like Sztainbok and Gajardo in this volume, I am visible as well as opaque both in the field and on the page. By *visible* I mean that my presence is known, and by *opaque* I mean that I am denied the position of the all-seeing, all-knowing Universal Subject at the same time as I refuse this position as part of an approach rooted in decolonial theory, critical race theory and women of colour feminisms. I am not an innocent interloper in the process of racialization I am studying, nor am I the objective and transparent subject of the text I am writing. In addition to leveraging tools of representation as I have been describing to tell an incomplete story, I am shaping the encounter as I am shaped by it. The tensions of my ambiguous position, both ascribed and claimed, mark my experience in the field, my data and my writing. This ambiguity is a familiar one as a mixed-race woman of colour; I am read in different ways in different contexts.

In the ethnographic part of my study, I am simultaneously partially whitened by my Canadian passport (that is, my citizenship status within a white settler colonial nation-state), English language/Anglo-Canadian accent, affiliation with University of Toronto. I am interpellated as a student and non-autonomous, non-adult by the Canadian elite school teachers. And I am read as a Brown woman outsider by the elite school group, and a Brown woman insider by South Asian elites at the local elite school with which the group partnered. As a whole, travelling on a Canadian passport and as an academic researcher had some whitening effects for me and enabled me to travel with the elite school group at the same time that I am/was also racialized as an ambiguously Brown woman.

In terms of researching race while being racialized I was not generally regarded by the elite school group as a person who had a right to know. For example, this meant being read as untrustworthy and a threat to the experience of the group of elite school students. As a Brown/Northern woman watching white and racialized/Northern girls and women watching Black South African children, the elite school teachers suspected and challenged my gaze. While I had some power as a Northern researcher affiliated with a respected research university, as well as five years' experience as a former elite school teacher and administrator, I was a graduate student, and I was repeatedly made to know this by the teachers in charge of the group. At the same time, my status as a researcher at a Canadian university heightened participants' uneasiness about what I might be seeing and reporting back, an uneasiness that was accentuated by my being an institutional outsider to the school group, although I have some degree of elite school affiliation as a former elite school teacher. Certainly, while my Canadian passport, university funding, and overall academic privilege enabled me to be in that encounter, not sharing the whiteness of the teachers elevated my outsider status and rendered my gaze more suspect.

This dynamic is familiar in that as a woman of colour, I am frequently not being regarded as someone who is knowledgeable or who has a right to know. For example, following the trip to South Africa, the elite school teachers made a formal complaint to the school administrators who organize these programs, saying that it was a burden to have an additional person to be accountable for on the trip. In other words, I wasn't regarded as someone who adds value, but rather someone who, like the students, must be taken care of. This ejection from the category of autonomous adulthood, or, infantilization, has clear racial and colonial underpinnings (see Sintos Coloma 2016 for an analysis in the Filipino context of American imperialism). Taking their cues from the teachers, the students read me through this lens and interacted with me as a peer with whom they shared stories about dating, their feelings about their school and teachers, etc. In some ways, this eviction from the category of Knowing Subject created possibilities for the students to confide in me as a perceived younger person and in so doing, my visibility and opacity as a Brown woman both foreclosed and opened pathways for the research.

I was simultaneously in the power position of studying the group, framed as somewhat of a risk by embodying a gaze that was not to be trusted, at the same time as I did not stake out any claim to being the Subject Who Knows and was strategically evasive about what I was observing. Being watched in an encounter was uncomfortable for everyone, especially for the white/Northern subjects-in-process. While visiting one South African township school, a white Canadian elite school teacher asked me, "Are you getting good data? I'm thinking about everything through your eyes." While it is unclear how this teacher imagined my gaze, the anxiety suggested by this comment is important and demonstrates how my gaze is suspect in that I may interpret and report things about the group in an unfavourable light. My presence, and my presumed gaze, actively shaped the voluntourism encounter. I observed this anxiety several times throughout the trip, learning to take field notes after the fact, and responding to another teacher who wanted reassurance that the work they were doing "was good, wasn't it?" I awkwardly dodged this question, a reflex that only seemed to increase participants' anxiety that my gaze was not to be trusted (see Razack 2000, 186 on "the inevitable duplicity of people of colour").

While I did not recognize this awkward dodging of the question as a methodological choice at the time, I suggest that it is productive to recognize such moments as ways to engage (or not) in a politics of accountability. Certainly, this looks different in elite school research of over-privileged populations versus when conducting research with marginalized communities. Can we be vulnerable with our racially dominant research participants and share our observations about the processes of racial becoming in which we are engaged in order to interrupt them as they are taking place? Or does the vulnerability reside in being okay with being the outcast who is not to be trusted, the Brown woman without a right to know, whose gaze is not reliable? My decision to dodge these questions distanced and helped protect me from research participants who I ultimately found to be hostile. Additionally, this decision gave me ongoing access to participants' observations. My critique, shared with the school in a report, was deferred until I was no longer dependent on the hospitality of my research participants.

These are the structural parameters of ethnographic research that ask for our compliance: as women of colour researching race we are caught between the harm of experiencing racism during our work and the harm of allowing racism to unfold uninterrupted as we navigate our precarious and tentative place as guests. This is precisely the methodological bind that I experienced in the following scenario.

During the trip, at times I was witness to "just us" conversations among white elites (parents and other adults involved in the trip) and at other times I was witness to similar "just us" conversations among South Asian elites. While these individuals were not participants in my study, they shaped the elite school students' context. Certainly, my shifting racialization as a mixed-race Brown woman, combined with my Northern capital and university researcher status, seemed to help this sliding back and forth between being Brown and being whitened by Northerness and class privilege. Where these conversations converged was on the topic of anti-Black racism, for example, the affirmative action admissions policies in South African universities that aim to correct the systemic under-representation of Black students. White and South Asian youth and adults expressed anti-affirmative action views while I was in the room; they wished to restrict the admission of Black students using a framework of ability, thus creating more spaces for non-Black students to be admitted.

Economic class privilege correlates with whiteness and greater academic achievement (Parekh, Brown & Robson 2018). A small, Black South African elite notwithstanding, ability-based arguments further privilege white and wealthy groups. While recent Black-led, anti-colonial student protests have confronted the institutionalized whiteness of South African universities (South African History Online n.d.), these institutions have a long road ahead to address institutionalized anti-Blackness.

With both white and South Asian elite parents, the conversation centred on the inordinate stress experienced by non-Black students given the affirmative action admissions policies to recruit Black students. These conversations never took place with Black people in the room. One white South African man described his oppression in terms of being "in the minority as an English-speaking white male." A white woman spoke of the stress of retaining her wealth and privilege on stolen land in South Africa and how she kept various passports and foreign currency handy, knowing that she may have to leave with a moment's notice. There seemed to be a fear and resentment of being displaced, a fear of losing what was rightfully theirs.

I felt harmed by the white supremacy that I witnessed and was subjected to during this study, and this took an emotional toll. At the same time, by saving my voice for the page rather than questioning those around me, how am I participating in white supremacy and anti-Blackness? Is it enough to retain my opacity as a shield in the field, document the violence, and save my critique for when I cannot be harmed by those involved in the study? Does an interjection even make a difference?

At the time of the study, I didn't feel I had the capital to ask questions that undermined dominant subjects' presumed right to be in African space and regulate Black bodies. And I didn't know how much more of their racism I could manage. Complicating things further, I understood my role in participant observation as that of a being non-disruptive presence. Given all of these considerations, I chose to save my critique for the page. My small contribution to denormalizing and unhinging anti-Black racism is in documenting it and writing other subjects into my research narratives.

Given this structural bind of ethnographic research on race, if we choose visibility during research instead of opacity, as racialized researchers of race we might interject in these moments, questioning those we encounter in order to interrupt and contest their racism, and documenting the process. Can we fail spectacularly at white femininity and still be granted access to these spaces as researchers? What happens if we are bad and ungrateful guests? At the very least we can write about failure and ejection.

Throughout my work, I strive to fashion the author as subject, the woman of colour that I offer to readers. In navigating vulnerability, conjunctions, and the new human (the non-dominant subject), part of my reaching for a politics of accountability is to make my presence visible in the text as someone grappling with this work. Because I know for myself that encountering Black, Indigenous and women of colour writers who strive for a politics of accountability helps to ground, orient and animate me. Accordingly, part of my work is to leave this trace for others to find, a trace that might assist other researchers to find their own way.

Final Thoughts

Given the structural and institutional conditions in which we operate as academics, many of us find ourselves in the position of invaders and imposters. Doing this work of accounting for racial violence and being visible by speaking about and against it is, to say the least, hard. Given these conditions, and in light of the ways in which we are invited to testify for white supremacy and anti-Black racism, how do I ethically enter into this triad of Brown researcher, white/Northern elite school students, and Black South African host community? Is an ethical position possible?

I have been suggesting that an ethical position is one that strives for a politics of accountability where this politics demands that we confront how we are simultaneously heir to/complicit with and/or penalized by systems of domination and oppression. A politics of accountability refuses to let violence be normalized, even and especially when our very presence is enmeshed in that violence.

Notes

1. For the second wave of critical whiteness studies that identifies the limitations of dominant approaches and engages with critical race theory in the context of white teacher identity formation, see Jupp & Lensmire (2016), Tanner (2017), and Kempf (2020).

2. My thesis as a whole theorizes the racialized and gendered process of constituting elite subjects at Canadian elite schools. I show that whiteness is integral to elite status and that becoming white (a process that all elite subjects, both white and of colour, must pass through) is at the heart of elite school programs and policies for multiculturalism and humanitarianism. I demonstrate how these institutional initiatives, whose stated objective is the creation of national and global leaders, sell whiteness. People of colour are relegated to the sidelines of elite schools, whether as beneficiaries of aid or as the foci of diversity discussions in the curriculum (Gaztambide-Fernández 2009), while whiteness remains crucial to consolidating the elite status of schools and subjects.

3. The slipperiness here is *not* to make oppression okay by narrating agency (Hartman & Wilderson 2003). There are risks to telling both the story of violence and the story of resistance against it. However, as I have been arguing, both stories are intertwined, necessary, and never free from representational violence.

4. The dilemma that this child, like all South Africans in this encounter, are not the focus of my study (since I was studying how white/Northern subjectivity mobilizes the children in townships as objects), and I did not have approval from the Research Ethics Board at my university to collect data about these children. That these children were not participants in my study was by design on my part; given that I had no prior relationship with them and could not communicate with them in Zulu, I did not feel that there was any way to include these children as participants that was not colonial and that would not contribute even more harm than that caused by the foreigners' presence. Still, I insist on the importance of these children having a presence as subjects in my work; I strive to narrate the violence of the encounter in a way that tells the story of Black subjecthood.

References

Ahmed, Sara. 2000. *Strange Encounters: Embodied Others in Post-Coloniality.* London: Routledge.

Angod, Leila. 2015. *Behind and Beyond the Ivy: How Schools Produce Elites Through the Bodies of Racial Others.* Doctoral dissertation, University of Toronto, Toronto, ON. hdl.handle.net/1807/69729.

___. Forthcoming. "Learning to Enact Canadian Exceptionalism: The Failure of Voluntourism as Social Justice Education." *Equity & Excellence in Education.*

Angod, Leila, and Rubén Gaztambide-Fernández. 2019. "Endless Land, Endless Opportunity: The Coloniality of Elite Boarding School Landscapes in Germany, the United States, and Canada." *Zeitschrift für Pädagogik (Journal for Pedagogy* 65, 2: 227–241.

Benjamin, Lorna Akua. 2003. "The Black/Jamaican Criminal: The Making of Ideology." ProQuest Dissertations Publishing.

Dei, George J. Sefa. 2021. "Foreword." *Curriculum Inquiry* 51, 1: 1–14. doi.org/10.1080/03626784.2021.1847533.

Dei, George J., Josephine Mazzuca, Elizabeth McIsaac, and Jasmin Zine. 1997. *Recon-*

structing 'Dropout': A Critical Ethnography of the Dynamics of Black Students' Disengagement from School. Toronto: University of Toronto Press.

Dumas, Michael J. 2016. "Against the Dark: Antiblackness in Education Policy and Discourse." *Theory Into Practice* 55, 1: 11–19. doi.org/10.1080/00405841.2016.1116852.

Fanon, Frantz. 1986 [1967]. *Black Skin, White Masks,* translated by C.L. Markmann. New York: Grove Press.

____. 2004 [1963]. *The Wretched of the Earth,* translated by R. Philcox. New York: Grove Press.

Gaztambide-Fernández, Rubén. A. 2009. *The Best of the Best: Becoming Elite at an American Boarding School.* Cambridge: Harvard.

Gaztambide-Fernández, Rubén, and Leila Angod. 2019. "Approximating Whiteness: Race, Class, and Empire in the Making of Modern Elite/White Subjects." *Educational Theory* 69, 6: 719–743. doi.org/10.1111/edth.12397.

Gordon, Avery. 1997. *Ghostly Matters: Haunting and the Sociological Imagination,* second ed. Minneapolis: University of Minnesota Press.

Grewal, Inderpal. 1996. *Home and Harem: Nation, Gender, Empire, and the Cultures of Travel.* Durham: Duke University Press.

Hartman, Saidiya. 1997. *Scenes of Subjection: Terror, Slavery, and Self-Making in Nineteenth-Century America.* New York: Oxford University Press.

Hartman, Saidiya V., and Frank B. Wilderson III. 2003. "The Position of the Unthought." *Qui Parle* 13, 2: 183–201.

Hill Collins, Patricia. 1990. *Black Feminist Thought: Knowledge, Consciousness, and the Politics of Empowerment.* Boston: Unwin Hyman.

Jupp, James C., and Timothy J. Lensmire. 2016. "Second-Wave White Teacher Identity Studies: Toward Complexity and Reflexivity in the Racial Conscientization of White Teachers." *International Journal of Qualitative Studies in Education* 29, 8: 985–988.

Kempf, Arlo. 2020. "If We Are Going to Talk About Implicit Race Bias, We Need to Talk About Structural Racism: Moving Beyond Ubiquity and Inevitability in Teaching and Learning About Race." *Taboo: The Journal of Culture and Education* 19, 2: 114–132. digitalscholarship.unlv.edu/taboo/vol19/iss2/10.

Ladson-Billings, Gloria. 2006. "From the Achievement Gap to the Education Debt: Understanding Achievement in U.S. Schools." *Educational Researcher* 35, 4: 3–12.

Lowe, Lisa. 2015. *The Intimacies of Four Continents.* Durham: Duke University Press.

Mahrouse, Gada. 2014. *Conflicted Commitments: Race, Privilege, and Power in Transnational Solidarity Activism.* Montreal: McGill-Queen's University Press.

McKittrick, Katherine. 2014. "Mathematics Black Life." *The Black Scholar* 44, 2: 16–28.

Parekh, Gillian, Robert S. Brown, and Karen Robson. 2018. "The Social Construction of Giftedness: The Intersectional Relationship Between Whiteness, Economic Privilege, and the Identification of Gifted." *Canadian Journal of Disability Studies* 7, 2: 1–32.

Patel, Leigh. 2015. *Decolonizing Educational Research: From Ownership to Answerability.* New York: Routledge.

Pratt, Mary Louise. 1992. *Imperial Eyes: Travel Writing and Transculturation.* New York: Routledge.

Razack, Sherene H. 1998. *Looking White People in the Eye: Gender, Race and Culture in Courtrooms and Classrooms.* Toronto: University of Toronto Press.

____. 2000. "'Simple Logic': Race, the Identity Documents Rule and the Story of a Nation Besieged and Betrayed." *Journal of Law and Social Policy* 15: 181–209. digitalcommons.osgoode.yorku.ca/jlsp/vol15/iss1/6.

___. 2004. *Dark Threats & White Knights: The Somalia Affair, Peacekeeping, and the New Imperialism.* Toronto: University of Toronto Press.

Rodney, Walter. 1981. *A History of the Guyanese Working People, 1881–1905.* Baltimore: Johns Hopkins University Press.

Said, Edward. 1979. *Orientalism.* New York: Vintage Books.

Simpson, Audre. 2007. "On Ethnographic Refusal: Indigeneity, 'Voice' and Colonial Citizenship." *Junctures: The Journal for Thematic Dialogue* 9: 67–80.

Sintos Coloma, R. 2016. "Becoming a Problem: Imperial Fix and Filipinos under United States Rule in the Early 1900s." *Postcolonial Directions in Education* 5, 2: 241–264.

South African History Online. n.d. "Student Protests in a Democratic South Africa." sahistory.org.za/article/student-protests-democratic-south-africa.

Tanner, Samuel Jaye. 2017. "Permission to Be Confused: Toward a Second Wave of Critical Whiteness Pedagogy." *Journal of Curriculum and Pedagogy* 14, 2: 164–79. doi.org/10.1080/15505170.2017.1297745.

Tuck, Eve. 2009. "Suspending Damage: A Letter to Communities." *Harvard Educational Review* 79, 3: 409–427.

Walcott, Rinaldo. 2014. "The Problem of the Human: Black Ontologies and 'the Coloniality of Our Being.'" In *Postcoloniality – Decoloniality – Black Critique: Joints and Fissures,* edited by S. Broeck and C. Junker (93–105). University of Chicago Press.

Warren, Chezare A., and Justin A. Coles. 2020. "Trading Spaces: Antiblackness and Reflections on Black Education Futures." *Equity & Excellence in Education* 53, 3: 382–398. doi.org/10.1080/10665684.2020.1764882.

5

Racialized Discourses

Writing against an Essentialized Story about Racism as a Practice of Ethics

Harjeet Kaur Badwall

> Only when we come to be very clear about how race is lived, in its multiple manifestations, only when we come to appreciate its often hidden epistemic effects and its power over collective imaginations of public space, can we entertain even the remote possibility of its eventual transformations. (Alcoff 2002, 267)

This chapter[1] is concerned with the ethics of knowledge production when conducting research on racial injustice. I specifically examine the ethical dilemmas that arise from the assumptions that constitute insider/outsider debates in research, specifically the assumptions about sameness within communities. I make the argument that assumptions about sameness, essentialism or universality pose significant risks to research that negate an examination of interlocking oppressions and the different ways racialized people experience white supremacy and racism. I contend that the assumptions shaping insider research are at risk of effacing power differences between researchers and participants by assuming sameness and consequently producing an assumption about innocence on the part of researchers. The discussion draws upon my research, in which I interviewed twenty-three racialized[2] social workers in Toronto, Canada, about their encounters with racism in the workplace. The study focused on the ways in which racialized workers negotiate professional practice within a white-normed profession, with a specific emphasis on the ways in which racial injustice manifests in everyday social work.

I am a racialized woman of colour and at the time of the study, I was also a practising social worker who had experienced many encounters similar to those shared by the participants. I entered the research with an understanding that I could not escape my own histories and relationships to whiteness, racism and social work. My multiple subject-positions were in the room and did not live outside of the interviews with the social workers. Instead, during the interviews with the participants, our subject-positions and complicated histories of racism were dependent upon each other in documenting the narratives about whiteness and racism and social work. Upon reflection, many years later, I question the assumptions that shaped the interdependent relationship across our narratives. What did this dependency hinge upon to create a larger narrative about dominance in social work? Did the interdependent relationships across the narratives rely on assumptions of insider-ness or sameness? Or did they come together around a shared goal to counter white supremacy in social work?

Although the workers and I shared experiences of racism, I could not assume "sameness," nor could I adopt an authentic voice about how "we" (racialized social workers) negotiate the violent terrain of everyday racism. I agree and support that foundational, shared experiences can be shaped by intimate connections to communities of belonging across ethnicity, race, culture and common experiences of marginalization (Chavez 2008; Dywer & Buckle 2009; Fisher 2015), but, I also attempted to follow Scott (1992) who cautions that identity (and experience) are contested terrains in which multiple and conflicting ideas will operate. It was critical that I paid attention to the similarities, but also the differences between the participants. In this research, this analysis meant that I attempted to write against a single story about racism or an essentialized representation about how race is experienced by racialized communities.

I begin this chapter with a background on the study and briefly discuss my theoretical frameworks for the research with a focus on the significance of race research to address issues of power and materiality. Next, I present literature on insider–outsider debates in research that aim to complicate and disrupt the binary between insiders and outsiders. Finally, I examine the importance of intersubjectivity and reflexivity when conducting insider–outsider research. My hope is to contribute to a larger discussion about the research ethics involved when our work attempts to function as a counter-narrative to domination. How do we engage the political project without simplifying and universalizing how communities negotiate and resist injustices? This chapter is interested in complicating our assumptions about insider research.

Background of Research

My research examined how workers' narratives about racism rupture and serve as counter-narratives to hegemonic practices of whiteness that run in and through social work knowledge production about its values and practices. Social workers participated in semi-structured, qualitative interviews that explored social work values, practices and their experiences with racism in the field. Of concern were their encounters with racial violence in everyday practice moments with white clients and the lack of support from co-workers and managers in the organizations where they worked. The stories shared by participants describe intense and complex forms of racism. The workers shared narratives telling how white clients would refuse to work with them, utter racist comments toward them, and in some situations, used physical violence (Badwall 2014). Furthermore, co-workers and managers offered very little professional support, which often resulted in no action. The participants' stories reveal the ways in which social work values of helping, empathy and client-centred practice silence the operation of white dominance and collude with racism. It was important to me to share these stories in a manner that exposed practices and structures of white dominance in social work while at the same time demonstrating the complex and multiple relations of power between workers and the communities that they engage. I purposefully traced the ways that racism was made invisible in these organizations through various discourses and practices of whiteness. In addition, I wanted to know how institutional whiteness remained centred in the exact moments that racial violence was dismissed.

To gain this understanding, I had to understand how white dominance in social work was historically established through "helping discourses" (Heron 1999; Valverde 1991) and look for the ways in which the desire to be "good" and "moral" remain intact in contemporary social work education and practice. Therefore, my research explored how social work values and practices are historically produced through colonial constructions of whiteness that define not only who the social worker is, but also how they are to perform (Jeffery 2002). The research revealed a troubling paradox: social work values committed to social justice ideals are at risk of colluding with everyday practices of racism (Badwall 2014). In the contemporary, colonial continuities remain intact through our desires to be "client-centred," empathic and critically reflexive (Badwall 2014). The research illustrates how racialized social workers cannot be seen as good workers, because when they name ra-cial violence in the workplace, they cannot maintain the profession's im-peratives to be client-centred and empathic. The participants' narratives reveal stories of overarching dominance in addition to the specificity of how racism takes place in everyday practice. The narratives shared by the workers required a methodology for analysis that explored the dis-cursive production of white dominance and also the materiality of racial injustice.

Stories about racism are discursively codified to allow certain nar-ratives about racism to be told and not others (Razack 2004). Razack argues that deconstructing narratives requires "separating the experi-ences of individuals from the way their stories are assembled for our consumption" (18). In other words, what do certain stories "do"? What are the taken-for-granted assumptions that underlie truth claims in our stories? How might uneven relations of power between researchers and participants assemble knowledge production? These questions invite an analysis that moves away from naturalizing certain claims and instead pays close attention to how discourses are assembled and organized through complex practices of power. Linking Razack's argument back to my research, I looked closely at the signifiers within the narratives that produced certain understandings about the dominant values and practices of the profession. Some of these signifiers included words such as helping, social justice, empathy, care, and so forth. However, I also understand Razack to be arguing that the signifiers are never outside of power and practices of domination. Therefore, discourses of helping, care and empathy signify particular forms of authority in social work through white femininity and I examined their moralizing and regula-tory effects on the professional practices of racialized workers.

Similarly, Carter (2000) argues that we need to move beyond an anal-ysis that examines the construction of differences to include the ways in which very specific discourses are "contested, reproduced or resigni-fied" (49) by certain subjects. He contends that we must examine who is doing the contesting or resignifying. The analysis of discourses cannot solely examine the role of language in the production of social reality, but must also examine how discourses inform the material conditions that shape social reality (Hook 2001). Carter (2000) contends that we must pay attention to the ways in which discourses produce material conditions that socially mark bodies: "How we present ourselves physically, and how our physical, corporeal self is interpreted by others, is, to a greater or lesser extent, a product of the ways in which our subjectivities are determined by various moral technologies" (29).

The analysis of racism and the operation of whiteness in this research could not be divorced from the ways in which societal norms are produced through visual markers of difference (Alcoff 2002). In this sense, subject-positions are personified through a set of power relations that are predicated upon notions of civility and degeneracy (Goldberg 1993), in which the body is made by power (Butler 2005). The material effects on differently racialized communities are varied, as "Difference is imprinted on bodies in uneven ways, with very real material consequences for those that emerge as bodies working outside of hegemonic normalcy" (Voronka 2016, 193). When the participants in the study told stories of white clients refusing to work with racialized workers, I avoided an analysis that viewed these events as unusual or infrequent or the actions of a few "bad" individuals. Instead, I situated these events within moralizing scripts of civility, where people of colour do not signify the normalized identity of the social worker in their professional settings. The work of race scholars assisted me with questions of method and analysis to shape a non-essentializing engagement with the data while, at the same time, to write a complex story about racism. However, the practice of conducting the research invited dilemmas that I did not expect. Most of the time, these dilemmas were shaped by my investments in telling a particular tale about racism and I realized that I could not escape my own assumptions about "insider-ness."

Insider–Outsider Innocence: Dangers of Universalism

Frankenberg (2004) argues that all research is situated, and researchers require a reflexive engagement about how they are positioned within a study. She states that the position of the researcher must be accounted for, as there is no objectivity "or an all-seeing glance" (106). My subject-positions as a social worker (at the time of the study) and as a racialized Brown woman needed attention during the research process. The analysis of the data evoked questions about the ways in which my multiple subject-positions (race, gender, class, sexuality, age, education and language) were influencing the conversations with participants and the interpretation of the data (Fine 1994; Foster 1994; Frankenberg 2004).

The social workers I interviewed identified feelings of urgency and relief in talking about the racism they were experiencing. For some, the interview was the first time they were disclosing stories about the racist environments in which they were employed. During the interviews, I recalled the moments in which I felt connected to participants, when there was an assumption of shared experience. In other moments, disconnection would appear when a participant was describing an understanding of racism that was outside of my frames of reference. It was not until I began reading the transcripts that I became aware of the specific moments in which my own reactions may have shaped the unfolding of the storylines within the research. I was also a social worker in a counselling role at the time of the interviews, conscious of my practices as a researcher slipping into a counselling response, and I wondered if the participants also expected this of me. The stories being shared were emotionally dense and, although I did not enter a formal "counselling" role, I was aware that my roles as researcher, counsellor, and racialized person were blurred and overlapping. Looking back, I question how my (and the participants') assumptions about insider-ness influenced the stories about social work and racism. I also question how these assumptions both aided and potentially limited the analysis.

Considerable literature has been written about the insider–outsider debates in research (Chavez 2008; Fine & Vanderslice 1992; Greene 2014). Insider research has been simply defined as the study of one's own social group or society (Naples 2003, as cited in Greene 2014). Many assumptions circulate in the literature about the ease with which "insiders" may conduct research with their communities. These assumptions include ideas about possessing pre-existing knowledge, understanding the emotional and psychological precepts of participants, creating more nuanced insights, and assumptions about safety and trust (Chavez 2008; Fisher 2015; Greene 2014). Some have also argued that insider research aims to "support political action to highlight injustice and inequity" (Fisher 2015). Insider research relies upon the notion of "lived experience" as truth, authority and political will — designed to counter the ways in which "othered" communities have been treated as objects of study in western, hegemonic epistemologies (Voronka 2016, 190).

The usefulness of insider research is connected to the importance of marginalized communities conducting research that challenges domination as a political project. Shared experiences between researchers and participants may strengthen political action that supports resistance practices and movements against domination. When writing against domination and injustice, narratives of shared experiences can serve to trace the historical and present-day constitution of violence as well as practices of resistance. In this study, the workers were negotiating racism across their cultural, social and political histories, as well as negotiating professional institutions of social work practice. These factors contributed to the specificities surrounding the ways in which multiple forms of racism infiltrated their work lives. Furthermore, there exists an embodied experience of racialization (Alcoff 2002).

Although individual subjects have varied meanings about racialization and its negotiation, embodiment is critical to insider research, largely because our world continues to be assessed through colour-lines (Alcoff 2002). Consequently, very real material effects can take place for racialized people (Carter 2000; Hook 2001). For example, in my study, social workers' responses to racial violence were influenced by long and complicated histories of racism in their lives. Therefore, racial violence, both inside and outside of social work, shaped the meanings that workers attached to these encounters. It was important to illuminate these factors and not dilute their influence. There is great value in exploring shared experiences among equity-seeking groups. Participant narratives in my study brought into focus forms of racial violence in social work that had not been previously acknowledged in social work education, in particular, racism from client populations in social work practice (Badwall 2014). Insights from this research raise serious questions about social work education and its collusion in structural and everyday racism. Therefore, insider research has the potential to bring awareness to various forms of domination that contribute to larger narratives of systemic violence and marginalization. However, we cannot assume that insider-ness is a straightforward or stable process. Problematic assumptions may circulate within these discourses about who is an insider and who is an outsider. Oftentimes, essentialism is espoused (Bettez 2014). To complicate insider–outsider relations, I turn to the work of scholars such as Bettez (2014) and Greene (2014), who theorize these relations across a complex continuum of identity-making processes.

One of the grand ideas promoting insider research is sameness between researcher and participants (Chavez 2008). Assumptions may circulate among insider group members about shared characteristics or homogenous understandings about how racism is defined, lived and resisted. Furthermore, these assumptions can raise questions about the ethics involved in our research. Mainly, that the assumptions shaping insider research are at risk of effacing power differences between researchers and participants by assuming sameness and consequently producing an assumption about innocence on the part of researchers. The assumptions about sameness and innocence produce risks to research that result in evading an interlocking analysis about how racialized violence is a deeply shaped historical condition that is also embedded in other forms of subject making. My study examined the ways in which racialized discourses are shaped by an interlocking analysis of power, committed to examining how various forms of violence "help to secure one another" (Razack 1998, 13). An interlocking analysis explores how subject-formation and practices of domination are never outside of one another, but instead depend on one another. This analysis does not suggest that all forms of violence are equal; on the contrary, what matters is their specificity, but also relationship to one another. In my research, this analysis meant that I attempted to write against a single story about racism or an essentialized representation about how race is experienced by racialized communities. My challenge was to pay attention to the complexity of different forms of racism, multiple whiteness projects and their relationship to other forms of violence (gender, class, etc.), while at the same time, not diminishing a larger narrative about racial injustice.

I also stand with racialized scholars who speak about our complicity in power when producing knowledge (Angod in this volume; Macías 2012: Sztainbok & Gajardo in this volume). These scholars remind us that research from the north is laced with colonial practices of data collection, categorization of communities, and extraction of knowledge. Because research is shaped by practices of categorization, it is imperative that we look closely at how we are organizing and co-creating the data with the communities we consult. Hence, a commitment to ethical research practices is a political commitment (Macías 2012) to denaturalize the operations of violence (Sztainbok & Gajardo in this volume), while also documenting racialized violence and demanding accountability from dominant groups (Angod in this volume). While power relations can shape research, my engagement with ethics points to the dangers of assuming a view towards innocence on the part of researchers when we are writing, analyzing, living out similar stories of injustice as the participants in our research projects. Therefore, my cautionary notes about insider research point to the ways in which assumptions about innocence and sameness may silence the complexity of the narratives being shared by participants.

Universalizing understandings of race and racism fail to examine the ways in which race is socially produced differently amongst Indigenous, Black and racialized communities. Insider research may also blur the historical specificities of racism across different communities, and the fluidity of racial meanings within communities (Alcoff 1991, 182). Although my theoretical entry points into the research were grounded in post-structuralism, I was not immune to the seductive promises of insider-ness in research. I was at risk of assuming that participants shared a global meaning or understanding of how racism effects communities. Furthermore, I could not rest comfortably on an assumption that our shared subject-positions (as racialized social workers) and "experience" guaranteed comfort for the participants. There may have been moments of connection and shared understanding, but they were not stable or consistent.

The workers interviewed for this study embodied a diversity of subject-positions across gender, class, sexuality, immigration status and age. Each of these differences needed attention to understand how they intersected with each other in their narratives. Furthermore, these narratives were also influenced by the social and historical context of the workers' lives. The participants, depending on their ethno-cultural subject-positions, experienced racism differently. I needed to give attention to the differences across anti-Black, anti- Indigenous, anti-Brown or anti-Asian racisms. These differences were very much a part of the meaning making those participants shared about their encounters with racism in professional settings. Social workers who identified as new immigrants had a different set of challenges about racial oppression than workers who were born in Canada or had lived here for many years. For example, participants who identified as new immigrants described situations in which their competency was continually questioned due to the presence of an "accent" when they spoke. In one situation, a male immigrant social worker was eventually fired from his job due to minor mistakes in his case notes and he was told that he did not have enough Canadian experience. In another example, a Black social worker described situations in which their competency was constantly questioned by white clients. In this worker's narrative, their manager "shadowed" them on the job, making sure they were performing optimally but framed this support as "help" and looking out for this worker. Looking back at this example, years later, I wonder how this worker's narrative also gives voice to larger forms of anti-Black racism. I wish I had explored with the participant the specificity of identifying as a Black worker and how ongoing anti-Black racism was shaping their experience of this workplace. There were also key differences across the institutional practice settings in which the workers were employed. For example, how racism was expressed in smaller grassroots organizations was different from the ways in which it was expressed in hospitals or school boards where larger bureaucracy and professionalism influenced its operation. Therefore, the institutional context was strongly present within their narratives about what constitutes good, competent professional practice. The differences in workplace settings also provides us with an understanding of how white supremacy and racism are organized differently. In other words, we must also examine the complexities that shape dominance.

Participants' narratives were not singular accounts of racism (Britzman 2003), but as Henderson (1994) states, they were constituted through a simultaneity of discourses in which their speech and practices included the discursive arrangements of many other voices, ideas and values. Bettez (2014), drawing on the work of Puar (2007), uses the term assemblage to denote a collection of subject-positions that shape partial and unfinished positionalities (4–5). Bettez argues that researchers need to critically reflect on the various assemblages that constitute identity making so that we may pay attention to difference between researchers and participants. Bettez (2014) asserts that a reflexive engagement with our multiple subject-positions can minimize "potential tendencies to essentialize others and ourselves and maximize our awareness of multiplicities of difference, particularly as they relate to structures of oppression" (5). Drawing on Razack (2004) and Carter (2000), I would add that attention to differences is linked to relations of power between researchers and participants in which knowledge production is codified to tell some stories, and perhaps not others.

My assumed insider-ness revolved around shared experiences of being a racialized social worker. I entered the research assuming "we" spoke a similar social work language — this was untrue. There were great variances across our understandings about social work. For example, participants who had graduated from their education over thirty years ago drew on ideas that are quite different from the dominant anti-oppressive, critical discourses of more recent graduates. On reflection, these concerns were also true about my own shifting positionalities (Greene 2014) as researcher, cis-woman, and racialized social worker; I had to reflect on the moments when I was deeply affected by stories of racism or when my responses were shaped by my social worker positionality or that of a researcher, etc. Therefore, insider-ness is not a fixed or static state of being (Chavez 2008; Trowler 2011) and our shifting subjectivities are never complete, but partial and in an ongoing state of "becoming" (Bettez 2014). I agree with Chavez (2008), who argues that we are partial insiders and partial outsiders, as our subjectivities are dependent on varying contexts and histories.

As researchers working on race and racism, are we at risk of creating a hierarchy of racism in which certain forms of racial violence are prioritized in our research over other forms, based on our own histories and frames of reference? The ethical considerations for writing against a single, essentialized story about racism serve to talk back to the colonial foundations of research that position researchers as speaking with "authentic" voice or becoming unproblematized representatives of the issues they are exploring (Sztainbok & Gajardo, this volume). Denaturalizing the operations of dominance and oppression requires that we engage with the contradictions and tensions within our analyses and commit ourselves to examining ambiguity in our research, as a political act.

The Third Space: Intersubjectivity and Reflection

Dwyer and Buckle (2009) propose the notion of the *third space* between the insider–outsider binary. They advocate for "a dialectical approach that may explore the complexity of similarities and differences" between researchers and participants (60). The third space, according to the authors, is a site in which "paradox, ambiguity, and ambivalence" can take place (60) and researchers can engage as a part of the research process. Contradictions and uncertainties can bring into focus our assumptions about sameness as "insiders." The third space opens an exploration of the many ways we can be insiders and outsiders in relationship to the research process. Engaging the third space also allows for the exploration of difference or points of disconnection. For example, my own biases regarding cultural competency models became apparent when interviewing a participant who was very invested in these approaches. For them, the antidote to institutional racism was education on culture. The third space would allow me to explore the tensions with this narrative. I could examine why cultural competency was important to this participant, in addition to raising questions about my doubts or uncertainties or why cultural competency was limited. In other words, I did not have to take an either/or positioning within the body of the research, but instead I could explore a space that could open up debates and questions about cultural competency or how we resist and negotiate racialized discourses.

Holloway and Jefferson (2000) argue that narratives are a site of "intersubjectivity" (44) in which the production of storylines is a mutually constitutive process. I expected that certain biases, differences and shared experiences of racism would shape my exchanges with the participants and my interpretations of these exchanges. Young (2004), drawing on Reinhartz (1997), suggests that our multiple selves (i.e., race, gender, class, sexuality, age) as researchers can influence the dynamics of research at any given time, whereby "respondents and informants may react to any of these in ways that foster, hinder, or dramatically affect the research" (191). Therefore, the researcher and participants are in a mutually constitutive relationship in which the researcher is also a co-participant (Chavez 2008, 476). However, the mutual constitution of the research relationship is not devoid of power relations. As researchers, we have the power to interpret the research and present the overarching narratives in ways that participants may not possess. Attention to ethics as political action requires researchers to examine the relationship between the reader and the text, as well as the power that is enacted in knowledge production (Macías 2012, 3).

I engaged the research interviews as narratives and storylines. Davies (2000) states that the discursive production of subject-positions is formed through jointly produced storylines that are "organized conversations and around various poles such as events, characters, and moral dilemmas" (93). The idea that researchers are also co-participants is an important alternative to positivist research that assumes researchers are objective and stable. In efforts to support inter-subjectivity, I made the decision to be interviewed for the research and my narrative is included among the stories analyzed. Although accounts from my narrative are dispersed minimally throughout the research, the decision to include my storyline was motivated by an understanding that my subject-position(s) were influencing the interpretation of the data.

The decision to include my narrative was also motivated by a commitment to remain critically reflexive on power relations during the research process and carefully engage the various ways in which my insider–outsider status informed the theoretical entry points and the interpretation of the interviews. The role of the researcher can re-inscribe relations of dominance. There is no innocent knowledge on the part of the researcher. Therefore, I emphasized my own multi-vocality and sought to avoid reinscribing an authentic voice for all racialized people. In this sense, not only was I speaking with and to the narratives provided by the participants, but I was also speaking with my own multiple narratives as well. However, I was neither speaking as an objective outsider looking in nor as a "knowing insider," but instead as a multifaceted subject whose stories and analysis were informed by many socially and historically produced discourses. This commitment to complexity was not simple or straightforward. And I can see now many years later that there were many gaps in the interpretation of the narratives. Reflexive practices can offer some support, but we cannot "fully see" the data, especially because the reflective process is individualizing. This process of reflexivity can only offer partial insights into the ways in which our diverse narratives co-construct meaning, especially where tensions exist across the meaning making, we prescribe to these events.

During the process of facilitating the interviews, I kept a journal to keep track of the reactions and assumptions that I experienced following each meeting. The reflective journal highlighted to me the production of tensions and questions I experienced, especially to the stories of racialized violence or assumptions about identity making. The journal also supported me to examine the messy examples when my values or understanding of the narratives differed from the participants. The goals of reflection should not support self-indulgence or transcendence. Hamden, drawing on Pillow, argues that reflexivity as a practice should push researchers toward sites of unfamiliarity and discomfort and issues a call for "a positioning of reflexivity not as clarity, honesty, or humility, but as practice of confounding disruptions" (Pillow 2003, as cited in Hamden 2009, 381). The notion of confounding disruptions is valuable towards our commitment to ambiguity in research, as it provides a space to question our assumptions and trace the social and historical influences that shape our ideas. This act of disrupting is strongly on the side of de-essentializing our work on violence.

While there are common themes about racism present among my interviews with social workers, adding my own narrative challenged me to purposely look for sites of tension and differentiation about how racism is experienced by racialized communities and its operations. It was ethically important to avoid marking my encounters with racism as the definitive signs of how race is experienced. Although my narrative functioned as a reflexive tool (as disruption) in the interpretation process, it did not fully resolve power imbalances (Heron 1999). The power afforded to me as a researcher was maintained insofar as I determined the selection of the accounts and my interpretation (however complex) shaped how participant narratives appeared in my writing. The overall presentation of the study was determined by my role as a researcher, in which I had "the power to reinterpret and hence authorize the experiences and voices of others in ways that may clash or not resonate with the lived experiences they seek to explore" (Britzman 2003, 38). This position was unavailable to the participants of this study; there was no site of innocence that could rescue me from the ways in which my subject-positions as a researcher, social worker, and racialized person operated throughout the formation of the research. I remain concerned with this practice and have questions about how researchers can reduce harm in our interpretation of narratives. Although gaps will exist, and while I did not produce stable and fixed understandings of racism, I still argue that the decision to include my own narrative was important to the process and to fostering a reflexive relationship about the power knowledge axis in our research.

Conclusion

Recognizing a multiplicity of voices, truths and subject-positions means we cannot examine the operation of racialized discourses in ways that fix their expression or denote authenticity. In this chapter, I have explored the assumptions underlying insider–outsider research projects. I have explored what is useful about insider research, along with the ethical risks of homogenizing the experiences of insider groups in our work. The focus of this chapter has not been to establish a position strongly for or against these approaches, but instead to highlight some cautionary notes. I suggest that there is no stable or innocent place to stand when we are creating research and inevitable risks are involved. Our commitments to ethical practices dictate that we seek out and create methods that reduce the potential of harm. This chapter is a reflective account of how I negotiated these concerns during the research.

The movement away from fixed truths about oppression can invite worries about how to make particular truth claims. In some respects, my worry about how to speak to dominance was alleviated by Valverde's (2004) reassurance that we do not have to abandon truth telling in our efforts to examine the production of discursive subject-formation, but we "can consider the possibility that there are many different practices of truth telling and, therefore, many different kinds of selves, and that these can easily coexist, even in the same person" (73). However, I also consider the intervention of Dixson and Rousseau (2005), who state that although there is no one voice for people of colour, "there is a common experience of racism that structures the stories of people of colour" (11).

Our choices as researchers will inevitably influence a dominant storyline within the body of our research. What we include and leave out is directly related to relations of power and our values, histories and subjectivities (Hamden 2009, 379). I end this chapter following Humphrey (2013), who states that the aim in our work is to become risk-aware as opposed to risk-averse, given the impossibility of eliminating risks (Humphrey 2013, 582). Although we cannot resolve all dilemmas fully, the practice of seeking and addressing them can be movement towards ethical practice.

Notes

1.   This chapter is an updated version of my article "Racialized Discourses: Writing against an Essentialized Story about Racism," *Intersectionalities: A Global Journal of Social Work Analysis, Research, Polity, and Practice* 5, no. 1 (2016): 8–19.
2.   The term racialized reflects Indigenous, Black and people of colour.

References

Alcoff, Linda. 1991. "The Problem of Speaking for Others." *Cultural Critique* 20: 5–32.
____. 2002. "Towards a Phenomenology of Racial Embodiment." In *Race*, edited by R. Bernasconi (267–283). Oxford, UK: Blackwell.
Badwall, Harjeet Kaur. 2014. "Colonial Encounters: Racialized Social Workers Negotiating Professional Scripts of Whiteness." *Intersectionalities: A Global Journal of Social Work Analysis, Research, Polity, and Practice* 14: 1–23.
____. 2016. "Racialized Discourses: Writing against an Essentialized Story about Racism." *Intersectionalities: A Global Journal of Social Work Analysis, Research, Polity, and*

Practice 5, 1: 8–19.

Bettez, Silvia Christina. 2014. "Navigating the Complexity of Qualitative Research in Postmodern Contexts: Assemblage, Critical Reflexivity, and Communion as Guides." *International Journal of Qualitative Studies in Education*, 1–23. Advance online publication. doi.org/10.1080/09518398.2014.948096.

Britzman, Deborah. 2003. *Practice Makes Practice: A Critical Study of Learning to Teach.* New York: State University of New York Press.

Butler, Judith. 2005. *Giving an Account of Oneself.* New York: Fordham University Press.

Carter, B. 2000. *Realism and Racism: Concepts of Race in Sociological Research.* London, UK: Routledge.

Chavez, Christina. 2008. *Conceptualizing from the Inside: Advantages, Complications, and Demands on Insider Positionality.* Qualitative Report 13, 3: 474–494.

Davies, Bronwyn. 2000. *A Body of Writing, 1990–1999.* Walnut Creek, CA: AltaMira Press.

Dixson, Adrienne, D., and Celia K. Rousseau. 2005. "And We Are Still Not Saved: Critical Race Theory in Education Ten Years Later." *Race, Ethnicity and Education* 8, 1: 7–27.

Dwyer, Sonya Corbin, and Jennifer L. Buckle. 2009. "The Space Between: On Being an Insider-Outsider in Qualitative Research." *International Journal of Qualitative Methods* 8, 1: 54–63.

Fine, Michelle. 1994. "Distance and Other Stances: Negotiations of Power Inside Feminist Research." In *Power and Method: Political Activism and Educational Research*, edited by A. Gitlin (13–35). New York: Routledge.

Fisher, Karen T. 2015. "Positionality, Subjectivity, and Race in Transnational and Transcultural Geographical Research." *Gender, Place & Culture* 22, 4: 456473.

Foster, Michele. 1994. "The Power to Know One Thing Is Never the Power to Know All Things: Methodological Notes on Two Studies of Black American Teachers." In *Power and Method: Political Activism and Educational Research*, edited by A. Gitlin (129–146). New York: Routledge.

Frankenberg, Ruth. 2004. "On Unsteady Ground: Crafting and Engaging in the Critical Study of Whiteness." In *Researching Race and Racism*, edited by M. Bulmer and J. Solomos (104–118). London, UK: Routledge.

Goldberg, David. 1993. *Racist Culture: Philosophy and the Politics of Meaning.* Malden, MA: Blackwell Publishers.

Greene, Melanie J. 2014. "On the Inside Looking In: Methodological Insights and Challenges in Conducting Qualitative Insider Research." *The Qualitative Report* 19: 1–13.

Hamden, A. 2009. "Reflexivity of Discomfort in Insider–Outsider Research Education." *McGill Journal of Education* 44, 3: 377–404.

Henderson, Mae Gwendolyn. 1994. "Speaking in Tongues: Dialogics, Dialectics and the Black Woman Writer's Literary Tradition." In *Colonial Discourse and Post-Colonial Theory*, edited by Williams, Patrick, and Laura Chrisman, 269–280. London: Routledge.

Heron, Barbara. A. 1999. "Desire for Development: The Education of White Women as Development Workers." Unpublished doctoral dissertation, Ontario Institute for Studies in Education, University of Toronto.

Holloway, W., and T. Jefferson. 2000. *Doing Qualitative Research Differently: Free Association, Narrative and the Interview Method.* London, UK: Sage.

Hook, Derek. 2001. "Discourse, Knowledge, Materiality, History: Foucault and Discourse Analysis." *Theory and Psychology* 11, 4: 521–547.

Humphrey, Caroline. 2013. "Dilemmas in Doing Insider Research in Professional Education." *Qualitative Social Work* 12, 5: 572–586.

Jeffery, Donna. 2002. "A Terrain of Struggle: Reading Race in Social Work Education." Unpublished doctoral dissertation, Ontario Institute for Studies in Education, University of Toronto.

Macías, Teresa. 2012. "'In the World': Toward a Foucauldian Ethics of Reading in Social Work." *Intersectionalities: A Global Journal of Social Work Analysis, Research, Polity, and Practice* 1, 1: 1–19.

Pillow, Wanda. 2003. "Confession, Catharsis, or Cure? Rethinking the Uses of Reflexivity as Methodological Power in Qualitative Research." *International Journal of Qualitative Studies in Education* 16, 2: 175–196.

Puar, Jasbir K. 2007. *Terrorist Assemblages: Homonationalism in Queer Times*. United Kingdom: Duke University Press.

Razack, Sherene H. 1998. *Looking White People in the Eye: Gender, Race, and Culture in Courtrooms and Classrooms*. Toronto, ON: University of Toronto Press.

___. 2004. "Those Who 'Witness the Evil': Peacekeeping as Trauma." In *Dark Threats and White Knights: The Somalia Affair, Peacekeeping and the New Imperialism* (15–39). Toronto, ON: University of Toronto Press.

Reinharz, Shulamit. 1997. "Who Am I? The Need for a Variety of Selves in the Field." In *Reflexivity and Voice*, edited by Rosanna Hertz. India: Sage Publications.

Scott, Joan. 1992. "Experience." In *Feminists Theorize the Political*, edited by Judith Butler and Joan Scott. Taylor & Francis.

Trowler, Paul. 2011. "Researching Your Own Institution: Higher Education." *British Educational Research Association*. March 31. bera. ac. uk/researchers-resources/publications/researching-your-own-institution-higher-education.

Valverde, Mariana. 1991. *The Age of Light, Soap and Water: Moral Reform in English Canada 1880s–1920s*. Toronto: McClelland and Stewart.

___. 2004. "Experience and Truth Telling in a Post-Humanist World: A Foucauldian Contribution to Feminist Ethical Reflections." In *Feminism and the Final Foucault*, edited by D. Taylor and K. Vintges (67–90). Urbana, IL: University of Illinois Press.

Voronka, Jijian. 2016. "The Politics of 'People with Lived Experience' Experiential Authority and the Risks of Strategic Essentialism." *Philosophy, Psychiatry, & Psychology* 23, 3–4: 189–201. doi.org/10.1353/ppp.2016.0017.

Young, Jr., A.A. 2004. "Experiences in Ethnographic Interviewing About Race." In *Researching Race and Racism*, edited by M. Bulmer and J. Solomos (187–202). London, UK: Routledge.

6

Mad Epistemologies and Maddening the Ethics of Knowledge Production

Brenda A. LeFrançois and Jijian Voronka

> Mad methodology resists rote positivism and defies the cult of
> objectivity; it listens for ghosts, madpeople, outcasts, and dis-
> embodied voices that trespass, like stowaways, in modernity;
> it perceives the expressive potential in the so-called rants and
> raves of madpeople; it is poised to find message within messi-
> ness and philosophy within "pathology"; and it respects the pe-
> culiar vantage points of those who are askew. Whereas ration-
> alists tend to discredit and depoliticize the madperson, a mad
> methodology centers that madperson within projects of critique
> and liberation. (Bruce 2017, 306)

In this chapter, we disrupt the typical approach to studying "mental illness" within both medical and social science research. The dominance
of biomedical epistemological assumptions within mainstream psy system (Rose 1990) research into madness urgently requires interrogation,
as do the resultant oppressive and ethically questionable forms of knowledge production, knowledge transfer, and service models that it creates
and perpetuates. Committed to social justice approaches to meaning
making, we proffer a Mad Studies and Critical Disability Studies–informed mad theory as methodology, which centres mad epistemologies
and where mad people[1] and mad cultural production occupy its analytical core. The process and practice of maddening research, however
emancipatory on some levels, is not wholly devoid of many of the issues
of power and privilege that saturates social justice informed researchers'
concerns about ethics. The possibilities and the problems are numerous

and we approach this chapter as not providing definitive and exhaustive answers to the thorny issues surrounding psy politics, mad epistemologies, and the ethics of knowledge production, but instead to open up the conversation about anti-sanist and anti-racist research ethics.

We come together for the writing of this chapter as mad activist academics and critical social work educators. Our overall aim is to provide a Mad Studies and Critical Disability Studies lens, informed by transnational feminist, critical race and postcolonial theories to the conversation of power and the ethics of knowledge production in "mental health." We hope that this lens will serve to broaden the methodological and ethical conversations that typically take place within social work and other social science disciplines. Our approach here is one that embraces an ethics of unruliness, which is subversive through its focus on maddening research and unsettling the dominance of the (white) academy as the hegemonic source of knowledge production. Arguably, Mad Studies, at its most maddening and unruly, serves to resist normalcy and disrupt the dominant sanist and racist definitions of madness typically used in "mental illness" research whilst calling into question enlightenment notions of rationality (Mills & LeFrançois 2018). It also calls out and disrupts the very processes and methods of producing those neoliberal knowledges that aim to contain, cure and profit from those deemed mad. Accordingly, it is armed with this subversive and activist stance that we engage in this meditation on the ethics of knowledge production and the maddening of research.

Maddening Ethics

This chapter flows in ways that mirrors Foucault's body of scholarship. As his early work does, we attend to the current social processes that identify abnormality and take action on difference through practices of normalization (both materially and discursively). As we expand in this section, we show how mental illness epistemes dominate research production and re/create subjugation through hermeneutic injustice. In this way we explore how "society creates people as particular sorts of subjects, for the particularity of individuals depends on the disciplinary apparatus(es) to which they are subjected" (Frank & Jones 2003, 182). Yet Foucault's later scholarship attends to how people create their own possibilities for subjectivity (Foucault 1994). This includes the freedom to forge resistant identities and counter knowledge against the defining norm of Reason. We expand on the ways in which the (always) unstable production of mad subjectivity, epistemology and methodology offers a radical rupture (Foucault 1990) in thinking about the ethics of research and knowledge production through a maddening of such practices. In this way, we show the dominance of current regimes of truth that dictate sanist logics, as well as what transgressive potential mad praxis offers when applied to research/ethics.

In *Force of Law*, Derrida (1990) brings us to a discussion of ethical decision making, after having been accused of elaborating a method of deconstruction that has nothing to contribute to ethics. Here, he argues that it is in the suspended moment prior to making a decision — what he calls a moment of madness — where justice lives. It is in this moment when engaging in ethical decision making that all decisions are necessarily impossible, until they are made. It is in this suspended moment, in this altered state of mind, that all ethical (im)possibilities may be deliberated, even the many unheard-of impossibilities. And yet, for Derrida (1990), this moment is devoid of rules, of logic, of Reason, of rationality, but instead is characterized as a moment of suffering, of torment, of suspense, of anxiety, of irruptive violence, and is a (terrifying) ordeal. However, it is also the only moment from which radical transformations and social justice may begin to take place and which demands taking political and ethical responsibility. Ethics cannot follow rules or formulas, but instead necessarily involves a continuous singularity of decision making taking place through and in madness. Although we question Derrida's (1990) omitting to deconstruct the dominant notion of *madness,* we nonetheless take up his theorizing of decision making as inherently contingent, unstable, and lacking in rationality. So much so that in applying it to the context of research, we suggest that any ethical decision making is always already mad and marked as unruly, despite attempts by positivists to render research ethics as a stable, rational, universal and objective process. As we shall see, however, this mad unruliness does not imply, support, nor belie claims to innocence on the part of mad research(ers).

We elaborate an ethics of unruliness that we understand to have emerged from the margins as a critique of and resistance to simplistic rule-based normative ethics, which focuses on rational, logical understandings of universal ethical rules and which dominate social science and medical research. It is important to consider that the term *unruly* contains a multiplicity of meanings that are important for our purposes here. Moreover, as a term it is unstable, indeterminate and polysemic. For instance, *unruly* may imply to be without rules or to reject formulaic, predetermined or universal laws. From a perspective of (forced) psychiatric treatment, to be unruly may imply the refusal to be controlled, managed, regulated and governed, including resisting and out-rightly refusing treatment. At the same time, and also of reclaimed importance in our analysis, the psychiatric gaze deems mad people as unruly in the sense of being read as "unstable," "disordered," "unpredictable," violent, dangerous and lacking in rationality. From an activist perspective, to be unruly may imply civil disobedience, rebelliousness, recalcitrance and a refusal to be ruled. Regardless of the context, unruliness always contains the suggestion of acceptance of the disorderly or an adamant refusal to follow orders. Writing in the context of literary theory and ethical criticism, Zalloua calls for an ethics of the unruly that embraces its "ungovernable character" (2014, 2) and does not try to harmonize contradictions by instead "exploring their productive tensions" (2014, 3). Indeed, for us, an ethics of unruliness in the context of social science research is not to be confused with allowing for misrepresentation of research participants. Instead, it argues for a radical departure from the urge to make mad subjects both knowable and governable, or to *make sense* of that which cannot and should not be reduced to the rationalist's desire for uniformity, consistency, universality and conformity to the dominant logics of the sanestream.

With this departure in mind, like Derrida (1990), we reject purely rule-based formulaic understandings of ethics, including, for our purposes here, those ethical rules outlined by research ethics boards that eschew any deeper meditation on the unknowns, the messiness, and the "madness" of ethical decisions in research contexts. Although we must always comply with those rule-based approaches to gain approval to conduct research, our understandings must necessarily move beyond such tidy and simplistic approaches and grapple with — or bask within — the disorderliness and unruliness inherent to instances of ethical dilemmas, as well as questions of what constitutes benevolence and maleficence in the moment of each of its encounters. In addition to rejecting these western ethical formulae, the ethics of unruliness also calls for a decolonial commitment to unveil and disrupt colonial ways of knowing — and colonial ways of making the other knowable — in order to open spaces for that which is unspeakable within western epistemes. We take issue with Derrida's lack of commitment to anti-colonial and anti-racist theorizing and actions, and attempt here instead to combine his thinking on ethics with a commitment to deconstructing the violence of colonialism and racism.

This ethics of unruliness links somewhat with Sztainbock and Garjado's (in this volume) exposé of Anzaldúa's ethics of ambiguity. Here there is a "call to be an epistemic dissident," where decoloniality is centred and where there are moves "toward the possibility of generating undisciplined and undomesticated knowledges that value speaking with and from 'wild tongues'" (Anzaldúa 2007 [1987], cited in Sztainbok and Gajardo, this volume) . Hence, what we are ultimately proposing is the maddening of ethics that is recalcitrant, unruly, uncontainable, disorderly, unstable, ungovernable and resistant to rule-based definition, whilst obstinately defying and eschewing dominant neoliberal, colonialist and positivistic/racist understandings of knowledge production about madness.

Mainstream Psy System
Research & Epistemic Injustice

The mental health industry continues to grow and operate based on knowledge produced within the psy system (Gorman & LeFrançois 2018). The psy system comprises not just biomedical psychiatry but also all allied disciplines that adhere to and practice biomedical psychiatric understandings of madness (LeFrançois, Beresford & Russo 2016; Rimke 2016) and that serve to govern and control individuals and populations (Rose 1990). These psy politics, for the most part, argue that madness is an illness that must be treated primarily with psychotropic drugs and sometimes also with electroshock. The dominant knowledges that the psy system produces gained authority and achieved its privileged position from modern biogenetic psychiatry's insistent association with medicine, despite the weak scientific evidence base, the lack of physical markers of disease, and the lack of objective tests for diagnoses — all which radically distinguishes psychiatry from medical science (Burstow 2015).

The attempts of psychiatry to gain acceptance, authority and power through science is further evident in its historical attachment to scientific racism and the role it played — and in many ways continues to play — in propagating colonial logics. Scientific racism and psychiatry both emerged through a common history and their ongoing articulation continues to be intertwined (Howell 2018). The scientific explanation and expansion of the notion of the "normal curve," for example, has reproduced hierarchies of power by constituting psychiatrically disabled people as abnormal (Campbell 2009; Chapman 2014; Davis 1995). These hierarchies of privilege and subordination intersect with other "abnormal markers" based on socially constructed notions of race, gender, class, sexuality, disability and age, leaving the unmarked white mind and body holding the superordinate position (Gorman & LeFrançois 2018). The scientific racism that dichotomized white bodies as superior and racialized others as primitive and inferior was the main doctrine that fueled imperialist gains and justified the violence of colonialization (Césaire 1972; Fernando 1992; Tuhiwai Smith 1999). Thus, as Bruce notes, "any critical investigation of madness and modernity must confront the matters of blackness and antiblackness in the foundation of modern Reason" (2017, 304).

Psychiatry as a science developed within the context of these socio-scientific epistemologies that allowed colonizers and slave traders to assert racist ideologies labelled as the benevolent goals of masters in their supporting of "primitive peoples" who were understood as lacking in self-control and rational thought (Fernando 1992; Gorman & LeFrançois 2018). The colonial project used the scientific method as a racist tool to make *the other* knowable from the perspective of white authority, which also includes psychiatric authority. And yet initially, psychiatry and its colonial scientists found very low incident of "mental illness" amongst those who were colonized (Cohen 2014; Fernando 2014; Fernando 1992; Oda, Banzato & Dalgalarrondo 2005), allowing some to argue that it is the experience of being in captivity that protected colonized people from "mental illness" (Fernando 2014), a discourse that validated the vested capitalist interests of the colonial project. The slave trade was then directly bolstered by psychiatry when it named runaway slaves as suffering from the "mental illness" called "drapetomania" (Bruce 2017; Chrisjohn & McKay 2017; Kanani 2011; Fernando 2014; Fernando 1992). Psychiatry then further psychopathologized Black slaves as being resistant and lazy due to the mental illness "dysesthesia aethiopica" (Adjei 2016; Bruce 2017; Chrisjohn & McKay 2017), a disease that was said to be more prevalent after emancipation and once they were without the "protective factor" of white care and authority (Fernando 2014).

Cures for these "mental illnesses" in slaves included strenuous outdoor manual labour and whipping (Chrisjohn & McKay 2017; Jackson 2002), again clearly reinforcing the capitalist colonial agenda.

With the success of classifying and treating unruly colonized people thus, and with the continued reliance on scientific racism, psychiatry continued to diagnose racialized and colonized people at higher rates and with varied forms of "mental illness," to the point where they became and continue to be grossly overrepresented within mental health services in the Global North (Cohen 2014; Fernando 1992; Fernando et al. 2012; Gorman & LeFrançois 2018; Metzl 2009; Voronka 2013). Indeed, Chrisjohn & McKay (2017) note that current capitalist interests intertwine with the (pseudo) scientific psy agenda of diagnosing Indigenous peoples in Canada with disorders characterized as personal defects, in order to circumvent addressing the inhumane and oppressive consequences of dispossession and continued settler colonialism.

With this historical attachment to the scientific method, it is not surprising that current research within the mental illness industry is most wholly quantitative, with randomized controlled trials being understood as the gold standard in the field (Beresford 2009; Donskoy 2015; Fernando 2014; Fischer 2010). In this way, mad bodies are made knowable from the perspective of (white) psychiatric authority in that mainstream mental illness research plays a leading role in the formation of regimes of truth that govern madness. In this process, people deemed mad are subjected to the objectifying forms of codifying behaviours read as abnormal and disabling, as well as the testing of biochemical reactions aimed to eradicate such forms of human difference. From a social justice perspective, these methodological adherences are at best ethically questionable and at worst oppressive. This is the case not just for mad research subjects undergoing scrutiny and experimentation (Burstow 2016), but perhaps more importantly for the large number of psychiatrized people who are subjected to the resultant practices within mental health services and other interconnected programs within the psy system, all of which are informed by the mental illness research industry.

Not only are these methodological adherences within mainstream mental illness research violent and sanist (Meerei, Abdillahi and Poole 2016; Poole et al. 2012), they rely on and reproduce a form of epistemicide (Mills 2013; de Sousa Santos 2012) or epistemic injustice (Donskoy 2015; Fricker 2007; 2010; Leblanc & Kinsella 2016) that remains hidden as it both erases and reshapes identity of mad subjects. Always assuming a pathological view of madness, deemed as an illness rooted in the brain, the mental illness research industry may be understood as sanist in its denial of social and structural causes (Leblanc & Kinsella 2016) of mad thoughts, behaviours, and feelings. Mad people's own explanations of their experiences are mostly subjugated when they do not conform to pathological and biogenetic perspectives (Donskoy 2015). Mad people of colour's explanations of their experiences are held as especially suspect, as racist stereotypes of irrationality or "feeble-mindedness" (Fernando 2014) reproduce and mutually constitute sanist stereotypes of irrationality (Bruce 2017). We question this obsession with the concept of rationality and the ways in which it is used by the powerful, including the capitalist state and its institutions, to dominate and subjugate those deemed mad and/or *othered* through colonization and systemic racism. Marking bodies and minds as ir/rational is a violent tool that also enables and legitimizes sane-identified peoples' refusal to try to understand or to simply disallow for alternative forms of meaning making that do not follow the narrow articulations of logic (Burstow 2015) that are ultimately based on hegemonic, positivistic, Eurocentric, racist/colonialist notions of Reason (Bruce 2017) and scientific epistemology. Indeed, Bruce (2017) observes: "The fact is that far more modern violence has been perpetrated under the aegis of Reason than committed by rogue madmen and madwomen" (307).

Both Donskoy (2015) and Leblanc & Kinsella (2016) elaborate on Fricker's (2007; 2010) analysis of epistemic injustice, as testimonial injustice and hermeneutic injustice, by applying these notions to the mad community as well as to mad subjects in the context of research and knowledge generation. Leblanc & Kinsella (2016) indicate: "The subjugation of Mad persons' experiences raises questions concerning power and knowledge, in particular, what constitutes valid knowledge(s), who are the legitimate knowers, and whose knowledge should count?" (60). This subjugation is made possible through testimonial injustice whereby stereotypes of mad people are directly set into motion as not just irrational, but also as intellectually inferior, untrustworthy, untruthful, lacking in credibility, lacking insight and downright dangerous (Leblanc & Kinsella 2016) and whose perspectives — if they are even able to be articulated — are necessarily biased, subjective, anecdotal and unrepresentative (Donskoy 2015). As Gorman (2017) succinctly summarizes, "the mad person in Western representation is read through the 'aesthetic of absence' — as the quintessentially nonconscious" (310).

In addition, subjugation through hermeneutic injustice includes more indirect systemic prejudices at play at structural levels, which remains more difficult for the mad community to point to and make intelligible (Leblanc & Kinsella 2016), despite the very real and harmful experiences it produces in everyday life. Lack of access to modes of interpretation, platforms to be heard, and the ability to be understood, along with the dominance of medical discourse that bars other interpretations of madness, are encapsulated within the experience of hermeneutic injustice for mad subjects. Hermeneutic injustice produces the subjugation and dismissal of mad theory and other forms of mad knowledge production because they do not conform to and rely on dominant psy system hermeneutic resources.[2]

And yet, epistemic injustice as it is experienced by those deemed mad has been understood by neither mainstream nor social justice–oriented researchers as being a "profoundly damaging ethical wrong" (Leblanc & Kinsella 2016, 72). Instead, the direct views and analyses of mad subjects continue to be rarely solicited within mental illness research while mad subjects continue to be scrutinized through observation and objectification. We remain subject to methodological violence through epistemic injustice, which not only includes the denial of mad people as knowers, the silencing of alternative articulations of the meaning of mad experiences, and systemic hermeneutic prejudice, but it also, on a very practical level, includes being subject to sanist research designs and sanist methods of data collection and analysis. Yet, even when direct participation of mad citizens is sought in the act of knowledge production, epistemic objectification often occurs where mad subjects provide information that nonetheless remains captured within the strict confines of the (sane-identified) researchers' epistemological, ontological, and methodological assumptions (Leblanc & Kinsella 2016; Donskoy 2015).

Mad Theory as Methodology

Understanding the epistemic violence and other forms of harm produced within the mainstream mental illness research industry, we advocate a reorientation to stronger ethical conversations in research and a paradigm shift, where mad theory as methodology is foundational and where comfort with unruliness may open up possibilities for a subversive ethics that eschews epistemological/methodological sanism and racism. Mad theory is well positioned to provide focus and new energy to counter mainstream mental illness research, where mad people and mad cultural production occupies its analytical core (Gorman & LeFrançois 2018). This is methodology that centres mad epistemologies, that embodies epistemic justice within mad communities, and that challenges both biomedical psychiatry and the neoliberalism that bolsters it, as it provides an alternative maddened discourse. In its most subversive and recalcitrant form, it is methodology that denies essentialized notions of madness and mad identity at the same time that it centres mad cultural production and the very mad politics that have risen up in response to the violences endemic to the mainstream mental illness research industry. It is research as social action, where activist researchers are committed to social change from a mad social justice perspective. What we advocate here is not new but emanates from the history of activism, theorizing, survivor research, and other forms of knowledge production from within mad movements. This has been developing over decades within different mad spaces in Canada and elsewhere.

Beginning in the early days of mad and psychiatric survivor organizing, the work done to analyze and re-historicize histories of madness and psychiatric violence has provided foundational contributions to a newly emergent mad theory as methodology. Indeed, "(i)t is through the perseverance of activists and scholars who have struggled for a mad people's historiography, and through the strength of antiracist and anti-colonial contributions to mad historiography by Black and Indigenous people and people of colour, that we are in a position to speculate on possibilities for Mad Theory" (Gorman & LeFrançois 2018). While transnational, critical race, and post-colonial analyses have informed Mad Studies from its beginnings,[3] mad theory as methodology requires the continued disruption of the epistemic erasure of mad people of colour within psychiatry and within mad movements. Although this includes exposing and combating the violence towards and the overrepresentation of racialized and colonized mad bodies within psychiatric institutions, it also demands interrogating "the suppressing and erasure of the experiences of racialized mad people (that occurs) even more so than those of white mad subjects" and "exposing the interconnections between the history of racism and the history of bio-medical psychiatry" (Gorman & LeFrançois 2018). Mad epistemology and methodology thus require the centring of psychiatrized bodies and those bodies whose experiences remain most marginalized not just within mainstream psy powers but also within mad movement spaces where overarching social relations of racism and colonialism are reproduced. Here and elsewhere psychiatric violence, sanism and racism play themselves out in complex ways — including by other service users, leading to what has been denounced as anti-Black sanism (Meerei, Abdillahi & Poole 2016) perpetuated against Black and other mad people of colour.

Through mad theory as methodology, and an ethics of unruliness with its decolonial commitments, possibilities open up to develop and entrench politicized ethical practices within research that openly consider and counter racism and (anti-Black) sanism, especially, but not only, in the form of the erasure of marginalized psychiatrized bodies and minds within all aspects of knowledge production. These practices must necessarily remain the active and continuous focus of researchers, as the singularity of context makes general rules impossible to formulate. Moreover, these ethical practices go beyond simple notions of beneficence and maleficence (or "to do no harm"), which tend to be interpreted within mainstream research using neoliberal notions of harm/benefits, and where industry benefits are intimately tied but generally remain unspoken. Instead, an ethical imperative is to unveil and disrupt colonial ways of knowing in order to make visible "the unheard of" and to allow for (racialized) mad knowledge production. This is a space where accountability is necessarily political and where ethical decisions are necessarily terrifying in their moment of uncertainty and impossibility; that is, where all decisions are always and already mad, or they are not ever decisions at all (Derrida 1990).

In the UK, directly involving service users in mental illness research has become mainstream policy over the last two decades (Omeni et al. 2014). As such inclusive policy and practice unfold, so do critiques of the limits of "broad church" approaches to inclusive and collaborative manners of research (Wallcraft, Schrank & Amering 2009). Importantly, in this context of accepting all views, including those that adopt a pathologizing biogenetic approach, strong statements about psychiatric violence cannot be made (Sweeney 2016a). Moreover, the dangers of continued epistemic violence loom large within these so-called inclusive approaches, as mere inclusivity essentializes the *representative* mad body/mind, mostly in ways that are completely devoid of any semblance of mad politics. As alternatives to this type of mainstream service user research, survivor research and Mad Studies offer methodological imperatives that centre epistemes beyond psychocentrism and the remit of medical authority (Donskoy 2015; Sweeney 2016a; Sweeney 2016b). Survivor research is conducted by psychiatric survivor–researchers and is "explicitly rooted in the political movement of people who have been subjected to psychiatric treatment" (Russo 2012, 2). Here, too, however, Russo (2016a) deconstructs how the risk of essentializing mad identity through the "survivor–researcher" branding remains problematic and, we would add, takes place oftentimes without any attempt to resolve the claim to innocence suggested through even the use of strategic essentialism. Nonetheless, in the last two decades survivor research has rapidly grown and there is much to be learned from the problems and the successes of survivor research in the West.[4]

Early scholarship outlining the ethical practices of research conducted by survivors is found in Faulkner's (2004) *The Ethics of Survivor Research: Guidelines for the Ethical Conduct of Research Carried out by Mental Health Service Users and Survivors*. These guidelines were developed specifically for survivor–researchers as a tool to help guide them through their own research, as well as when working in larger research teams. Ethical guidelines for conducting survivor research include clarity and transparency to all of those involved in the research, including theoretical approach to the research. Faulkner (2004) notes that in the development of these guidelines "it was members of black and minority ethnic communities who most supported the importance of transparency about the theoretical underpinnings of research" given "that black communities have in the past been damaged by research carried out on them which was fundamentally incompatible with their own beliefs about mental illness and/or about the dominance of racism and oppression within society" (6). Other ethical practices include, following emancipatory research, ensuring that research adopts an agenda for change and that research is accountable to local and broader service user/survivor communities (Faulkner 2004).

And yet, there remains no absolute strategies within mad methodology and survivor research that absolve or render us innocent of the risks in relation to essentialism and epistemic violence. Any attempts to produce knowledge with/about mad subjects and/or mad communities must remain transparent on these points, with strong commitments to render visible any fault lines in relation to conceptual generalizations, for example, and other forms of power relations that arise. We must also continue to think through and openly discuss the ways in which the (mad) knowledge that is generated may be taken up and used to harm on both practical and epistemological levels. Mad theory as methodology does not guarantee violence-free research processes, practices, findings and intervention applications, regardless of its roots in rising up to combat the violences endemic to mainstream mental illness research. Exposing the singularity of each instance of ethical decision making, which necessarily eschews rules and universal laws, makes visible the potentiality for resultant harms. Indeed, Derrida (1990) points out that once a decision is made, there is no longer any justice, it is only in the suspended moment of (mad) contemplation that justice and ethics flourish. This moment, however, should (but will not always) lead us to choose in a politically responsible manner both despite and because of the unruly state of mind that precedes our choices.

Similarly, Sweeney, Beresford, Faulkner, Nettle & Rose's edited collection *This Is Survivor Research* (2009) traces survivor research ethics, practices, and politics as well as methods and methodologies congruent with survivor research in the UK. What continues to be articulated through literatures on survivor research is that it is informed by principles that underpin the service user/survivor movements (Sweeney 2009; Faulkner 2009). A defining component to survivor research is "a commitment to making change in line with the interests and rights of service users at individual level (empowerment) and at broader levels (political and social change)" (Beresford 2009, 184). More recently, Landry (2017) offers a review of Canadian survivor research over the last twenty-five years. She maps both the developing politics behind survivor research in Canada, as well as the epistemic principle emerging through this work. Survivor research in Canada attends to the politics of research production: questioning what counts as evidence, relational elements of support, and service provision, and querying the research process. Some principles of research production include resisting psychiatry, engaging and disengaging from recovery frameworks, and reclaiming madness (Landry 2017).

Donskoy (2015) suggests that survivor research may be understood as a form of epistemic justice in and of itself. It is a deeply political undertaking that both uses and builds mad theory. Characterized as nomads, survivor–researchers "explore forbidden territories and texts …, sift through, trace pathways, (and) contest the rejection of subjective truths," all which may be understood as "a poetics of resistance" (Donskoy 2015, 117–118). This poetics of resistance, when enacted through the maddening of research, the embrace of a subversive mad politics, and an acceptance of an ethics of unruliness, may very well illustrate the ongoing praxis and potentialities of mad people as insightful knowers and the mad community as a source of hermeneutic pride, both despite and because of the instability, polysemy and indeterminacy of these constructs.

At the same time, Mad Studies scholarship continues to explore the dangers of essentializing and constructing notions of mad identity as a cohesive subject/ivity with an accompanied unified collective politics (Diamond 2013; Essien 2009; Gorman 2013; Tam 2013). Risks to essentializing experiences and professing a singular strain of mad identity include how it elides the asymmetries within the lived experience of heterogeneously constituted subjects (Pattadath 2016, 205). When we make moves that belie the interstices between us through strategic essentialism, dangers include "whitewashing how madness lands and is graphed on bodies differently. Depending on other 'essences' that are always operating in collusion with madness, including race, class, sexual and gender-identity, citizenship, and so on, universalizing lived experience risks erasing how systems of power require one another, and the material consequences" of how such biopower organizes and impacts the lives of individuals (Voronka 2016, 197). Like Badwall (in this volume), we suggest the importance of opening the "third space" beyond the insider–outsider dichotomy within survivor research specifically, and Mad Studies scholarship generally, where the multiplicity of complex experiences is attended to and where similarities and differences are actively explored and interrogated within the heterogeneity of mad experiences and reactions to (anti-Black) sanism. This strategy is important in guarding against any tendency from mad researchers to articulate a singular and essentialized story of the experiences of mad people, mad communities, and mad cultural production.

Given the origins of Mad Studies, mad theory, and mad methodology within psychiatric survivor and mad movements, we would like to underscore that "the most important potential sources for Mad Theory continue to be collective interventions into ways of knowing that come from outside the academic industrial complex, or that challenge its boundaries and authority" (Gorman & LeFrançois 2018, 111). The academy is hierarchical, competitive and driven by neoliberal goals that are at odds with the ethics of (mad) knowledge production (Sweeney 2016b). Mad methodology requires a commitment to remain connected to the everyday lives of those deemed mad and to the grass roots organizing that spring from violent psy encounters. Sweeney (2016a) argues that whilst we must work from within to madden the academy and counter the violence inherent to the mental illness research industry, we must continue to seek paths outside the academy and remain connected to and accountable to our mad communities, including the survivor-led organizations found within them.

A sustained challenge to Mad Studies must be to decentre whiteness, western and Eurocentric logics within community activism, research, and knowledge production (LeFrançois 2015), where mad spaces are simultaneously made white places and where, for instance, the "outright silencing and de-centring of Blackness by mad folk wanting less 'dissention'" is common (Meerei, Abdillahi and Poole 2016, 27). Further, work that moves beyond simple inclusion and diversity tactics in collective practices, collaborations, citation politics, curricula, and collective theorization should be prioritized (Kalathil & Jones 2016). Kalathil and Jones argue that survivor research depends on recognition of the self as a survivor and individual identity construction and, thus, mad/survivor research production is often constituted through encounters with western/colonial psychiatry. Hence, survivor research itself is a western method/ology that depends on conditions whereby individual experience takes priority in identity formation, a markedly western logic. They note that in sites where conceptions of survivor research may not reach, be relevant, or indeed be experienced as an imported western episteme, this does not mean that critical scholarship on madness doesn't occur. Rather, "the constructs 'user/survivor research' and 'Mad theory' may not capture forms of mad counterculture and knowledge production in contexts where the presence and influence of psychiatry are tenuous … [and] even where the legacy of western colonial psychiatry's influence dominates discourse, an individualized notion of the 'user/survivor' may not follow" (Kalathil & Jones 2016, 186). Thus, as we further the project of Mad Studies methods and methodologies — including the maddening of research ethics — we need to be mindful that we don't reproduce the imposition of frameworks as imperialist paradigms on others (Nabbali 2013) while simultaneously recognizing the value of counterhegemonic work that continues to take place globally in a variety of forms. It is here that an ethics of unruliness entrenched with decolonial commitments remains so important in opening spaces for social and epistemic justice.

Maddening Research

By claiming epistemic justice through a politics of Mad theory as methodology, and perhaps through a poetics of resistance (Donskoy 2015), we move to further madden research by highlighting the devising of (mad) research designs, the incorporating of (mad) research methods, and the working through of other research issues in ways that are consistent with our ontologies, epistemologies and ethics. The unruly nature of mad knowledge production suggests that mad methods and mad research designs cannot be pinned down to a definitive list. Our creativity is boundless and in this section, it is not our aim to constrain the exploration of different or new designs and methods. Instead, we note some of the methods and designs marked as important by mad activist scholars and survivor–researchers. Indeed, the significance of the experiences of survivor–researchers is crucial to the project of maddening research, as Sweeney (2016a) points out that the pragmatism inherent to these experiences balances out what may be seen at times as a heavily theorized Mad Studies.

One of the possibilities that maddening research offers is alternatives to the ways in which survivor–researchers and community members are often engaged by research. Community-based participatory research practices are a common method whereby mad people are conditionally invited in to contribute to research and, as Janes' chapter (in this volume) so effectively argues, such methods end up conducting the conduct of community collaborators. Participatory and inclusionary research methods in psy complex research pose specific ethical dilemmas for those being included. They invite mad people to enjoin into systems of knowledge production that sustain our subjection; turn experience into essentialized identities; and reduce collective politics to individual traits. Ultimately, the condition of such collaboration is the replication and solidification of psy complex knowledge production (Voronka 2016).

In contrast, mad approaches to research have included those that are critical, reflexive and politically driven, with an exploratory, emancipatory and social justice–oriented vision (Sweeney 2016b). Typical methods may include direct interviews and/or focus groups, usually semi or unstructured in order to learn from the knowledges of mad participants. Observation of psy violence in situ (LeFrançois 2007; Rosenhan 1973) and/or document analysis of policies (Finkler 2013; 2014), psychiatric charts (Daley, Costa & Ross 2012), and historical records (Reaume 2000; St. Amand & LeBlanc 2013) may be used, all of which turn the gaze away from the psychiatrized and onto the system of oppression. From the humanities, Wolframe's (2013) method was that of a mad reading of text. Others have engaged in performance and arts-based methods (Rice et al. 2017), autoethnographies (LeFrançois 2013; Gorman 2011), and ethnographies of peer work (Voronka 2019b). Although the methods used vary, the questions that these methods aim to answer tend to be focused on issues that are outside of the interests of the psy system and instead focus on questions of importance to mad communities (Donskoy 2015). For instance, these are methods where "we explore our priorities, our perspectives, our views on what heals and harms, (ideally) without censorship" (Sweeney 2016a, 38).

The issue of censorship, however, is a fraught one and one that occurs in several ways. Most notably, the lack of funding opportunities for radical scholarship that challenges psy orthodoxies remains an ongoing problem (Burstow & LeFrançois 2014; Sweeney 2016a). The biomedical dominance that characterizes the review of funding applications is widespread. In Canada, the Social Science and Humanities Research Council (SSHRC) ceased to fund mental health or madness-related research several years ago, diverting social science and humanities-based faculty researchers to bid for funds from the medical-oriented Canadian Institute for Health Research (CIHR). Since this change occurred, to our knowledge, there have been no Mad Studies applications that have received funding from CIHR. Obtaining funding from national granting agencies or even from other sources usually means changing language to comply with biomedical understandings and minimizing or eliminating mad politics not only in the writing up of grant applications, but also in the prior publishing of articles that are needed in order to bolster such eventual grant applications. The knowledge that is subsequently produced tends to uphold the status quo within the mental illness research industry rather than allowing for the establishment of mad activist knowledge production. This type of subtle or hidden censorship is an example of hermeneutic injustice, whereby funding bodies do not allow for episte-mological or methodological challenges to the status quo. This injustice links directly to the concrete politics of knowledge production that have been infused with capitalist neoliberal agendas. Pharmaceutical indus-try ties remain central to those politics within funding bodies in relation to mental health research. Although mad theory–informed research continues to take place mostly unfunded, in order to more effectively engage in the maddening of research, the ethics of knowledge produc-tion demand that these structural barriers to obtaining research funds be knocked down.

Censorship issues may also play themselves out within research teams. In the types of large research teams that are more likely to be funded, the principal investigator (PI) or research lead is often not a mad scholar or survivor–researcher (Sweeney 2016a). The lead or PI may not even be an ally or mad-positive but may instead have simply sought out partnering with mad scholars or survivor–researchers in order to satisfy service user involvement policies, such as those in the UK, or to satisfy other neoliberal "inclusive" research strategies that fold us — and often bind us — into mainstream (read: sanestream) agendas. As such, mad perspectives may be sought by the lead or PI but then subsequently silenced if those perspectives articulate issues beyond either the mainstream agenda or the limited reformist agenda of the research. For instance, Sweeney (2016a) gives the example of mainstream research questions that ask about how mental health ser-vices could be improved rather than asking the more insurgent ques-tion of what is harmful to service users within mental health services. The distinction is not subtle, nor are the likely findings and subsequent policy and practice implications. What is key here is not mad identity so much as mad politics foregrounding the ways in which members of research teams contribute to and control the parameters of research designs, including the methodologies, methods, ethics and overall vision of the research. Sweeney (2016a; 2016b) urges that survivor control of research teams and the generation of politically driven and activist knowledge that comes from and is owned by mad communi-ties is vital in countering censorship and sanism within the research process. Such collective ownership issues are strongly consistent with Mad Studies understanding of mad activist knowledge production (Gorman & LeFrançois 2018) including an ethics of unruliness, where dominant epistemes are not allowed to regulate, order, rule over and erase mad politics and mad responsibilities.

Ownership issues become complex within collective approaches advocated by Mad Studies, perhaps more so than in other forms of collective knowledge generation or participatory research. We suggest this to be the case given that research ethics boards tend to view mad community folk as "vulnerable" and in need of protection from, rather than be fully implicated with and credited by/as, researchers. If the mad folk in question also come from other marginalized populations, such as children, people of colour, Indigenous people, or queer communities, research ethics boards tend to be even more unlikely to sanction their complete participation as co-researchers. Ironically, none of these "vulnerability" issues tend to have much of an impact on the granting of ethics approval for mad people's involvement as experimental subjects in clinical trials of new psychiatric drugs (Mitchell & LeFrançois 2016) or clinical trials of electroshock (Burstow 2016). Regardless of the difficulties in getting clearance to engage in collective and participatory approaches to research, such research that does get permission to be conducted then needs to navigate difficult issues around ownership, credit and anonymity. An issue that is often raised, for example, is the ethics of using participants' names instead of pseudonyms where credit for one's own words and ideas is desired. Research ethics boards often will not allow for such crediting and instead force a protectionist stance through anonymity that is not only disrespectful toward mad participants, but also represents another form of what Leblanc and Kinsella (2016) have discussed as testimonial injustice against mad people. Other examples include the crediting of the research as a whole to mad communities. Funding agency rules tend to limit those who can be named as co-applicants or collaborators on research grants to those who have particular academic credentials, thus barring many mad community members as fund holders and denying them ownership as official research partners.

That being said, collectivity in the maddening of research does not mean that we cannot engage in independent research, but when we do, strong links to our communities should be maintained, beyond tokenistic advisory boards. Also, research dissemination and access to scholarly products must remain open beyond academe or to those who can afford independent access. We all have a politically informed ethical responsibility in actively fighting censorship and the copyright issues that stop the public in general, and the mad community in particular, from accessing research for us and about us. Faulkner (2004) notes that along with traditional academic publications, disseminating written content in accessible reports, offering summaries of findings, making them available online, and circulating them in service user newsletters and to service user organizations are ways of making research knowledge public knowledge (28). Other strategies include an ethics of dissemination that entails academic publishing only in online open access venues, although in many academic institutions, doing so works against mad scholars' and survivor–researchers' abilities to be promoted. Nonetheless, we encourage dissent — or an unruly recalcitrance — that may include the uploading of full articles to online sites such as academia.edu or within online spaces that covertly share copyrighted publications. This form of activism and the risks attached to it are important to combat the corporate university and the publishing industry that feeds off of it through exclusivity.

Conclusion

In this chapter, we open up a discussion about anti-sanist and anti-racist research ethics and the politics of mad knowledge production. We have traversed the terrain of power and oppression in mainstream mental illness research, exposing its interconnectedness to positivism, rationalism, and scientific racism, as well as the resultant epistemic injustice and structural violence inflicted on mad communities, bodies and minds. Necessarily without being exhaustive in our analysis of the issues and tensions between dominant psy politics and mad epistemologies, we proffer Mad Studies as an unruly and subversive source of mad theory as methodology and the maddening of research. We hope that what we have produced here will further conversations and lead to the development of more deepened understandings of and approaches to a mad ethics of knowledge production, including an ethics of unruliness.

Notes

1. When we use the term "mad people," we are not suggesting an essentialized being that *is mad*. Instead, we use this term to refer to those people who have been both a) deemed mad by sanists (usually a professional somewhere within the ever-expanding psy system), and b) have reclaimed the term "mad" and "mad identity" as a form of political resistance to sanism. Most mad people do not understand them-

selves as essentially different from sane-identified people, other than having experienced psychiatric oppression due to having thoughts, feelings, and behaviours that do not fit into the narrowing socio-cultural definition of "normal" deployed in the Global North.

2. See, for example, the following volumes: Aho, Ben-Moshe & Hilton 2017; Aubrecht & La Monica 2019; Ben-Moshe, Chapman & Carey 2014; Beresford & Russo 2021; Breckenridge & Kathait 2019; Bruce 2021; Daley, Costa & Beresford 2019; Green & Ubozoh 2019; Gottstein 2020; Kalathil & Jones 2016; Kilty & Dej 2018; LeFrançois, Beresford & Russo 2016; LeFrançois, Menzies & Reaume 2013; Linton & Walcott 2018; Pickens 2019; Rimke, Gray & Croft 2016; Russo & Sweeney 2016; Spandler, Anderson & Sapey 2015; Voronka & Costa 2019.

3. See, for example: Gorman 2013; Gorman et al. 2013; Gorman & LeFrançois 2018; Gorman & Udegbe 2010; Haritaworn 2013; Joseph 2015; Kanani 2011; LeFrançois 2013; Mills 2013; Mills & LeFrançois 2018; Nabbali 2013; Patel 2014; Tam 2013; Voronka 2008; Voronka 2013.

4. See, for example, and to name only but a few: Sweeney et al. 2009; Carr 2016; Beresford 2009; Donskoy 2015; Faulkner 2017; Faulkner 2009; Faulkner 2004; Kalathil 2011; Kelly 2016; Landry 2017; Rose, Ford, Lindley & Gawith 1998; Russo 2016a; Russo 2016b; Russo 2012; Sweeney 2016a; Sweeney 2016b.

References

Adjei, Paul B. 2016. "The (Em)bodiment of Blackness in a Visceral Anti-Black Racism and Ableism Context." *Race, Ethnicity & Education* 21: 275–287.

Aho, Tanja, Liat Ben-Moshe, and Leon Hilton. 2017. "Mad Futures: Affect/Theory/Violence." Special forum editors, *American Quarterly* 69, 2: 291–302.

Anzaldúa, Gloria. 2007 [1987]. *Borderlands/La Frontera*. San Francisco: Aunt Lute Books.

Aubrecht, Katie, and Nancy La Monica. 2019. "Survivals, Ruptures, Resiliences: Perspectives from Disability Scholarship, Art and Activism." *Canadian Journal of Disability Studies* 8, 4: 1–390.

Ben-Moshe, Liat, Chris Chapman, and Allison C. Carey. 2014. *Disability Incarcerated: Imprisonment and Disability in the United States and Canada*. New York: Palgrave Macmillan.

Beresford, Peter. 2009. "Control: User-Controlled Research." In *Handbook of Service User Involvement in Mental Health Research,* edited by Jan Wallcraft, Beate Schrank and Michaela Amering (181–198). West Sussex, UK: Wiley-Blackwell.

Beresford, Peter, and Jasna Russo. 2021. *The Routledge International Handbook of Mad Studies*. London: Routledge.

Breckenridge, Jhimil, and Namarita Kathait. 2019. *Side Effects of Living: An Anthology of Voices on Mental Health*. Speaking Tiger Publishing Pvt Ltd & Women Unlimited.

Bruce, La Marr J. 2017. "Mad Is a Place: Or, the Slave Ship Tows the Ship of Fools." *American Quarterly* 69, 2: 303–308.

___. 2021. *How to Go Mad without Losing Your Mind: Madness and Black Radical Creativity*. Durham, NC: Duke University Press.

Burstow, Bonnie. 2015. *Psychiatry and the Business of Madness: An Ethical and Epistemological Accounting*. London: Palgrave Macmillan.

___. 2016. "Legitimating Damage and Control: The Ethicality of Electroshock Research." *Intersectionalities* 5, 1: 94–109.

Burstow, Bonnie, and Brenda A. LeFrançois. 2014. "Impassioned Praxis: An Introduction to Theorizing Resistance to Psychiatry." In *Psychiatry Disrupted: Theorizing Resistance and Crafting the (R)evolution,* edited by Bonnie Burstow, Brenda LeFrançois and Shaindl Diamond (3–15). Montreal: McGill/Queen's University Press.

Campbell, Fiona K. 2009. *Contours of Ableism: The Production of Disability and Ableism.* London: Palgrave Macmillan.

Carr, Sarah. 2016. "Narrative Research and Service User/Survivor Stories: A New Frontier for Research Ethics?" *Philosophy, Psychiatry, & Psychology* 23, 3/4: 233–236.

Césaire, Aimé. 1972. "Discourse on Colonialism." In *Discourse on Colonialism* (1–24). New York: Monthly Review Press.

Chapman, Chris. 2014. "Five Centuries' Material Reform and Ethical Reformulations of Social Elimination." In *Disability Incarcerated: Imprisonment and Disability in the United States and Canada,* edited by Liat Ben-Moshe, Chris Chapman and Allison Carey (25–43). New York: Palgrave Macmillan.

Chrisjohn, Roland D., and Shaunessy M. McKay, with Andrea O. Smith. 2017. *Dying to Please You: Indigenous Suicide in Contemporary Canada.* Penticton, BC: Theytus Books.

Cohen, Bruce M.Z. 2014. "Passive-Aggressive: Maori Resistance and the Continuance of Colonial Psychiatry in Aotearoa New Zealand." *Disability and the Global South* 1, 2: 319–339.

Daley, Andrea, Lucy Costa, and Peter Beresford (eds.). 2019. *Madness, Violence & Power: A Critical Collection.* Toronto: University of Toronto Press.

Daley, Andrea, Lucy Costa, and Lori Ross. 2012. "(W)righting Women: Constructions of Gender, Sexuality and Race in the Psychiatric Chart." *Culture, Health and Sexuality* 14, 8: 955–969.

Davis, Lennard J. 1995. *Enforcing Normalcy: Disability, Deafness, and the Body.* London: Verso Press.

de Sousa Santos, Boaventura. 2015. *Epistemologies of the South: Justice Against Epistemicide.* United Kingdom: Taylor & Francis.

Derrida, Jacques. 1990. "Force of Law: The Mystical Foundations of Authority." *Cardozo Law Review* 11, 5–6: 919–1045.

Diamond, Shaindl. 2013. "What Makes Us a Community? Reflections on Building Solidarity in Anti-Sanist Praxis." In *Mad Matters: A Critical Reader in Canadian Mad Studies,* edited by B.A. LeFrançois, R. Menzies, and G. Reaume (64–78). Toronto, ON: Canadian Scholars' Press.

Donskoy, Anne-Laure. 2015. "Not so Distant Voices or Still Lives: Paying Attention to the Voice of the Psychiatric Service User and Survivor Voice in Research." *Cultural Disability Studies* 1: 103–132.

Essien, Karan. 2009. "Identity Issues in Mental Health Research." In *This Is Survivor Research,* edited by Angela Sweeney, Peter Beresford, Alison Faulkner, et al. (63–70). Ross-on-Wye, UK: PCCS Books.

Faulkner, Alison. 2004. *The Ethics of Survivor Research: Guidelines for the Ethical Conduct of Research Carried out by Mental Health Service Users and Researchers.* Bristol, UK: The Policy Press.

___. 2009. "Principles and Motives for Service User Involvement in Mental Health Research." In *Handbook of Service User Involvement in Mental Health Research,* edited by Jan Wallcraft, Beate Schranks and Michaela Amering (13–24). West Sussex: Wiley-Blackwell.

___. 2017. "Survivor Research and Mad Studies: The Role and Value of Experiential

Knowledge in Mental Health Research." *Disability & Society* 32, 4: 500–520.

Fernando, Suman. 1992. "Roots of Racism in Western Psychiatry." *OpenMind* 59: 10–11.

___. 2014. *Mental Health Worldwide: Culture, Globalization and Development.* London: Palgrave Macmillan.

Fernando, Suman, Jayasree Kalathil, Philip Thomas, and Jan Wallcraft. 2012. "Questioning 'Schizophrenia.'" *OpenMind* 172: 12–13.

Finkler, Lilith "Chava." 2013. "They Should Not Be Allowed to Do This to the Homeless and Mentally Ills: Minimum Separation Distance Bylaws Reconsidered." In *Mad Matters: A Critical Reader in Canadian Mad Studies,* edited by Brenda A. LeFrançois, Robert Menzies, and Geoffrey Reaume (221–238). Toronto, ON: Canadian Scholars' Press.

___. 2014. "'We Do Not Want to Be Split Up from Our Family': Group Home Tenants amidst Land Use Conflict." In *Psychiatry Disrupted: Theorizing Resistance and Crafting the Revolution,* edited by Bonnie Burstow, Brenda A. LeFrançois, and Shaindl Diamond (96–113). McGill/Queen's: Montreal.

Fischer, Daniel B. 2010. "Politics of Research in Mental Health." In *Handbook of Service User Involvement in Mental Health Research,* edited by Jan Wallcraft, Beate Schrank, and Michaela Amering (227–242). West Sussex, UK: Wiley-Blackwell.

Foucault, Michel. 1990. *The History of Sexuality (Vol. 1): An Introduction,* translated by Robert Hurley. New York: Vintage Books.

___. 1994. *Ethics: Subjectivity and Truth. The Essential Works of Foucault, 1954–1984* (Vol. I), edited by P. Rabinow. New York: The New Press.

Frank, Arthur W., and Therese Jones. 2003. "Bioethics and the Later Foucault." *Journal of Medical Humanities* 24, 3/4: 179–186.

Fricker, Miranda. 2007. *Epistemic Injustice. Power and the Ethics of Knowing.* Oxford: Oxford University Press.

___. 2010. "Replies to Alcoff, Goldberg, and Hookway on Epistemic Injustice." *Episteme* 7: 164–178.

Gorman, Rachel. 2011. "'Obama's My Dad:' Mixed Race Suspects, Political Anxiety and the New Imperialism." *ThirdSpace: A Journal of Feminist Culture & Theory* 10, 1: 1–15.

___. 2013. "Thinking through Race, Class, and Mad Identity Politics." In *Mad Matters: A Critical Reader in Canadian Mad Studies,* edited by Brenda A. LeFrançois, Robert Menzies, and Geoffrey Reaume (269–280). Toronto, ON: Canadian Scholars' Press.

___. 2017. "Quagmires of Affect: Labor, Whiteness, and Ideological Disavowal." *American Quarterly* 69, 2: 309–313.

Gorman, Rachel, and Brenda A. LeFrançois. 2018. "Mad Studies." In *Routledge International Handbook of Critical Mental Health,* edited by B.M.Z. Cohen (107–114). London, UK: Routledge.

Gorman, Rachel, annu saini, Louise Tam, et al. 2013. "Mad People of Color — A Manifesto." *Asylum* 20, 4: 27.

Gorman, Rachel, and Onyinyechukwu Udegbe. 2010. "Disabled Woman/Nation: Renarrating the Erasure of (Neo)colonial Violence in Ondjaki's Good Morning Comrades and Tsitsi Dangarembga's Nervous Conditions." *Journal of Literary and Cultural Disability Studies* 4, 3: 309–325.

Gottstein, James. 2020. *The Zyprexa Papers.* Alaska: self-published.

Green, L.D., and Kelechi Ubozoh. 2019. *We've Been Too Patient: Voices from Radical Mental Health — Stories and Research Challenging the Biomedical Model.* Berkeley, CA: North Atlantic Books.

Haritaworn, Jin. 2013. "Beyond 'Hate': Queer Metonymies of Crime, Pathology and Anti/Violence." *Jindal Global Law Review* 4, 2: 44–78.

Howell, Alison. 2018. "Forget 'Militarization': Race, Disability and the 'Martial Politics' of the Police and of the University." *International Feminist Journal of Politics* 20: 2: 117–136.

Jackson, Vanessa. 2002. "In Our Own Voice: African-American Stories of Oppression, Survival and Recovery in Mental Health Systems." dulwichcentre.com.au/wp-content/uploads/2014/08/In_Our_Own_Voice_African_American_stories_of_oppression_survival_and_recovery_in_mental_health_systems.pdf.

Joseph, Ameil J. 2015. "The Necessity of an Attention to Eurocentrism and Colonial Technologies: An Addition to Critical Mental Health Literature." *Disability & Society* 30: 7: 1021–1041.

Kalathil, Jayasree. 2011. *Recovery and Resilience: African, African-Caribbean and South Asian Women's Narratives of Recovering from Mental Distress*. London: Mental Health Foundation.

Kalathil, Jayasree, and Nev Jones. 2016. "Unsettling Disciplines: Madness, Identity, Research, Knowledge." *Philosophy, Psychiatry, Psychology* 23, 3/4: 183–188.

Kanani, Nadia. 2011. "Race and Madness: Locating the Experiences of Racialized People with Psychiatric Histories in Canada and the United States." *Critical Disability Discourse* 3: 1–14.

Kelly, Timothy. 2016. "Heterogeneities of Experience, Positionality, and Method in User/Survivor Research." *Philosophy, Psychiatry, & Psychology* 23, 3/4: 229–232.

Kilty, Jennifer, and Erin Dej. 2018. *Containing Madness: Gender and 'Psy' in Institutional Contexts*. New York: Palgrave Macmillan.

Landry, Danielle. 2017. "Survivor Research in Canada: 'Talking' Recovery, Resisting Psychiatry, and Reclaiming Madness." *Disability & Society* 32, 9: 1437–1457.

Leblanc, Stephanie, and Elizabeth A. Kinsella. 2016. "Toward Epistemic Justice: A Critically Reflexive Examination of 'Sanism' and Implications for Knowledge Generation." *Studies in Social Justice* 10, 1: 59–78.

LeFrançois, Brenda A. 2007. *Psychiatric Childhood(s): Child-Centered Perspectives on Mental Health Inpatient Treatment and Care*. Unpublished PhD dissertation. University of Kent at Canterbury, United Kingdom.

___. 2013. "The Psychiatrization of Our Children, or, an Autoethnographic Narrative of Perpetuating First Nations Genocide through 'Benevolent' Institutions." *Decolonization: Indigeneity, Education & Society* 2, 1: 108–123.

___. 2015. "Acknowledging the Past and Challenging the Present, in Contemplation of the Future: Some (Un)Doings of Mad Studies." Paper presented at the *Making Sense of Mad Studies Conference*, October 1, 2015. Durham University, UK.

LeFrançois, Brenda A., Peter Beresford, and Jasna Russo. 2016. "Destination Mad Studies." *Intersectionalities* 5, 3: 1–11.

LeFrançois, Brenda A., Robert Menzies, and Geoffrey Reaume (eds.). 2013. *Mad Matters: A Critical Reader in Canadian Mad Studies*. Toronto: Canadian Scholars' Press.

Linton, Samara, and Rianna Walcott. 2018. *The Colour of Madness: Exploring BAME Mental Health in the UK*. London: Skiddaw Books.

Meerei, Sonia, Idil Abdillahi and Jennifer M. Poole. 2016. "An Introduction to Anti-Black Sanism." *Intersectionalities* 5, 3: 18–35.

Metzl, Jonathan. 2009. *The Protest Psychosis: How Schizophrenia Became a Black Disease*. Boston: Beacon Press.

Mills, China. 2013. *Decolonizing Global Mental Health: The Pyschiatrization of the Ma-*

jority World. London: Routledge.

Mills, China, and Brenda A. LeFrançois. 2018. Child as Metaphor: Colonialism, Psy Governance, and Epistemicide. *World Futures* 74: 503–524.

Mitchell, Richard C., and Brenda A. LeFrançois. 2016. *Rights-Based Ethics and Adoption of ERIC in Canadian Research with Children & Young People.* Presentation given to the Secretariat on Responsible Conduct of Research, July, Government of Canada, Ottawa, ON.

Nabbali, Essya M. 2013. "'Mad' Activism and Its (Ghanian?) Future: A Prolegomena to Debate." *Trans-Scripts* 3: 178–201.

Oda, Raimundo M.G., Claudio Banzato, and Paulo Dalgalarrondo. 2005. "Some Origins of Cross-Cultural Psychiatry." *History of Psychiatry* 16, 2: 155–169.

Omeni, Edward, Marian Barnes, Dee MacDonald, et al. 2014. "Service User Involvement: Impact and Participation: A Survey of Service User and Staff Perspectives." *BMC Health Services Research* 14, 491: 1–13.

Patel, Shaista. 2014. "Racing Madness: The Terrorizing Madness of the Post-9/11 Terrorist Body." In *Disability Incarcerated: Imprisonment and Disability in the United States and Canada*, edited by Liat Ben-Moshe, Chris Chapman and Allison C. Carey (201–216). New York: Palgrave Macmillan.

Pattadath, Bindhulakshmi. 2016. "Experience as 'Expert' Knowledge: A Critical Understanding of Survivor Research in Mental Health." *Philosophy, Psychiatry, & Psychology* 23, 3/4: 203–205.

Pickens, Their Alyce. 2019. *Black Madness: Mad Blackness.* Durham, NC: Duke University Press.

Poole, Jennifer M., Tania Jivraj, Araxi Arslanian, et al. 2012. "Sanism, Mental Health, and Social Work/Education: A Review and Call to Action." *Intersectionalities* 1: 20–36.

Reaume, Geoffrey. 2000. *Remembrance of Patients Past: Patient Life at the Toronto Hospital for the Insane, 1870–1940.* Toronto: Oxford University Press.

Rice, Carla, Eliza Chandler, Jen Rinaldi, et al. 2017. "Imagining Disability Futurities." *Hypatia* 32, 2: 213–229.

Rimke, Heidi. 2016. "Mental and Emotional Distress as a Social Justice Issue: Beyond Psychocentrism." *Studies in Social Justice* 10, 1: 4–17.

Rimke, Heidi, Mandi Gray and Lacey Croft. 2016. "Mental Health and Distress as a Social Justice Issue." *Studies in Social Justice* 10, 1: 1–146.

Rose, Diana, Richard Ford, Peter Lindley, and Libby Gawith. 1998. *User-Focused Monitoring of Mental Health Services in Kensington & Chelsea and Westminster Health Authority.* London: The Sainsbury Centre for Mental Health.

Rose, Nikolas. 1990. *Governing the Soul: The Shaping of the Private Self.* Florence, KY: Taylor & Frances/Routledge.

Rosenhan, David. 1973. "On Being Sane in Insane Places." *Science* 179, 4070: 250–258. web.archive.org/web/20041117175255/http:/web.cocc.edu/lminorevans/on_being_sane_in_insane_places.htm.

Russo, Jasna. 2012. "Survivor-Controlled Research: A New Foundation for Thinking about Psychiatry and Mental Health." *Forum: Qualitative Social Research [Sozialforchung]* 13, 1: Article 8.

___. 2016a. "Towards Our Own Framework, or Reclaiming Madness Part Two." In *Searching for a Rose Garden: Challenging Psychiatry, Fostering Mad Studies*, edited by Jasna Russo and Angela Sweeney (59–68). Wyastone Leys: PCCS Books.

___. 2016b. "In Dialogue with Conventional Narrative Research in Psychiatry and Mental Health." *Philosophy, Psychiatry, & Psychology* 23, 3/4: (215–228).

Russo, Jasna, and Angela Sweeney (eds.). 2016. *Searching for a Rose Garden: Challenging Psychiatry, Fostering Mad Studies.* Wyastone Leys: PCCS Books.

Spandler, Helen, Jill Anderson, and Bob Sapey. 2015. *Madness, Distress and the Politics of Disablement.* Bristol: Policy Press.

St. Amand, Nérée, and Eugène LeBlanc. 2013. "Women in 19th-Century Asylums: Three Exemplary Women; A New Brunswick Hero." *Mad Matters: A Critical Reader in Canadian Mad Studies,* edited by Brenda A. LeFrançois, Robert Menzies and Geoffrey Reaume. Toronto: Canadian Scholars' Press.

Sweeney, Angela. 2009. "So What Is Survivor Research?" In *This Is Survivor Research,* edited by Angela Sweeny, Peter Beresford, Alison Faulkner, et al. (22–37). Ross-on-Wye, UK: PCCS Books.

___. 2016a. "Why Mad Studies Needs Survivor Research and Survivor Research Needs Mad Studies." *Intersectionalities* 5, 3: 36–61.

___. 2016b. "The Transformative Potential of Survivor Research." In *Searching for a Rose Garden: Challenging Psychiatry, Fostering Mad Studies,* edited by J. Russo and A. Sweeney (49–58). Wyastone Leys: PCCS Books.

Sweeney, Angela, Peter Beresford, Alison Faulkner, et al. (eds.). 2009. *This Is Survivor Research.* Ross-on-Wye, UK: PCCS Books.

Tam, Louise. 2013. "Wither Indigenizing the Mad Movement? Theorizing the Social Relations of Race and Madness through Conviviality." In *Mad Matters: A Critical Reader in Canadian Mad Studies,* edited by Brenda A. LeFrançois, Robert Menzies, and Geoffrey Reaume (281–298). Toronto: Canadian Scholars' Press.

Tuhiwai Smith, Linda. 1999. *Decolonizing Methodologies: Research and Indigenous Peoples.* New York: Zed Books.

Voronka, Jijian. 2008. "(Re)Moving Forward? Spacing Mad Degeneracy at the Queen Street Site." Special Issue on Decolonizing Spaces, *Resources in Feminist Research* 33, 1/2: 45–62.

___. 2013. "Rerouting the Weeds: The Move from Criminalizing to Pathologizing 'Troubled Youth' in *The Review of the Roots of Youth Violence.*" In *Mad Matters: A Critical Reader in Canadian Mad Studies,* edited by B.A. LeFrançois, R. Menzies, and G. Reaume (309–322). Toronto: Canadian Scholars' Press.

___. 2016. "The Politics of 'People with Lived Experience': Experiential Authority and the Risks of Strategic Essentialism." *Philosophy, Psychiatry & Psychology* 23, 3/4: 189–201.

___. 2019a. "Slow Death through Evidence-Based Research." In *Madness, Violence, & Power: A Critical Collection,* edited by Andrea Daley, Lucy Costa, and Peter Beresford (80–96). Toronto: University of Toronto Press.

___. 2019b. "The Mental Health Peer Worker as Informant: Performing Authenticity and the Paradoxes of Passing." *Disability & Society.* doi.org/10.1080/09687599.2018.1545113.

Voronka, Jijian, and Lucy Costa (eds.). 2019. "Disordering Social Inclusion: Ethics, Critiques, Collaborations, Futurities." Special Issue in *Journal of Ethics in Mental Health* 10.

Wallcraft, Jan, Beate Schrank, and Michaela Amering. 2009. *Handbook of Service User Involvement in Mental Health Research.* West Sussex, Wiley-Blackwell.

Wolframe, PhebeAnn. 2013. "Reading through Madness: Counter-Psychiatric Epistemologies and the Biopolitics of (In)Sanity in Post-World War II Anglo-Atlantic Women's Narratives." PhD dissertation, McMaster University, Hamilton.

Zalloua, Zahi. 2014. *Reading Unruly: Interpretation and its Ethical Demands.* London: University of Nebraska.

7

Less Dangerous Collaborations?

Governance through Community-Based Participatory Research

Julia Elizabeth Janes

Community-based Participatory Research[1] (CBPR) is consistently held up as a benchmark for socially just knowledge production. Calls for the intensification and further institutionalization of CBPR[2] indicate the discursive value of community-engaged research, but its material benefits to community collaborators are unclear. CBPR's claims to socially just research relations and outcomes remain largely uninterrogated and the everyday participatory practices under-documented and theorized. As a practitioner of CBPR for over a decade, I have a sustained commitment to working with communities toward social change. However, I hold this commitment in tension with the multiple ways that inclusion of communities in knowledge production, not only as research participants but as co-researchers, operates as a form of governance and counter governance. The space in between the often oppressive practices of CBPR and the liberatory possibilities of collaborative knowledge production is the site of my research.

My research on community/university collaborations is guided by two conceptual anchors. The first is Foucault's (1984) contention that everything is dangerous and, therefore, requires a pessimistic activism. Dangers inhere to all knowledge production projects, but are obscured by CBPR's liberatory claims and therefore are difficult to bring into view. I aim to foreground the dangers that inhere to CBPR without seeking to identify bad practices or propose better practices. The second conceptual anchor is Cahill, Quijada Cerecer, and Bradly's (2010) position of critical hope, which recognizes that equitable collaborative knowledge production with divergent constituencies is both impossible and essential. Embracing the impossibility of the claims of CBPR marks the beginning of an ethics of collaborative knowledge production.

I take up the ethics of collaborative knowledge production, following on Macías' chapter in this volume, as a performative, political practice never free of the violence of representation. Following on Mignolo (2000; 2009), I argue that epistemic governance is an exercise of dominance, a symbolic and material violence, and a site of ethical and political contestation. I contest epistemic dominance through an interrogation of "what is unseen, under-theorized and left out of knowledge production" (Mohanty 2003, 230). Tracing the well-concealed operations of epistemic privilege in collaborative knowledge work is central to my research and this chapter.

This chapter draws from my research on the social relations of Community-based Participatory Research. The quotes[3] embedded in the following sections of this chapter emerged from primarily group interviews with twenty-nine academic, community-based professionals, and peers who collaborated on CBPR projects in the Greater Toronto Area. In this chapter, I focus on one strand of analysis from this study, which traced participatory practices that constitute communities as targets and techniques of governance through the promise of community-wide benefit. I propose that this largely unmet promise of benefit to collaborating communities constitutes an ethical trespass and colludes with neoliberal politics of commodifying knowledge and knowers.

The first section of this chapter situates CBPR within the broader context of community as a site of governance in the knowledge economy. The next section takes up micro participatory practices that target community collaborators and exploit their labour to gain access and data. I then zoom out to the macro governmental rationalities that make such participatory practices thinkable. And because governance is never total, the final section puts forward counter proposals toward less dangerous university/community collaborations.

Governance through Community Participation and Partnership

I locate this inquiry into the politics and ethics of CBPR within the more general consideration of governance through community participation and partnerships. I understand participation and partnerships in

CBPR as exceeding that of research participant and extending "up the ladder" to responsibilities for recruitment, data collection and analysis, and dissemination. These more substantive community contributions are central to the claims of CBPR enacting equitable research relations. Following on Miller and Rose (2008), I understand the term governance as inclusive of state or sovereign government and governmentality, which Dean (2010) emphasizes operates through multiple sites of authority, desires, interests and everyday practices. While community as a concept predates advanced liberalism, Miller and Rose assert that it became governmental when statist notions of social welfare were coming under fire from all sides of the political continuum. Community was then put forward as a valourized antidote to the failings of the social.

Whereas the social is a singular site of state intervention, community is infinitely plural, and therefore, demands different forms of governance that rely on self-regulating, active citizens, working toward their improvement, as well as those of others who shared their affiliative bonds. Active, self-responsible, self-regulating citizens are, according to Miller and Rose (2008), cultivated through techniques of inclusion. CBPR operates as a technique of inclusion, which targets communities, renders them responsible for their social problems and appropriates their knowledge and labour with the promise of social solutions. Community in CBPR is constructed as largely unproblematic, harmonious and homogenous site of intervention and as a subject position in need of improvement. Furthermore, community as a site of intervention is produced through the logic of the project. We can see the production of community in the following quote by a peer researcher [2a]: "The community is nebulous ... but they do it to get grants and bamboozle poor people to think they're part of a particular community." The subjectivities of academic and community are similarly synthetic and constituted as a false binary that precludes that academics are part of communities and community members attend universities. These binaries are, nevertheless, reproduced in the study and this chapter, as the focus is on how these subject positions are understood by research collaborators and constituted through the core logic of CBPR: to intervene in and improve communities.

The rationalities that underpin governance through inclusion are mutually constituted by neoliberalism and neocolonialism. While neoliberalism privileges enterprise and competition, Venn (2009) argues that neoliberal austerity projects are rationalized through raced and (neo) colonial logics of extraction. CBPR leverages its inclusive politics to gain entry and extract the knowledges of the communities that are the target of its interventions in ways that mirror colonial projects, which appropriate the land and resources of the Global South. CBPR is not only colonial in its knowledge extractions but also, and uniquely, in its appropriation of the labour of community collaborators. While I take up the specific operations of coloniality in CBPR elsewhere (Janes 2017), this chapter foregrounds neoliberal rationales. Although CBPR is constituted as outside of — or in opposition to — governmental rationales of competition, commodification and individualism, after considering micro participatory practices, I outline the ways CBPR colludes with these neoliberal metrics.

Micro Governmental Practices: Community as a Target

Miller and Rose define governmental practices as those that "shape, normalise and instrumentalize the conduct, thought decisions and aspirations of others in order to achieve the objectives they consider desirable" (2008, 32). Scott (1995) questions what project are these new targets required for and what techniques are necessary to attain it? If the project of CBPR is to accumulate the knowledge and labour of communities, then access to communities is paramount. As I have argued (Janes 2016), participatory practices are an effective technique for gaining access to over-researched and research-resistant communities, which are often the target of CBPR.

Participatory practices instrumentalize community affiliations to gain entry to research resistant spaces, while obscuring histories and presents of exploitive research. In the quote below, an academic [9] outlines the strategic use of community recruiters, which is naturalized as a good research practice and celebrated openly by colleagues without consideration of ethical transgressions.

> You're talking about data that you would not be able to collect otherwise. Because these are people who would never fill out a survey. They have been screwed over by so many systems. But now you come back with a different approach, claiming that you are doing things differently. You come back with someone from

their own community who they recognize asking them to do the survey. So many of them [CBPR researchers] will talk about this when they are presenting at conferences: "We are able to get such amazing data. These people would have never shared this information otherwise."

Henkel and Stirrat (2001) and Simons, Masschelein and Quaghebeur (2005) caution that both old and new techniques of participation share similar extractive aims — to accumulate local knowledge. The extractive aims of CBPR are vividly depicted in the following quote by a community-based peer [1] who leveraged affiliative networks to amass survey data.

She [an academic] was absolutely amazed that I had access to a lot of people. They were expecting us to stand out in the middle of winter for four hours, begging our way in ... and I thought this is stupid. I went over to [an agency] asked if I could have the women come in and do the survey there.

The description of enduring hours in the cold and "begging" alert to the devalued, even dehumanized, status of the peer researcher who is expected to fail.

The practice of regulating community collaborators begins with delimiting norms for the conduct of community-based researchers, which we can locate in the following quote by a community professional [10a].

Everybody had to fit into that model no matter what their skills were. Sitting around tables, committee format, taking minutes, starting on time, ending on time, understanding the information that was flowing, and being able to bring that information back to others. There were various areas that [peers] weren't able to do that. And so communication broke down, which led to people thinking that information was purposely being withheld.

Prescribing the parameters of conduct, while breaking down local norms is a key governmental practice (Scott 1995). Moreover, norms for participation reflect what Jordan and Kapoor (2016) identify as an increasingly technical approach to participation. Once norms for participation take hold, they are, as this academic [9] found, difficult to critique.

They were so proud and they wanted to convince me of how great CBPR was.... These people don't want you turning around saying: "You're just doing surveillance, you're implicating yourself, these community-based organizations, people living with mental health issues, HIV, diabetes or cardiovascular illness — you are implicating all of them in the surveillance of others by bringing them into CBPR."

O'Connell, in Chapter 9 of this volume, outlines how challenges to normative discourses of "everything in plain sight" are circumvented through the implication that the critic has something to hide. Similarly, critiquing dominant discourses of the goodness of community engagement may be taken up as "anti-community" and preclude consideration of the ethics of peer researchers engaging in data collection as an act of surveillance of their own communities.

Micro Governmental Techniques: Appropriating Community Labour

As advanced in the introduction to this chapter, what makes CBPR a particularly effective site of governance is that it not only constitutes community as a target of intervention, but as a technique for acquiring a tertiary, subordinate labour force. Ilcan and Phillips (2008) and Olssen and Peters (2005) argue that participatory practices align with the aims of the knowledge economy to mobilize active, competent knowledge workers. The demand for an expanded knowledge workforce makes community co-researchers highly attractive, not the least for their cost efficiency. Research participants described the political economies of community labour. For example, a peer [2a] characterized her labour as analogous to working on a "chain gang," which brings into focus how participation regulates as it activates community labour. A community-based professional [10b] emphasized the need for competent peer researchers who are accountable and productive: "I certainly prefer working with people [peer researchers] who we've trained … we're doing over 400 interviews … it was really great to have people that we can count on." An academic [15] echoed the importance of engaging competent community-based peers: "I am not saying that we don't want inclusion, but I am saying that we should preselect community members that are capable of what we expect …" In these quotes, both the rationales of neoliberalism and inclusive liberalism are apparent through the production of responsible, subordinate, community labour.

Participatory research practices also regulate community labour through low/no compensation and precarity. Although occasional references to uneven compensation are noted in the CBPR literature (Guta et al. 2014; Pinto et al. 2015), consideration of how these practices reflect a more generalized devaluing of community, which transcend the provision of stipends, warrants further inquiry. The lack of discussion of the uneven compensation of community-based collaborators can be traced to egalitarian claims, which suggest that CBPR is already and always a site of equitable relations. However, the problematic economies were apparent to an academic [9] who commented that: "everyone loves a peer model because why would you pay $60,000 a year when you could pay a peer, if they are lucky, $30,000 to do not the same work, but very similar work." Nichols and colleagues (2014) attribute the poor compensation to community-based researchers to funding priorities to hire graduate students and to collective agreements, which protect student labour but lead to low wages and temporary labour conditions for non-student researchers. Unnoted in the literature is the absence of any labour rights for community collaborators who receive honoraria and are not formally employed.

Despite the troublingly low compensation to community collaborators, Bell and Salmon (2011) found that peer participants view their research work as an essential part of the informal economy. Similarly, a community professional [10b] noted that peer researchers in her organization are "pretty well paid compared to our social enterprises ... more or less $25 an hour — close to that of a research assistant." She went on to ascribe good compensation practices to other community organizations: "They want to be able to put honoraria in the pockets of their tenants ... and they are happy to pay peer researchers; I think they are trying to circulate that money back into the community." While a laudable gesture toward ameliorating community poverty, the political implications of attenuating the erosion of social welfare with short-term stipends warrants careful consideration.

A peer researcher [11c] was incredulous, not just at the uneven compensation, but at the differential contributions: "It astounds me that I am sitting in a room with people getting paid really good money who know much less than I do about the topic." Another peer [2a] extended the critique to how scarce compensation acts as a means of silencing dissent: "People sometimes don't want to speak because if they're getting something for coming, they're always scared if I say something wrong, maybe somebody won't invite me back." The politics of compensation not only regulate conduct but, as the same peer observed, reduced community contributions to a monetized exchange: "I'm going to say something really crass and mercenary right now. I have a child who is severely handicapped and if somebody says: 'Come to this group or facilitate this group…' I'm there in a minute." Community professionals and academics would be unlikely to characterize payment for their work in such reductive terms.

The preceding description of receiving payment as "crass" highlights that compensation is only natural for some. As a community professional [16a] observed: "I remember someone saying in an advisory committee 'you are all paid to be here, but this is my own time and my own energy, and that is the case all the time for me.'" While the unevenness of compensation is called into question in the preceding quotes, an academic [8] positioned the asymmetry in positive terms: "I see myself as a conduit for resources that I can bring: institutional review boards, grants, access to students, my free time." The unevenness, while implied, is normalized as a privilege that can allow work without direct compensation from the project. What is not made explicit is that many community professionals, and certainly peers, are not free to be "free" and rely on stipends built into the project.

The disparity in financial support to carry out the labour of CBPR was not always taken for granted by research participants and was sometimes a site for careful consideration. An academic [5b] identified funders as determining resource allocations, which signals the importance of challenging the institutional arrangements that instantiate the inequitable economies of collaboration.

> Peer researchers often have very few resources and their time is incredibly precious. We needed to make a lot of contact so that all the logistical things are in place. Trying to shape things so you could cover childcare and could provide a decent honorarium. It's often really difficult to do that depending on the funding source.

While many research participants troubled the disparities in compensation, a community-based peer [7c] framed it as discriminatory: "I see it as a stigma. She [a research consultant] got paid and we were volunteers, but we did a lot of the work." The disparity between contributions and compensation indicates the pervasiveness of volunteerism in CBPR. Community collaborators who are unpaid or paid by honoraria are outside of labour protections where such uneven compensation would, indeed, be considered discriminatory. Another community-based peer [1] linked the devaluing of community collaborators to erroneous assumptions regarding the possibility of peers having academic credentials.

> The ethics committee questioned why we're being paid so much, and that's discrimination right there: the fact that they had just assumed that nobody working on the team had a university education ... I said this is Canada. Poverty has a whole different face. I've got women from grade school to PhDs.

As noted earlier, the false binary of academe and community precludes community having academic histories and presents and academics being part of a community, and ignores neoliberal labour trends where higher educational attainment is not necessarily associated with a rise in socio-economic status.

In contrast, to peer researchers volunteering on CBPR projects is the employment model of CBPR, which formalizes the labour of the peer, but only for the duration of the project. The employment model enables the operations of the market, including short-term precarious labour conditions, to take hold of community collaboration. A community-based professional [14] was skeptical about the quality of project-dependent employment: "On paper, it sounds really good to say that our peer researchers have found other opportunities in research settings, but if they are getting stuck in one small project after another ... it does not make a lot of sense." In contrast, an academic [5a] described the employment approach to CBPR as a more equitable practice: "The employment model in some respects felt like a much less contentious way to assemble a team. And it felt more egalitarian and ... more like it could truly be a collaboration where it was all of our jobs to formulate the project." However, what goes unnoted are the hierarchical relations of employees and employers.

The problematics of short-term research employment are paradoxically at play, as a community professional [14] acknowledged, even in a CBPR project interrogating precarious employment. In the following quote, the risk that precarious employment will adversely impact the social assistance of a peer researcher is recognized, but positioned as intractable.

> We're constantly in a dilemma, especially on the very research projects that are focused on examining precarious employment … we're actually hiring peer researchers on short-term contracts. And then some of them are on social assistance, so we have to strategically work with their case worker to make sure that their social assistance money doesn't get cut. These are institutional barriers that every CBPR project will have to deal with.

A peer [1] further elaborated on the adverse consequences of precarious project-based income on disability benefits: "You have to take a look at each woman, if she's on ODSP [Ontario Disability Support Program], then you have to pay her in a different way." The peer added that this consideration of the impact to social assistance did not occur and a colleague "totally lost her daycare benefits for the next year." The ethical tensions of providing short-term income and precarious employment for peer researchers are rarely acknowledged in the CBPR literature (for an exception see Guta et al. 2014). However, the impact of an abrupt cessation of compensation at the end of a CBPR project is vividly captured as an ethical breach in this exchange between two peers [2a and 2b].

> Sustainability … I'm saying that people got used to a certain standard. 'Cause a couple of hundred dollars makes a big difference in your life. And then boom! It's gone, and I am wondering how people felt going off the money. That's an ethical concern, too. I know there are other people who had real issues … A couple of them actually got evicted.

Research participants critically engaged with the ethics of expecting community-based organizations (CBOs) and individual collaborators to labour in CBPR with little support, which presumes, as a community professional [11a] noted, that "people have the time … and the money to support participation." The devolution of responsibility, but not resources, is a hallmark of neoliberalism (Goldberg 2009). We can locate this devolution in the following quote by another community professional [14]: "Academics realize that if they partner with agencies they can download recruitment without the corresponding sharing of power, benefits, and resources." The ethical trespass of responsibilizing agencies and community members to engage in research with little support not only articulates to neoliberal austerity, but also ensures that shortfalls in recruitment are assigned to community-based partners.

As O'Connell's chapter in this volume argues, demands for greater participation, without consideration of the material supports required, devolve responsibility to individual participants and away from public institutions. A community professional [11a] challenged adding research responsibilities to already overextended agencies: "Research never allocates resources to support community-based organizations.... The expectation is your participation will be seamless.... Meanwhile, they're told to pick up this [research] as an extra activity on top of what they're doing on an everyday basis." The inattention to the ethical tensions of engaging under-resourced collaborators in research activities is made thinkable by dislocating CBPR from the social conditions in which it unfolds. The displacement of the social realities of community collaborators is activated by the macro neoliberal politics of individualism and competition that have taken hold of CBPR.

Macro Governmental Rationalities: The Neoliberal Politics of CBPR

Neoliberal governmental rationalities underpin the politics of community collaboration and make thinkable and doable the ethical trespasses of the participatory practices, discussed in the previous sections. Paradis (2015) maintains that neoliberal governance makes use of pre-existing discourses of dominance to rationalize and activate competition and individualism in all sectors of society. The primacy of these rationales in the knowledge economy has been explored by a number of governmentality scholars (Shore 2008; Thorpe 2009). However, this scholarship attends to how these rationalities impinge on academe rather than how they inflect university/community collaborations. CBPR's collusion with neoliberal aims warrants careful scrutiny because its operations are so well concealed by discursive claims to socially just research. Also troubling is that community engagement is increasingly deployed to attenuate anxieties around the neoliberalizing of the university (Dean 2015). The intensification and institutionalization of community-engaged scholarship re-secures the goodness of academe and its foundation in colonial, patriarchal, white, western conceptions of knowledge, while at the same time sustaining neoliberal metrics and managerialism.

Participatory practices are highly attractive to neoliberal aims to accumulate and commodify knowledge (Bourke 2013; Dean 2015). Trudeau and Veronis (2009, 1128) refer to this trend as "partnering-to-compete," whereby CBOs strategically collaborate to meet the demands of top-down state restructuring. A community professional [11b] identified neoliberal rationalities as transforming participatory approaches to research.

> It's certainly opposite of participatory governance starting from the ground up ... It's not random that whole neoliberal approach is trickling all the way down to how we're operating now.... We're having to be aligned to government funding priorities to partner; our culture is also morphing to that sort of model, and we are neglecting to reflect upon where it's going.

An academic [13a] similarly critiqued the infiltration of neoliberal rationales into CBPR, which induced divisiveness and a culture of fear: "People are secretive about it — they go around saying: 'Did you get the money?' It's classic neoliberal managerialism. It stays very quiet, very divided and if you challenge that system it puts you at risk ... creating a lot of fear and a lot of silence." The competitiveness of the funding field, as a community professional [16a] observed, adversely impacted collaborative relations: "As money gets tighter, people get much more competitive. So, the relationships don't work anymore because people are fighting over a smaller pot of funds. And that really is so antithetical to our way of working, but it's hard to keep from being drawn into it." Here, the paradox of the partnering-to-compete paradigm comes into view, as both requiring community collaboration but creating conditions that make these relationships difficult, if not impossible.

For some community collaborators, the politics of partnership were not only difficult to evade, but essential to the survival of CBOs. Salmon, Browne and Pederson (2010) maintain that CBOs are increasingly partnering with academics because grants offer an alternate funding stream for their social justice projects. An academic [9] observed how this trend coordinates the conduct of both community and academic partners.

> Program funding has been cut considerably but there seems to always be money for CBPR. So, people are participating in CBPR

projects to keep staff on board. The community partner needs the research dollars to keep the doors open and every university wants community-engaged research in some form so [they] need each other.

What is often unnoted in the CBPR literature is the ethical trespasses these partnerships introduce to the politics of disclosure and reporting. As the academic [9] quoted above expanded, the efficiencies of CBOS providing service while doing research pose ethical issues for staff, service users, and academic researchers.

> Program managers are supposed to be providing services, but they are also doing research at the same time. I don't know if you can do both ... I have been in situations where I have thought organizational mandates are creating conflict ... but many organizations are quite happy to blame the sector and other organizations that haven't adopted their anti-oppressive, anti-racist, sex positive framework.... How do you then say: "You're a part of this, too." There are research interviews where that stuff comes up but ... you can't go public with it because then you risk that relationship.

The ethical complications of conflating service and research relationships places service, and importantly the service user, at risk. The role duality of providing service at the same time as acting as a co-researcher is only beginning to be considered in the literature (Holian and Coghlan 2013), while the ways that community/university partnerships complicate what can be said and done receives less attention.

Neoliberal rationales of collaboration not only activate competition, corrode community/university social relations, and divert resources away from social programming, they also supplant social change. Research participants naturalized the trajectory from knowledge to action as the liberatory promise of CBPR, but at the same time acknowledged that it was unfulfilled. One way in which the gap between knowledge and action is maintained is through the legitimating outcomes of knowledge transmission. The prevalence of understanding action as dissemination was reported by Brown (2013) and Stoecker (2009). Stoecker found that the majority of applicants to a funding stream that required both community participation and actionable outcomes identified no action or action as dissemination, while Brown found a similar conflation in responses from CBPR practitioners. The framing of action as dissemination provokes the question of whether the production and consumption of knowledge stands in for social action. A community professional [3] questioned the entrenched rationales of knowledge transfer, as legitimating dissemination rather than social action as an outcome of CBPR.

> The struggle was when you ask: "What are the actions that came out of your work?" They reverted to talking about the things that were explicitly identified in their proposal. What they didn't talk about was the ways that action really forms in their community. We wanted to ask what has your project done five years on? What have been the ripple effects? But people are used to thinking about their actions in very limited ways: "We held a workshop, and we've produced some papers." So dissemination becomes action.

If social change and community benefit are held out as an outcome of community collaborations with academe, but are reconstituted as dissemination (i.e., publications, presentations) then the ethical trespass becomes clear. A community-based peer [11b] challenged the marketized logic of knowledge transfer, as well as the one-way transmission implied, which re-inscribes academe as the site of knowledge production and community as beneficiary consumers.

> For me the action piece was the important piece. The participatory is important, but the action piece gave it [CBPR] life. I'm disappointed at the new language that funders are using, which doesn't really see that part. Right now we're trying to do 'knowledge transfer' … seems like a generic term compared to action. Who's transferring what to who?… I've got knowledge that I'm transferring and … For how much an hour?

Paradoxically, both desires for CBPR to activate social change and its failures to do so are highly attractive to the rationalities of the neoliberal knowledge economy, where the focus on usefulness can be incrementalized within status quo relations of dominance. Missing from the discussion of whether CBPR activates or supplants social change is consideration of how these aspirations render collaborators responsible for realizing substantive impacts through single time limited projects.

Ambitions of social change, while laudable, constitute CBPR co-researchers as super agents: sovereign liberal subjects who can enact social transformation unencumbered by complex socio-political conditions. CBPR is, thus, configured as an impossible project and to preserve its goodness, it must carefully reconstruct its aims at the scale of the individual. The tensions of desires for impacts at the scale of the social and realities of scaffolding individual community collaborators toward greater social mobility are reflected upon by an academic [4].

> So on the individual level, we are trying to make things better by providing people with opportunities to build skills, to develop certain capacities. And at the community level to develop new insights that people can take up in their work. And at the policy level perhaps some of those insights inform policies. But I find that the easiest place to make change, the one that is more in my control, is at the individual level.

Another academic [8] explicitly laid out how the promise of social action is deployed instrumentally to secure participation and re-inscribe subordination.

> We [academics] come into these communities where they are very aware of being held back by a number of systems. And we promise them that we can change those things. But we do not have any activities built into what we're doing that will change those things. I think it's terrible that we reinforce the lack of power that these communities have by doing all of this work and at the end of it, we sign a petition....

Neoliberal rationales enable the reconfiguration of community benefit into community harm, social change into an individualist intervention, and social research into social programming. It is through these transformations that CBPR sustains status quo relations of dominance, while appearing to do just the opposite. However, governance through community collaboration is neither inevitable nor total. The final section of this chapter considers counter proposals to mitigate the dangers of community/university collaborations.

Proposals for Less Dangerous Collaborations

This chapter concludes with strategies of collaboration that reach toward "the art of not being governed quite so much" (Foucault 2003b, 265) and open up space to think differently about CBPR. These transgressive proposals are entangled with the ethical concerns outlined thus far and do not seek to exculpate CBPR through a better, more innocent practice. Rather, these counter proposals are understood as simultaneously resistant and reproductive of knowledge hierarchies. Among the many ways that research participants reimagined an ethics of collaboration, I put forward three counter proposals for consideration: practices of distance and refusal that resist desires for proximity and normative prescriptions for participation; decentring academe as the site of knowledge production through alliances with social movements; and transgressions of scale, which re-orient CBPR toward social and epistemic transformation to attenuate the creep of neoliberal individualism.

Ahmed argues for an ethical encounter that adopts a "stance of respectful distance" (2000, 157). According to Ahmed (2000), practices of distance take two paths: to step away or do a double turn, first toward yourself and then toward the other. An academic participant [8] echoed the urge to step away:

> We need to be stepping back and thinking really long and hard about what it means to create change.... to think very consciously about what we can accomplish, what engaging people in this process is going to do for them as individuals and what is the potential for the future change. And being very clear with everyone about what those possibilities are. And how difficult that change might be. Most of community members know, but sometimes they don't and they think that you're going to accomplish amazing things with one CBPR project.

Another way to practice distance, as suggested by a community professional [12], is to refuse the name and thus, the claims of CBPR: "I think that we need to separate ourselves from the label of CBPR, invest less in the label and more in the actual work that the label claims to be doing." Resistance to prescriptions for participation were also championed by a community-based peer [1]: "The funders want it, so they are saying they are doing it [CBPR] ... but they are going to find out that they're not going to have any of us involved. We are just saying no." The ethics and politics of refusal is taken up by Simpson (2007) and Tuck and Yang (2012) as a strategy of resistance and a site of ethical engagement.

An ethics of refusal can also be located in the rejection of the tyranny of full participation. In the following quote, an academic [8] unsettles the moral imperative of full participation: "I think sometimes the CBPR model that gets taken up is that we should all be doing everything together, all have the same skills rather than complementarity. Because it's grounded in a framework that says if you're not working in this way your work is unethical." As argued in the previous section, framing full participation as a socially just benchmark ignores the trespass of burdening under-resourced individuals and communities with the "invitation" to collaborate on a CBPR project. A return to principles and practices of complementarity challenges prescriptive norms that quantify and regulate participation through institutionalized audits.

Another strategy for disrupting institutionalized norms for collaboration was that of decentring academe as *the* legitimate site of knowledge production. Langdon and Larweh (2015) advocate for participatory research that is co-designed with existing social movements. Two academics [5a and 5b] reflected on different ways in which allyship with social movements might emerge. In both proposals, activist groups are constituted as epistemic leaders who determine when and how academe can participate. Rather than partnering-to-compete, this model of collaboration is community driven and reverses norms of instrumentalizing community networks to that of leveraging academic affiliations.

> The invited approach is very clear ... activist groups know what they want to do and what help they need to do it. For many of them there is a particular credibility attached to "research" that has an institution attached to it, which enables their work. It's strategic and useful to supporting their expertise.
>
> I think it's about being there in those spaces already. In my own experience, the farther outside that world I go the more invested I become in academia and the less time I dedicate to activist activities. Also, the less legitimate it would be if I just started hanging out in those spaces now.

Another proposal for revitalizing commitments of CBPR to social transformation can be located in Blackstock et al's call for a "multi-scalar imagination" (2015, 260), where CBPR pursues both individual and modest scales of social change. However, what Blackstock and colleagues miss are the epistemic possibilities of collaborative knowledge work. A community professional [14] argued, like Mignolo (2000; 2009) and de Sousa Santos (2014), that epistemic justice must come first: "The concept of knowledge democracy is very appealing ... that in order to promote social justice or economic equality you have to first promote cognitive justice." Decolonizing and democratizing knowledge production is imperative to realizing what de Sousa Santos refers to as "cognitive justice" (237), where valuing and engaging diverse knowledges and knowers is a prequel to our social justice struggles. A reimagining of CBPR's scale of impact that reorients toward social and epistemic transformations resists the governmental move of participatory research supplanting social programming and standing in for social change.

The possibilities of epistemic transformations were reflected upon by another community professional [12]: "When people talk about knowledge production, they usually begin with some French philosophers. But this guy — what he's talking about ... It's not only an east African thing; it's something we need right here in Toronto." The quote invokes de Sousa Santos' (2014) proposal that Global South epistemologies are required to challenge the dominance of Euro/western-centric knowledges. Indigenous scholarship offers important strategies toward engaging different ways of knowing and collaborating, which exceed the coloniality of western knowledge production (see for example, Absolon and Dion 2017; Battiste 2011; Kovach 2010; Tuck and Yang 2012).

Although CBPR may offer a rupture to western Eurocentric epistemologies, research participants' consideration of decolonized ways of knowing were rare. The scant inclusion of Indigenous and Global South epistemologies in CBPR literature is an absent presence throughout this chapter, which focuses on a particular distillation of collaborative research in a North American context. While different ways of knowing abound within these geographic boundaries, when taken up by the institutionalized CBPR interrogated in this chapter, they are transformed. It is my critical hope and current focus of my work to learn from Indigenous and other marginalized knowers' ways of co-creating and gathering knowledges with as little colonizing as possible.

Concluding Thoughts

This chapter interrogated CBPR's claims to socially just practices and outcomes through a theoretical and empirical engagement with community/university collaboration as a site of governance. I argued that CBPR has evaded a criticality that takes seriously the ethics and politics of collaboration through the naturalization of community inclusion as a socially just practice. By tracking the specific micro participatory practices that are activated and normalized by CBPR's claims to goodness, I advanced that community collaboration is both a target and technique of governance. Participatory practices target communities that have been ill served by research to gain access, devolve research responsibilities, and regulate community collaborators.

While the critique of extractive and regulatory research practices could be extended to social research in general, the appropriation of community labour as a technique of governance is unique to CBPR. The production of low-cost, competent, compliant community researchers is highly attractive to the needs of the knowledge economy. Practices of no compensation reify the community collaborator as a volunteer, while low compensation operates to regulate and monetize community contributions. The ascendant employment model consolidates the market logic of CBPR and introduces precarious labour conditions. My analysis troubles the exploitive conditions of employing peer researchers and the epistemic down grade of community collaborators from knowledge producers to labourers.

I proposed that the ethical transgression of inviting under-resourced community members and agencies to labour in social research without adequate support is made thinkable through neoliberal rationalities of competition, individualism, marketization and managerialism. CBPR is constituted as contesting these neoliberal rationales and is, therefore, situated as outside of or in opposition to knowledge capitalism and put forward as an antidote to anxieties surrounding the corporatization of the university. I argue that these discursive claims to socially just knowledge production obscure the neoliberal rationalities that find fertile ground in CBPR. I locate this paradox in the partnering-to-compete paradigm, which I traced to funding arrangements that simultaneously mandate and corrode the social relations of CBPR and induce CBOs to collaborate with universities to replace eroding program funding with research dollars. The ethical tensions of diverting resources away from social programming, while engaging in practices that are remarkably similar to programmatic interventions, warrant serious reconsideration. Further, marketized rationalities for knowledge commodification and transfer were linked to the conflation of social action with dissemination. This second shift enables CBPR's liberatory social justice aims to be supplanted with demands for more research dollars, evaluation, evidence, publications and unsustainable pilot programs.

And because governance is never total, I put forward counter proposals for thinking and doing CBPR differently. The proposals I advanced in this chapter included practicing distance and refusals; embracing a complementarity that takes seriously the diverse interests, investments and resources of collaborators; decentring academe through alliances with social movements; and re-orienting CBPR toward social and epistemic scales of transformation to mitigate neoliberal individualism. While these resistant proposals do not escape the ethical tensions raised, they do offer critical hope for less dangerous university/community collaborations.

Notes

1. Collaborative research between academe and communities is semantically and operationally diverse. I began my research with the terminology and commitments of Participatory Action Research. However, over time I settled on CBPR, as it is currently the most commonly used terminology in the context of collaborative research in Canada.
2. See for example Bourke (2013) and Janes (2017), who track the institutionalization of community-engaged scholarship in academe. Brown et al. (2015) note that almost every Canadian university has institutional support to CBPR including community-university engagement centres. For specific examples of the entrenchment of community-engagement as a marker of institutional excellence, see the strategic white papers of Ryerson University (2014), the University of Toronto (2008; 2012) and York University (2010).
3. The quotes from research participants are linked to the three self-identified positions (i.e., academics, community-based professionals and peers — community members directly impacted by the social issue under inquiry). The number in parentheses indicates the unique identifier of each participant.

References

Absolon, Kathleen, and Susan Dion. 2017. "Doing Indigenous Community-University Research Partnerships: A Cautionary Tale." *Engaged Scholar Journal: Community-Engaged Research, Teaching, and Learning* 3, 2: 81–98.

Ahmed, Sara. 2000. *Strange Encounters. Embodied Others in Post-Coloniality*. London and New York: Routledge.

Battiste, Marie. 2011. *Reclaiming Indigenous Voice and Vision*. Vancouver: UBC Press.

Bell, Kirsten, and Amy Salmon. 2011. "What Women Who Use Drugs Have to Say About Ethical Research: Findings of an Exploratory Qualitative Study." *Journal of Empirical Research on Human Research Ethics* 6, 4: 84–98.

Blackstock, Kirsty, Liz Dinnie, Rachel Dilley, et al. 2015. "Participatory Research to Influence Participatory Governance: Managing Relationships with Planners." *Area* 47, 3: 254–260.

Bourke, Alan. 2013. "Universities, Civil Society and the Global Agenda of Community-Engaged Research." *Globalisation, Societies and Education* 11, 4: 498–519. doi.org/1 0.1080/14767724.2013.834182.

Brown, Allannah. 2013. *Action and Research: Community-Based Research at the Wellesley Institute*. Toronto: Wellesley Institute.

Brown, Leslie, Joanne Ochocka, Sylvie de Grosbois, and Budd Hall. 2015. "Kamúcwkalha: Canadian Approaches to Community-University Research Partnerships." In *Strengthening Community University Research Partnerships: Global Perspectives*, edited by Budd Hall, Rajesh Tandon, and Crystal Tremblay (95–112). Victoria, BC: University of Victoria.

Cahill, Caitlin, David Alberto Quijada Cerecer, and Matt Bradley. 2010. "'Dreaming of … ': Reflections on Participatory Action Research as a Feminist Praxis of Critical Hope." *Affilia* 25, 4: 406–416.

de Sousa Santos, Boaventura. 2014. *Epistemologies of the South: Justice Against Epistemicide*. New York: Paradigm Publishers.

Dean, Amber. 2015. "Colonialism, Neoliberalism, and University-Community Engagement: What Sorts of Encounters with Difference Are Our Institutions Prioritizing?" In *Unravelling Encounters: Ethics, Knowledge, and Resistance*, edited by Caitlin Janzen, Donna Jeffery, and Kristin Smith (175–194). Waterloo: Wilfrid Laurier University Press.

Foucault, Michel. 1984. "On the Genealogy of Ethics: An Overview of Work in Progress." In *The Foucault Reader*, edited by Paul Rabinow (347–379). New York: Pantheon.

____. 2003a. "The Ethics of the Concern of the Self as a Practice of Freedom." *The Essential Foucault*, edited by Paul Rabinow and Nicholas Rose (25–43). New York: The New Press.

____. 2003b. "What Is Critique?" In *The Essential Foucault*, edited by Paul Rabinow and Nicholas Rose (263–278). New York: The New Press.

____. 2010. *Governmentality: Power and Rule on Modern Society*. London: Sage.

Goldberg, David. 2009. *The Threat of Race: Reflections on Racial Neoliberalism*. Malden, MA: Blackwell.

Guta, Adrian, Carol Strike, Sarah Flicker, et al. 2014. "Governing through Community-Based Research: Lessons from the Canadian HIV Research Sector." *Social Science & Medicine* 123: 250–261.

Henkel, Heiko, and Roderick Stirrat. 2001. "Participation as Spiritual Duty; Empowerment as Secular Subjection." In *Participation: The New Tyranny?* edited by Bill Cooke and Uma Kothari (168–184). London: Zed Books.

Holian, Rosalie, and David Coghlan. 2013. "Ethical Issues and Role Duality in Insider Action Research: Challenges for Action Research Degree Programmes." *Systemic Practice and Action Research* 26, 5: 399–415. doi.org/10.1007/s11213-012-9256-6.

Ilcan, Suzan, and Lynne Phillips. 2008. "Governing through Global Networks: Knowledge Mobilities and Participatory Development." *Current Sociology* 56, 5: 711–734.

Janes, Julia. 2016. "The 'Will to Participate': Governmentality and Community-Based

Participatory Research." *Intersectionalities, Special Issue: The Ethics and Politics of Knowledge Production* 5, 1: 110–125.

___. 2017. "Governance through Participation: An Inquiry into the Social Relations of Community-Based Research." PhD dissertation, York University.

Jordan, Steven, and Dip Kapoor. 2016. "Re-Politicizing Participatory Action Research: Unmasking Neoliberalism and the Illusions of Participation." *Educational Action Research* 24, 1: 134–149.

Kovach, Margaret. 2010. *Indigenous Methodologies: Characteristics, Conversations, and Contexts.* Toronto: University of Toronto Press.

Langdon, Jonathan, and Kofi Larweh. 2015. "Moving with the Movement: Collaboratively Building a Participatory Action Research Study of Social Movement Learning in Ada, Ghana." *Action Research* 13, 3: 281-297. doi.org/10.1177%2F1476750315572447.

Mignolo, Walter. 2000. *Coloniality, Subaltern Knowledges and Border Thinking: Local Histories/Global Designs.* Princeton, NJ: Princeton University Press.

___. 2009. "Epistemic Disobedience, Independent Thought and Decolonial Freedom." *Theory, Culture & Society* 26, 7/8: 159–181. doi.org/10.1177/0263276409349275.

Miller, Peter, and Nikolas Rose. 2008. *Governing the Present: Administering Economic, Social and Personal Life.* Cambridge, UK: Polity.

Mohanty, Chandra. 2003. *Feminism Without Borders: Decolonizing Theory, Practicing Solidarity.* Durham, NC: Duke University Press.

Nichols, Naomi, David Phipps, Stephen Gaetz, et al. 2014. "Revealing the Complexity of Community–Campus Interactions." *Canadian Journal of Higher Education* 44, 1: 69–94.

Olssen, Mark, and Michael A. Peters. 2005. "Neoliberalism, Higher Education and the Knowledge Economy: From the Free Market to Knowledge Capitalism." *Journal of Education Policy* 20, 3: 313–345. doi.org/10.1080/02680930500108718.

Paradis, Emily. 2015. "Do Us Proud: Poor Women Claiming Adjudicative Space at CESR." *Journal of Law and Social Policy* 24: 109–134.

Pinto, R.M., Anya Y. Spector, R. Rahman, and J.D. Gastolomendo. 2015. "Research Advisory Board Members' Contributions and Expectations in the USA." *Health Promotion International* 30, 2: 328–338.

Ryerson University. 2014. *Our Time to Lead. Academic Plan 2014–2019.* Toronto: Ryerson University.

Salmon, Amy, Annette J. Browne, and Ann Pederson. 2010. "'Now We Call It Research': Participatory Health Research Involving Marginalized Women Who Use Drugs." *Nursing Inquiry* 17, 4: 336–345. doi.org/10.1111/j.1440-1800.2010.00507.x.

Scott, David. 1995. "Colonial Governmentality." *Social Text* 43: 191–220.

Shore, Cris. 2008. "Audit Culture and Illiberal Governance: Universities and the Politics of Accountability." *Anthropological Theory* 8, 3: 278–298. doi.org/10.1177/1463499608093815.

Simons, Maarten, Jan Masschelein, and Kerlijn Quaghebeur. 2005. "The Ethos of Critical Research and the Idea of a Coming Research Community." *Educational Philosophy and Theory* 37, 6: 817–832. doi.org/10.1111/j.1469-5812.2005.00160.x.

Simpson, Audra. 2007. "On Ethnographic Refusal: Indigeneity, 'Voice' and Colonial Citizenship." *Junctures: The Journal for Thematic Dialogue* 9: 67–80.

Stoecker, Randy. 2009. "Are We Talking the Walk of Community-Based Research?" *Action Research* 7, 4: 385–404. doi.org/10.1177/1476750309340944.

Thorpe, Charles. 2009. "Capitalism, Audit, and the Demise of the Humanistic Academy." *Workplace: A Journal for Academic Labor* 15: 103–125.

Trudeau, Dan, and Luisa Veronis. 2009. "Enacting State Restructuring: NGOs as 'Translation Mechanisms.'" *Environment and Planning D: Society and Space* 27, 6: 1117–1134. doi.org/10.1068%2Fd0906.

Tuck, Eve, and K. Wayne Yang. 2012. "Decolonization Is Not a Metaphor." *Decolonization: Indigeneity, Education & Society* 1, 1: 1–40.

University of Toronto. 2008. *Towards 2030: A Third Century of Excellence at the University of Toronto.* Toronto: University of Toronto.

____. 2012. *Towards 2030: The View from 2012 – A Framework.* Toronto: University of Toronto.

Venn, Couze. 2009. "Neoliberal Political Economy, Biopolitics and Colonialism: A Transcolonial Genealogy of Inequality." *Theory, Culture & Society* 26, 6: 206–233.

York University. 2010. *Building a More Engaged University: Strategic Directions for York University 2010–2020.* Toronto: York University.

8

"Let Us Tell Our Story"

Deep Memory, Mnemonic Resistance,
and the Failure to Witness in Research
with Street Sex Workers

Caitlin Janzen and Susan Strega

> Through the years, five years and then one by one they're …
>
> [Name] died of natural causes.
>
> There was a lot of us.
>
> There's probably only four of us left so I'm going through the same thing again.
>
> [Name] was killed, [Name].
>
> Most of them were horrific.
>
> [Name] was found on Highway 8.
>
> [Name] was murdered by Portage la Prairie there.
>
> [Name] was found on the street anyway from a seizure after being massively beaten. [Name] was hammered in the back of the head, caved in.
>
> *Researcher:* Oh my goodness …
>
> Well, us as trannies, we're not even recognized.
>
> (Naomi, Winnipeg interviews)[1]

The excerpt above is a direct transcription from an interview conducted as part of the "Someone's Mother, Sister, or Daughter" research, a two-stage project that sought to understand the role of family relationships in the lives of women who work in street sex work, including their decisions to transition out of street sex work.[2][3] In the first stage, we conducted a discourse analysis of street sex work and street sex worker coverage in western Canadian newspapers (Janzen et al. 2013; Strega, Janzen et al. 2014). The research team then interviewed women involved in street sex work and family members of women involved in street sex work; in total, we interviewed ninety-nine people from Calgary, Edmonton, Regina and Winnipeg.[4][5] In this chapter, we explore the ethical responsibilities and challenges engendered by our work. More specifically, we analyze the role of memory in our interviews and the forms of "mnemonic resistance" enacted by participants as strategies of laying claim to participation in the production of knowledge about the lived reality of street sex work in Canada. Central to our analysis is the question of whether academic research can adequately respond to the testimonial address. In other words: What is the capacity of researchers to bear witness to the pain of others?

The "Someone's" research team comprised women who had either worked in the sex industry themselves or who had a family member who was working in street sex work. Half of the team was Indigenous, the other half white. In many cases, the embodied knowledge the researchers carried with them into interviews and our openness with the women we interviewed about this knowledge established a certain level of trust on the part of the interviewees. At the same time, it founded a complex form of empathy on behalf of interviewers. How to remain ethically reflexive about this empathy and trust is a serious concern for those who conduct research with participants, such as those we interviewed, who have been historically and systemically excluded from the production of knowledge about their own lives and experiences. While participant narratives were often punctuated by assumptions of shared knowledge between themselves and researchers ("you know what that's like, you've been there"), it would have been perilous to linger in this imagined common space.

As Harjeet Badwall (this volume) contends in the context of her research with racialized social workers, researchers must not "rest comfortably into an assumption that our shared subject-positions ... guaranteed comfort and safety for the participants. There may have been moments of comfort and shared understanding, but they were not stable or consistent." Badwall reasserts the need for researchers to examine socio-historical specificities through the prism of intersectionality as a counter to grand assumptions that insider research allows us access to deeper or more authentic forms of knowledge. It is a dangerous proposition to imply a sameness between the women we interviewed and us as academic researchers, who may have "been there," or at least somewhere nearby, at points in time. After all, the coordinates of where "there" is located are always in flux, dependent not only on the positionality of various research team members, but also on the various subject positions *within* each member of the research team, and identifications forged on the basis of them. Badwall draws upon Dwyer and Buckle's (2009) notion of a "third space" in research relations, one that exists between insider and outsider. In resisting the notion of identarian sameness, we maintain the necessity of exploring the dialogic space between inside and outside as well as between researcher and participant. In what follows, we engage with these complexities as we examine the role of shared (though not common) memory as a mode of intersubjective relationality in research.

Research, Ethics and Research Ethics

Because we sought to understand the social processes involved in transitioning out of street sex work, and in the family relationships of workers, our original intent was to conduct a grounded theory study via semi-structured interviews. After obtaining ethics approval from the University's Human Research Ethics Board, we worked closely with sex worker–serving agencies that were known to us, or with whom we had worked previously, to recruit participants who met our criteria: over 18 years of age; current or recent (within the past three years) experience in street sex work; or a family member of a street sex worker with current or recent experience. All interviews were conducted in sex worker support agencies; funds were provided to agencies so that support staff were available if women wished to debrief after their interviews.

From the first interviews, participants conveyed to us in a myriad of ways that they wanted and needed narrative sovereignty over their stories. Recognizing that the information we sought was not the knowledge our participants needed to impart, we correspondingly realized that we were being called upon to listen more than interview. In response, we re-conceptualized this phase of our work as a narrative analysis and storytelling, methodologies with which research team members were familiar (Strega, Brown et al. 2009; Thomas 2015). As DeVault (1999) notes, narrative has the potential to make the invisible experiences of the marginalized visible. Stories are embedded within political, social and cultural contexts; narrative analysis, when done critically, is intended to reveal the layered contexts and interactions of race, class and gender (Riessman 2002).

We situate the interview encounters discussed in this chapter within the context of colonial violence and systemic misogyny, a context in which sex workers are harmed, often with impunity. Moreover, founded as it is upon the control and management of the bodies and sexuality of Indigenous women (Lawrence 2003, 2008), the ongoing colonial legacy of what is known as Canada continues to endanger the lives of all Indigenous girls and women. Ongoing dispossession, structural poverty, misogyny and colonial racism form a particularly violent intersection for Indigenous women involved in street sex work in Canada (Hunt 2015/2016; Dean 2015; IACHR 2014; Amnesty International 2009).

Indeed, traumatic violence inscribed itself on many memories shared with us during the interviews. Trauma was sometimes woven into narrative, and at other times it resisted narrative assimilation, appearing instead in episodic flashes. These observations are consonant with the understandings put forth by those working within the framework of trauma theory. Hence, in this chapter, we draw upon the fields of trauma studies and memory studies to further articulate the workings of traumatic memory in the interviews as dialogue encounters. The European Holocaust serves as a key referent for both trauma and memory studies. In fact, as Andreas Huyssen (2000) argues in his discussion of dominant memory discourses, the globalization of memory studies has given an overdetermining function to the European Holocaust whereby the specificities of historical traumas (including the Shoah itself) are obscured when viewed through the assimilating lens of European history. Huyssen continues:

> It is precisely the emergence of the Holocaust as universal trope that allows Holocaust memory to latch on to specific local situations that are historically distant and politically distinct from the original event. In the transnational movement of memory discourses, the Holocaust loses its quality as index of the specific historical event and begins to function as metaphor for other traumatic histories and memories. (24)

In what follows, we heed this warning by attending to the geographic and cultural specificities of Canada's legacy of genocidal violence against Indigenous Peoples, and its resonances in national memory, legislation and social stratification. That said, the conceptual contributions of survivors of the European Holocaust such as Charlotte Delbo, as well as those who witnessed the testimonies of European Holocaust survivors (Langer 1991; Felman and Laub 1992), offer a theoretical frame for understanding the workings of traumatic memory and the complexity involved in offering an ethical response as interlocutor–researchers. Consequently, our discussion does also give a certain prominence to accounts of the Shoah.

Confronted with the traumatic memories of ninety-nine people, we soon realized that these interviews were in fact testimonies, and as such, they demanded an ethical response in excess of both the commitments and the capacity of most social science research. Hence, in this chapter, the analysis of our experience oscillates between the traumatic memories recalled by the participants, and the ethical demands — both ontological and institutional — made of academics as witnesses to traumatic testimony. It is this call to witness, and the inability of academic research to fully respond to testimony, that is of central concern in this chapter.

The excerpt we opened with illustrates one way in which the participant's right to have control over their own narrative is restricted by the academy. It is, of course, not truly a direct quote. In accordance with the *Tri-Council Policy Statement* that governs research in Canadian academic institutions, all identifying characteristics have been removed. The names of speakers have been replaced with pseudonyms and the names they speak have been removed altogether, or, as it is commonly referred to in transcription, "scrubbed clean" of identity. This means that even when she testifies about what it means to go unrecognized, even in her deliberation to speak the names of her disappeared loved ones, Naomi (who is not really Naomi at all) has her acts of memory expunged.[6] The severing of the subject from a name, especially one of her own choosing (Naomi is a self-identified trans woman) is, according to Derrida (1976), a form of "intersubjective violence" (127). We argue that this overwriting and deleting of names is just one of the ways that academics are, at best, institutionally constrained witnesses and, at worst (or perhaps, therefore), ultimately failed witnesses. In this cultural moment, we must also ask what it means that we continue to do so in the face of the insistent call from Black and Indigenous communities to "say her name" (Crenshaw and Ritchie 2015).

As we explain below, our impulse to give a rational and effective account of violent events was repeatedly troubled by the insurgence of what Delbo, in her memoir *Auschwitz and After* (1995) termed "deep memory," with its capacity to shatter tidy narrative frames. That nearly every woman we spoke with recounted violent events — sometimes many — that they experienced as traumatizing is evidence of the magnitude and ubiquity of violence perpetrated against street sex workers. And yet, unless carnivalized in the mainstream media, the disappearance and murders of women from the Downtown Eastside of Vancouver, the rural outskirts of Edmonton, the North End of Winnipeg, and throughout Canada, barely resound in the national consciousness, let alone reside in the national memory. As Razack (2007) pointedly argues, consuming narratives of pain without interrogating the power relations that sustain the suffering of others allows the privileged viewer/reader to maintain both a proximal distance and a "willful blindness about our collective history" (387). We feel good about feeling something; however, we are not moved to action. As Razack continues: "We have too often felt, rather than thought, and very little has changed" (ibid.).

Still the stories continue to be told and in fact, the telling of these stories is a form of what Margalit terms "mnemonic labor" (2002, 52). From the Greek, *mnēmonikos*, meaning "relating to memory" or "of memory," mnemonics are commonly understood as memory aides. Referring to Ancient Greek and Roman oration, mnemonic devices such as the "memory palace," or the method of loci, highlight the practice — indeed the art — of remembrance. In this chapter, we use the term "mnemonic" conceptually to illustrate the creative work involved in the strategic deployment of memory, whether for conservative or emancipatory ends.

In his book *The Ethics of Memory* (2002), Margalit distinguishes between what he calls "common memory" (a memory held by a large number of individuals) and "shared memory" (memory calibrated through a process of communication). Margalit conceptualizes the attunement of shared memory through the telling and retelling of events as "mnemonic labor" (52). He continues:

> In modern societies, characterized by an elaborate division of labor, the division of mnemonic labor is elaborate too … shared memory in modern society travels from person to person through institutions, such as archives, and through communal mnemonic devices … whether good or bad as mnemonic devices, these complicated communal institutions are responsible, to a large extent, for our shared memories. (2002, 54)

As with all divisions of labour in modern industrialized societies, the division of mnemonic labour is inequitable. As we discuss below, while state-led processes such as Truth and Reconciliation Commissions and formal inquiries represent a condensed end-product of decades of political struggle, the resulting reports are routinely endowed with the title of "Official History." In contrast, survivors of injustice and allied activists fight tirelessly to have their stories heard, never mind registered, in shared memory.

Beginning in the 1990s, sex worker activists, Indigenous and other community activists, testified publicly and regularly about violated, disappeared and murdered women at events such as the annual Downtown Eastside (DTES) Memorial March (Hunt 2013). As documented in Amnesty International's *Stolen Sisters* reports (2004; 2009), disappeared and murdered women are disproportionately Indigenous and disproportionately street and survival sex workers. These stories are not new; as Whitlock (2006) notes, long before the recent Truth and Reconciliation Commission in Canada, extensive documentation of colonial violences as well as Indigenous protests against residential schools and the abuses of the Sixties Scoop was collected and archived (Dussault and Erasmus 1996; Fournier and Crey 1997; Woolford 2009). These testimonies are now accompanied by demands from Indigenous communities, scholars, and activists, not only for public acknowledgment of these events and experiences, but for concrete action to redress the consequences of them. Our research was conducted in the midst of such demands for public acknowledgment, recognition and responsibility for change. But it was also carried out (and continues to be carried out, by acts such as the writing of this chapter) with the knowledge that the stories accumulated to date by us and by others, whether in their individual horror or in their staggering numbers, have thus far failed to galvanize actions that would bring an end to, or even a significant reduction in, violence. As quickly as these stories are told, they risk being forgotten by all except those to whom they are most intimately connected. Yet, in common with other academic researchers, the promise of change — one of the levers on which we rely to encourage, recruit, or elicit research participants — connects the telling of stories to this possibility. This is illuminated in the below excerpt from our "Information and Consent Form":

> A potential benefit of taking part in the research is the opportunity to tell your story and reflect on your experiences. Also,

your participation in this project may benefit future street sex workers and/or their families by contributing to a greater understanding of the experiences and supports needed by street sex workers and their families.

Nothing in these statements is ethically transparent about the aptitude of academic knowledge production to engender the transformational change survivors are rightfully demanding.

Perhaps the ability to forget about the ongoing violence perpetrated against street sex workers is unsurprising considering that who and what we remember has everything to do with where people are positioned within systems of power. Marginalized by gender and gender identity, processes of racialization, systems of colonization, poverty, and in many cases, addiction and disability, street sex workers are denied access to the means of dominant memory production. This is not to say, however, that they have not contributed "mnemonic labour" (Margalit 2002, 52) or to shared memory. For, as Ryan writes (glossing on Foucault's famous statement), "where there is power, there is [mnemonic] resistance" (Foucault, as cited in Ryan 2011, 165). In the latter part of this chapter, we identify strategies of memory insurgence as acts of resistance deployed by the women who shared their testimonies with us. More than acts of memorialization, these strategies work actively at the interface of individual and collective memory, constituting politicized demands for a place within national memory.

The task of the ethically responsive researcher is to amplify these strategic acts of memory, giving them conceptual precedence in a step towards epistemic justice for those who have not yet been heard. We take the words of Kwagiulth scholar Sarah Hunt (2013) seriously in this regard:

> we need to move away from positioning ourselves as advocates for, and saviours of, some disempowered sister–Other and instead facilitate a process that centres the voices of sex workers themselves. Otherwise we risk reproducing the discourses of colonialism that constitute Indigenous women as without agency. (87–88)

Hence, we argue that any mnemonic occupation of collective memory must occur on terms established by street sex workers themselves and take representational forms in which they can recognize their own lives and the lives of those they have lost.

Response-ability: Interviewing, Listening, Witnessing

To state that street sex workers are unremembered in collective memory may appear ill-informed in this cultural moment. Over the past fifteen years, women involved in street sex work have occupied a central space in Canadian public discourse. From the media maelstrom that came to surround the women disappeared from Vancouver's DTES, to recent prostitution law reform, to the consistent conflation of the systemic catastrophe of Missing and Murdered Indigenous Women with the sex trade, street sex work is again a fixture on the front pages of newspapers across Canada. And yet, as with the genocidal violence of colonization, occupying a place in national awareness is separate from holding an activating space — that is, a space that precipitates action — within the national memory. As many participants testified, the haunting figures residing in newsprint (virtual or physical), even while they share the same names and facial features, failed to adequately represent the loved ones they had lost. At best, these phantasmatic figures formed vacant outlines; at worst, they took the shape of uncanny imposters. One woman spoke about how women with full lives outside of sex work become abstracted through objectifying headlines, whereby lives are reduced to bodies and losses to statistics. Asked about her thoughts on how the media portrays sex workers, she replied:

> Well they don't, they just sit there "Oh, a woman's dead. They found a body wherever. She used to …" you know "Do drugs and alcohol." What was it this one time I seen in the paper, it so infuriated me because one week a white lady had … had been found. And it was "Oh and her grieving mother." And later, a working woman was found the next month or somethin'. "Oh this lady was known to be a … a known drug user." What about her grieving mother?

Another woman spoke about how her friend's death was covered in the media in such a way as to render her unrecognizable to those close to her. When asked how the media could have represented her life more fully, she stated, "Just represent her life. Period." Yet a third woman stated that in media coverage of sex workers, "their humanity is completely lost and it's all … it's all surface and there's no real."

The very name of the "Someone's Mother, Sister, or Daughter" project was an attempt to re-remember the women who were disappeared or murdered or violated. The title is taken from a direct quote from Rick Frey, who, in demanding justice for his murdered daughter, Marnie Frey, stated: "The Downtown Eastside women were portrayed as being prostitutes, hookers, drug addicts. They weren't — They were our daughters, our sisters, mothers" (*Vancouver Sun* 2007, A4). This and similar statements represent the emergence of a strong counter-discourse, which is itself mobilized in an ethically complex way. While heeding the call to complicate the subjectivities of the women they were writing about, journalists imposed a new framework whereby women became grieveable only through their relational ties to recognized family structures (Strega, Janzen et al. 2014; Dean 2015).

Violent, traumatic memories featured prominently in every interview; in many cases, almost as soon as recording began, women launched into life stories in which time was measured in intervals of violence at the hands of family members, foster parents, intimate partners, customers, as well as complete strangers. It was as if a gate had been opened with the first question, unleashing a flood of unstoppable memories. In retrospect, we believe two main factors contributed to this traumatic turn in the research: first, that members of the research team had experiential knowledge of the sex industry, some of it with street or survival sex work; and second, that in shifting from a semi-structured to a more narrative-inspired interview method, we opened a wide enunciative space, which participants filled with those memories they considered most significant.

That we, as researchers, had our own storehouse of similar or related memories from which to draw allowed us to assume membership in the "community of memory" (Margalit 2002, 69) formed by the women we were listening to, even if we did not remember the *same* episode of violence. This extension of Margalit's concept of shared memory is possible, we think, due to the extraordinary nature of the memories shared, combined with the intensity with which they are recalled, and in addition to the rarified and stigmatized social position one would have had to occupy to hold this "knowledge of the past" (14). Despite our assumption of a community of memory, however, there remains a measure of distance in our proximal relationship with these women, many of whom at the time of the interview were still working on the street, many of whom were living and struggling with addiction and serious health problems, most of whom were racialized as Indigenous (where half of the researchers were Indigenous), and almost all of whom were living in dire poverty. This subjective distance within a space of encounter cannot be narrowed with appeals to shared memory, whether implicit or explicit; it can be traversed with sensitivity and respect, but it remains structurally in place.

Drawing on the ethics of Emmanuel Levinas, Sara Ahmed (2000) holds that some modes of encounter are better than others. These better modes of encountering others are described through bodily sensations such as breathing and the caress. Levinas' ethics privilege ways of encountering that respect and uphold the otherness of the other, allowing for cohabitation instead of assimilation of the other into one's epistemic frame, or as Ahmed adds, fetishizing the strangeness of the stranger. We contend that the openness to and respect for difference central to Levinas' ethics is crucial for thinking through the ways in which proximity is negotiated based on a problematic insistence on shared experience and memories, both in academic research and in broader social relations.

Margalit (2002) makes a distinction between the abstract thin relations we share with distant strangers and those thick relations that bind us to those "near and dear" to us as they "are anchored in a shared past or moored in shared memory" (7). Where our thick relations are guided by ethics, Margalit argues, we are beholden to our thin relations only by a general morality. Ahmed also makes a clear distinction between morals and ethics. Importantly, however, unlike Margalit, Ahmed does not base this distinction on a tiered model of closeness and, therefore, responsibility. Quite contrary to this, Ahmed (2000) writes, "if we make our responsibility conditional then we are occupying the regulative order of morality — we are relying upon distinctions of worth (or worthiness) and need, by saying, I am responsible more for you ... than I am for the others" (146).

This Levinasian ethical stance, with its complex intersubjectivity, is unequivocal in comparison with Margalit's model, which, while seemingly concrete, depends upon an assumption of clear and fixed relations. Such clarity and permanency is rarely experienced in the messiness and fluidity of human relations. By contrast, Levinas offers us some lucidity:

we each have a responsibility, and, therefore, an ethical imperative to care and care deeply for the Other, full stop. This responsibility is pre-ontological, before knowledge of the Other and hence, prior to sociality. Margalit's tiered model of relations is, then, contrary to a Levinasian ethical position of being for and with others and strangers alike. And yet, while we adhere to Levinas' non-assimilative ethical imperative, the foundation of relationship on the basis of assuming shared memory complicated and disrupted this commitment at many points in the research process.

That some of us on the research team *got close* to the women we were interviewing through mobilizing our own memories, that we reduced the distance between self and stranger, does not automatically imply a sort of manipulation or insincere attempt to "build rapport." As interviewers, we sincerely *felt* close to the women we were interviewing. We aspired to convey a complex empathy that comes from a sense of living through shared struggles. And yet, as we discuss later, despite our good faith wishes, the space between *me* and *her* remains an ethically trepidatious zone in which good intentions are no guarantee against consumptive fantasies. Many participants were direct in resisting consumption, telling us that they expected action from us, that they were giving us their stories in the service of changing their own lives and the lives of other sex working women. But the dangers are evident, as Taylor, Sollange and Rwigema (2015) point out with reference to Rwandan survivors of genocide, "there is a real risk of testimony becoming an emotional commodity provided by the racialized survivor of violence for use in the academic and non-profit marketplace" (99). As academic "experts" in street sex work, we stand to reap many rewards "while paradoxically silencing and disempowering the survivor" (ibid.). Razack (2007) has used the phrase "stealing the pain of others" to argue that empathy can be an appropriative mode of consuming the other through annihilatory mechanisms of identification.

As noted, every person we spoke with (both women involved in street sex work and family members) told stories of trauma, loss and violence. This is especially notable considering our original interview schedule did not seek to elicit such narratives. However, we did begin interviews with the invitation: "Tell me your story." In extending such an invitation, one lets go of both the content and the context of the interview. With this invitation, the genre of the meeting was altered. Instead of research interviews, the encounters became venues in which women gave account of one's self, one's journey, and one's experiences, many of which were episodic recalls of traumatic violence. In other words, the interviews shifted genre from responses to testimonies while we, as actors, responded by shifting roles from researchers to witnesses.

With this transposed relationship comes a different ethical call, from a responsibility that is bifurcated between the research participants and the institution to a "response-ability" (Oliver 2000, 41) in the intersubjective present. No longer concerned with historical accuracy or verbal precision, the researcher as witness is called upon to attend to the performance of testimony. As Oliver writes,

> It is the *performance* of testimony and not merely what is said that makes it effective in bringing to life a repetition of an event; not a repetition of the facts of the event, nor the structure of the event, but the silences and blindness inherent in the event that, at bottom, make eye-witness testimony impossible. (39)

This impossibility of witnessing is more fully expressed in the work of Italian philosopher Giorgio Agamben (1999). For Agamben, witnessing constitutes an ethical challenge of remaining in the space of collapse between the human and inhuman. In this space of testimony, a space structured by what is missing from it, the speaking subject engages in the dual process of subjectification and de-subjectification. The very act of speaking one's self into being requires that the subject vacates or dismantles their self to speak of themselves. In the enunciative act of giving testimony, the *speaking* subject shifts into the subject *being spoken of.*

As it pertains to the current discussion, we conceive of ethical witnessing as a practice of listening vigilantly to the will and drive to *live*, of lending epistemic support to the subject who may begin to fade in the process of speaking their history into being in and through the practice of giving testimony. Ethically witnessing this testimony entails careful attention to subjectivizing processes that persist *in spite of* the State's unwillingness to protect some bodies, and its inability to deliver justice. In our analysis, we sought to explore the radical act of living in the "state of exception" (Agamben 2005) enacted by Canada's legal abandonment of street sex workers, who continue to be murdered with impunity.[7] After all, engaging in street sex work is most often a practice of survival, of staying alive by a necessary means. Thus, bearing witness to testimonies of loss and survival is much more than an attempt to retroactively bestow humanity upon those who were already human, despite having been denied their human rights.

Inherent in this ethics of witnessing is the call to remain open to that which strikes us as inconceivable, that which is beyond our frames of comparison. As Oliver (2000) states in her rejection of models of ethics based on recognition politics, "acknowledging the realness of another's life is not judging its worth, or conferring respecting or understanding or recognizing it, but responding in a way that affirms response-ability or addressability.... Ethics is possible only beyond recognition" (41–42). Oliver's ethics of witnessing is at the same time a theory of the subject. For in listening with "vigilance" to and for the dialogic performance that makes "openness to otherness possible" (2000, 39), our subjectivity, along with that of the speaker, is inaugurated in the intersubjective space between us. Oliver offers a deeply relational mode of subjectivity enacted in the intersubjective space that holds both address and response. The question remains, however, of the capacity of social science research to remain in this mode of intersubjective relationality and, therefore, this ethics of witnessing.

At this point, it important to note that it is we who came asking for testimony. As researchers, we actively recruited our participants and we did so with a specific purpose: to analyze and to theorize. To theorize for social change, yes; but it is nonetheless important to identify the direction of the ethical imperative to provide testimony, as it changes the dynamic of witnessing. This is not to imply that those who participated in the research did not find it somehow cathartic or empowering; indeed, many shared that speaking their stories was beneficial in precisely these ways. It is, however, to highlight the difference between witnessing done in the context of academic research and witnessing that originates from the desire of the speaking subject to give testimony.

Reclaiming Deep Memory

In his work with testimonies of Holocaust survivors, Dori Laub determined that any attempt towards recovering from trauma requires the production of a coherent narrative about the traumatic event. While we problematize both the capacity and imperative of imposing structure on trauma, many of the women who spoke with us disclosed that this was, in fact, the first time they had spoken about a particular traumatic event.

As Gloria stated, "I could never talk about my bad time with anyone. I still remember it like today though." If, as Langer suggests, "testimony is a form of remembering" (1991, 2), what operations of memory are involved in the testimonies given by the women we listened to?

In *Auschwitz and After*, Delbo differentiates deep memory from common memory. Deep memory is that which breaks through the "skin of memory" (Delbo quoted in Langer 1991, 5). Like all skin, the "skin of memory" serves as a boundary between inside and out, self and other. Also like skin, deep memory clings to the self so that even after Delbo, employing a serpentine metaphor, attempts to shed her mnemonic skin, she is left carrying a layer of deadened skin that "refuses to renew itself" (Langer 1991 xi). Deep memories are both etched upon and ingrained within the body, lodged beneath the surface, but only tenuously. As Delbo makes evident, deep memory threatens to break through at any point, "spill[ing] out and recaptur[ing]" the host (Langer 1991, 5). Affective spills, when they occur, interject into linear chronology, casting one back into the time and place of their traumatic event. The past, Delbo warns, never remains in the past. Instead, it holds the new self, the post-traumatic self, hostage to its return via an insurgence of deep memory. When asked by an interviewer if she continues to live with Auschwitz, Delbo responds, "No — I live beside it" (Langer 1991, 5). Like Delbo, Sharon, a woman we spoke with in Calgary, lives beside the tyranny of deep memory. She observes about her struggle:

> The things that I still have trouble living with … still have trouble remembering are things that I did to get drugs. Somehow those are harder memories for me to live with. Well though, of course, obviously, I'm living with them, but they're harder for me to live with.

Tania, another woman we spoke with, also testified to the injuriousness of her deep memories and her efforts to contain them. Speaking to her repressed memories of a near-death experience, Tania discloses, "I don't even remember what happened that night. I mean I do, but don't want to know. I am good not remembering what he did to me." Tania works to keep that traumatic night in the dark depths of her memory, because she knows that if such a memory were to resurface, it could forever shift the delicate balance between knowing and not-knowing what she endured.

Despite the agonizing struggle, one does continue to "live beside" this place of trauma. What allows one to go on living beside "a place beyond knowledge" (Delbo 1995, 230) is what Delbo refers to as "common memory." According to Delbo, common or "thinking" memory speaks in an altogether different voice from that of deep or "sense" memory; so distinct, in fact, it is as if the self has been split or doubled, as she reveals in the following passage:

> I have the feeling that the "self" who was in the camp isn't me, isn't the person who is here, opposite you. No, it's too unbelievable. And everything that happened to this other "self," the one from Auschwitz, doesn't touch me now, *me*, doesn't concern me, so distinct are deep memory and common memory. (Delbo as cited in Langer 1991, 5)

Victoria conveyed such doubling in our testimonies by stating, "I've been sleeping for the last few years and now that I'm awake and coherent — I know I've seen so much, but it's almost not me."

Common memories allow one to speak of trauma in a more or less rational way. When one speaks in the voice of common memory, time is once again a relief: "that was in the past. It is over now." As Langer finds in his account of Holocaust testimonies, in the act of giving traumatic testimony, individuals tend to "veer" (1991, 5) from common to deep memory as if engaged in a battle between the two selves. Indeed, we witnessed such a subjective battle in Mary's testimony:

> Last March on the 20th, I was beckoned over to a vehicle and I turned around to walk away and I was crossing the street and they revved up from behind me and smashed into me. The first hit fractured my hip, my pelvis, my body flipped forward and my face slammed into this ... the trunk of the car and broke my jaw and they hit the back of my head here too. But anyway, I'm laying on the floor and I'm telling you, this was a life-changing moment for me. It was in the middle of the night, it was dark and then a voice said "Move Mary." And I didn't even think about it at the time. But I just started moving, crawling with my elbows and I could hear like in my body, like I could hear in my head a crunch going all up my body but I still kept pulling myself. I got ... my upper body in between two parked cars and

I passed out. Well the guy had gone down a block, did a U-turn and came back and ran me over again.

[...]

Looking back, you know, I've had many, many emotions about this person that did that, did this. There was a driver and then there was a passenger and ... I've had many, many feelings about this driver and — oh I don't know, but right now I think in a weird sort of way I kinda owe him a debt of gratitude. My life has changed very much for the better since. I've been. I mean I can't hate him.

At the fore of Mary's testimony is her struggle to keep deep memory at bay through the introduction of an acceptable narrative frame. Indeed, she labours so intensely in saving herself from the return of this repressed memory that the redemptive reframing made possible through common memory is ironically less coherent than the attempted articulations of her sense memories. To be grateful to a man who ran her over twice and left her for dead is unimaginable — except as an alternative to the alienation of returning to that place of trauma on a swell of deep memory. Here the ethics of witnessing, which entails listening without imposing a frame of coherence, is seemingly at odds with feminist politics, which may seek to interrupt Mary's narrative in order to disrupt the misogynistic logic behind both the heinous act she recounts and the sense she is making of it.

For trauma theorists such as Caruth (1996) and Brison (2002), gaining some measure of narrative control over the possessive grip of deep memory is crucial to regaining subjective agency. For Culbertson (1995), the task "is to render body memories tellable" (179) by rearranging them into a coherent story. "In so doing," she continues, "it becomes possible to return the self to its legitimate social status as something separate ... undoing the grasp of the perpetrator and re-establishing the social dimension of the self lost in the midst of violation" (179). Equations such as these treat deep memory as something to overcome. Indeed, as Delbo illustrates, living in the throes of deep memory can be debilitating. Still, Langer reminds us that deep memories are also reservoirs of embodied knowledge that common memory can never possess.

Against this strand lies that of Indigenous scholars including Clark (2016) and Million (2013), who question the usefulness of trauma theory and therapy in attempts to understand and respond to the violent experiences of Indigenous peoples. As Million points out, the discourse of trauma has its own grip, locking Indigenous voices in echo chambers of psychological and legal victimhood. Million (2013) writes, "in the struggle to authorize trauma's discursive truth, Native voices authorize trauma, putting it into motion in their affective testimony.… They become empowered by trauma's discourse at the same time they become its subjects" (94). Clark reiterates this argument, adding that discourses of trauma can themselves be techniques of colonization. Clark (2016) writes:

> we need to suspend the ongoing creation of Western stories of damage and harm. Otherwise the statistics become toxic narratives of identity that are not situated within lives of resistance and strength, nor placed in historical and changing place and time.… It is vitally important in our listening and our witnessing that we do not continue to create narratives of risk and harm separated from the stories of strength, resiliency and survivance. (54)

Further, Million (2013) persuasively argues that the ethic of discharging traumatic memory through telling is a "convoluted undertaking" as "Canadian Aboriginal peoples, subjects of a history of colonial violence, are thickly ensconced in the intensities, logics, and languages of trauma, particularly now as they are called on to speak as subjects of 'truth and reconciliation'" (3). While many trauma theorists identify coherent, linear and rational as requisites for healing, the capacity of such narratives to deliver justice, as we shall see, is less promising.

Between Contested Memory and Revisionist History

In the excerpt that opens this chapter, Naomi is remembering and giving an (ac)count of her chosen family, a family of individuals who as street sex workers themselves did not count in life as life, and unless re-counted, will not come to matter in death. To go unrecognized, as Naomi is aware, means that at an intimately material level, your memories are not stored in dominant collective memory and you yourself will likely fail to figure as part of national memory. For those street and/or survival sex workers who are Indigenous — and in western Canada, the site of our research, survival and street sex workers are disproportionately Indigenous — this fate is inextricably linked to ongoing attempts to remove Indigenous peoples, both physically and symbolically, from land and from national narratives (Barman 2007; Freeman 2010; Regan 2010).

For example, during the 2017 sesquicentennial, many settlers were startled by persistent and varied expressions of Indigenous resistance to celebrating Canada's "150th birthday"; most could not recognize that the celebration required (again) the erasure of Indigenous peoples' long and well-documented tenure in the physical landscape. Because white Canada's existence as a nation-state is intricately bound up with genocidal violence and dispossession directed at Indigenous peoples, memory falls into a "paradoxical space between the inability to forget and the inability to remember" (Lozanski 2007, 224). It must occupy this space, for if it did not, white Canadians would be visibly implicated in the ongoing colonial violence project that is Canada. In the case of survival and street sex workers, the international and internal valorization of Canada as a safe country is inextricably tethered to a ubiquitous silence on the gendered and racialized violence to which sex workers are routinely subjected. This often-lethal violence, though not formally recognized, continues to haunt the boundaries of national memory. At the same time, it cannot be formally remembered, for the recognition that comes with remembering would implicate us in accepting violence and in allowing violence to continue.

This struggle between collective memory and officiated history as it relates to violence against street sex workers is illustrated by *Forsaken*, the report issued by BC's Missing Women Commission of Inquiry.[8] Tasked with collecting testimony from municipal and Royal Canadian Mounted Police forces, as well as from families of disappeared women, non-profit groups, and the community at large, the Inquiry was a battleground over the means of mnemonic production and the power to declare contested memory History proper.

The report endeavours to convey care and compassion by, for example, listing all sixty-seven of the women who were disappeared from the Vancouver area between the years of 1997–2002. Read alongside Margalit's criteria for ethical memory, however, *Forsaken* is a historical document that goes no further than its moral obligations to the women. Although the Commission heard some testimony from family, friends, and others in thick relation to the disappeared women, the report is written in the language of thin relations. Part I opens thusly:

> Most of us never have to be concerned about being forsaken. We have permanent homes, we have family doctors, we have jobs where we work daily with others, we have children who rely on us, we have medication if we are sick, we are not victims to extreme violence, we are not engaged in any activity that would cause us to hesitate to notify the police of our presence. (Oppal 2012, 4)

Rather than appeal to shared attributes of geography, memory or national identity, *Forsaken* widens the distance between the disappeared women and the imagined reading public. This proximal distance renders not just the suffering, but also the very existence of street sex workers unimaginable to the exclusionary collective.

Forsaken attempts to silence the ghosts that haunt Canadian society by putting them to rest in the past. The Inquiry endeavoured to sedate the trauma of abandonment by creating a cohesive narrative about the lives of the disappeared women, beginning with clear antecedents and ending with definitive answers about the police investigations. In her work on the Chilean Torture Commissions, Macías (2013) explains the process as "the reduction of complex personal experiences to manageable information that can be included in the national narrative in a non-threatening manner" (126). Despite the formalized imperative to remember through thinking memory, however, Delbo reminds us that sense memories have other plans. Deep memory tells the collective conscious that the violent disappearance and murder of sex workers "is an abyss that we cannot pass over with equanimity into the future" (Langer 1991 xiii).

Politicizing Deep Memory

It is through the non-linear temporality of deep memories that the women who gave their testimonies as part of the "Someone's" project rejected the imaginary figures constructed through dominant means of memory production. Ryan (2011) uses the term "mnemonic resistance" to refer to "the methods by which the individual resists the encroachments of a powerful dominant memory, which is enabled by both the individual's or repressed group's interpretative agency and also the collective memory's necessarily vague characters" (155). The women we spoke with exercised highly interpretive forms of agency to reject the versions of memory circulated by the mainstream media. They advocated for an uprising of deep memory capable of breaking through dominant narrative frames that dehumanized and misremembered their loved ones. Tina articulated this in the excerpt below:

> Let us tell our story. You know, they can't change what we tell them to fit the public's eye. We have to be able to say our own words without them putting in their edits and this and that. It's not right, 'cause then it's not the truth. And I think our truths have to be told, you know? From the inside. And maybe people will start to listen and start to care more, because we are people. We hurt. We bleed. We feel. We have families. We have kids. And they gotta understand that.

The significance of remembering on their own terms was one that resounded throughout the testimonies. The women we spoke with contested dominant memory in concentrated and sometimes public ways. Shirley, for example, was actively writing her memoirs as a mode of intergenerational memory transmission, while Patricia wrote back to the journalist who covered her friend's death, publicly contesting the dehumanizing treatment of her memory. Said Patricia:

> My girlfriend, [Name] was on the front page when she was murdered. And the picture they put on there. They didn't have to put that kind of picture. Like they made sure they fucking zoomed in on the beer bottle that was on the table behind her. And she had her feet up. So, I wrote to the paper, I wrote to the reporter. They should be accountable. These women have families and friends. [I wrote] did you have to use that kind of picture? It was as if they were saying "she's a crack whore. Easy come, easy go."

In contesting representations that mis-represent and mis-remember those within their community of memory, the women insisted upon a "hospitable memory" for their loved ones — a memory founded upon a responsibility "beyond all living present, before the ghosts of those who are not yet born or who are already dead, be they the victims of wars, political or other kinds of violence" (Derrida 1994, xix). Gordon (1997) adds that we will continue to live in a society haunted by ghosts so long as the political conditions to blame for the corporeal disappearance of our ghosts remain in operation. "We must reckon with [our ghosts] graciously," Gordon writes, "attempting to offer [them] a hospitable memory *out of concern for justice*. Out of concern for justice would be the only reason one would bother" (64, emphasis in original).

Conclusion

Just as our encounters with women involved in street sex work often ended in a call to action, we conclude this chapter with some remarks on the capacity of academic researchers to act as witnesses. Turner (2012) argues the ontological conditions necessary for witnessing are that the witness be present, available, and that they provide a strong representation of what they have witnessed. Being present, in Turner's theorization, does not require that one be at the actual site. To witness, he writes, "is then not so much about co-location or contemporaneity," but requires an anticipatory stance, a readiness to witness and to recall what they have witnessed in another time or place. "Witnessing," Turner continues, "can then be recognized as a mode of being in the world" (6). On this count, there is nothing to preclude academic researchers from being effective witnesses. Indeed, Margalit also realizes the import of a network of witnesses beyond the first-hand witness for carrying the significant event into the future.

It is Turner's condition of availability that forms the greater barrier to the concept of research as an act of witnessing. Beyond the instrumentality of being "ready-at-hand," availability in witnessing requires an offer, an invitation to witness. Though not explicitly identified by Margalit, his use of the concept of communities (of morality and of memory) also relies on an invitation. Inclusion in any voluntary community is contingent upon acceptance. As we illustrated in this chapter, as researchers with experiential knowledge and shared memories of sex work, we temporarily assumed membership into the community of memory shared by the women we interviewed. As the exchange below demonstrates, this was, in many ways, a wrongful assumption.

Evelyn: Well, I'm scared but ... you know, it's good that people like you actually, you know, care.

Researcher: Mmm.

Evelyn: I mean you want to hear our stories, and you take the time out. 'Cause it takes, you know, I can see the look in your eyes and I can tell, like you're really listening, you know what I mean? Like you're listening and you know — you're listening …

Researcher: Mmmhmm.

Evelyn: And it's like something that takes a lot, you're actually sitting here like doing this interview is like you care.

Upon first reading, Evelyn's statement appears to be a simple statement of gratitude. The more we read it, however, the more complex her address becomes. For example, her phrase "people like you," radically undercuts any assumption we researchers may have held of belonging to a "natural community of memory" (Margalit 2002, 69) with the women we were listening to. In fact, much like Delbo's account, Evelyn's address is as much a challenge as it is a call to witness. She gets to the crux of testimonial ethics, saying by implication, "you are listening, but can you *hear* me?" Or, "I look in your eyes and it is *like* you care, but what will you *do*?" We worry that just like in the encounter itself, we will fail to respond ethically to her testimony.

Above all, the women we spoke with wanted us, the researchers, to record their stories, steeped as they were in deep memory, and to share them with the full weight of their affective resonance. And how might we respond to this call? The mandate of academic research (most especially social science research) is to sort through human experience in search of generalizable themes, dominant discourses, or narrative frames. Stories are fragmented into excerpts, severed from speaker and context, and compiled into codes or themes. Even more, they are stripped of names and identifying features to conform to institutional research ethics, which are long on legalities, but short on justice. In other words, that which was given as testimony may well be returned as data unless we work hard to convey the women's words in ways that honour and convey all the affective resonance with which they were experienced and shared.

In his discussion of witnessing, Margalit (2002) maintains that moral witnessing is "all about taking risks" (157). We contend that one risk we must take (particularly those of us in the social sciences) is to admit that in the role of academic researchers, we are not capable of acting as moral witnesses and that we do not often offer a hospitable memory to those who have been disappeared. Instead, we assume (and oftentimes consume) the stories of those we encounter and rewrite them in our own words and for our own purposes. In so doing, we risk further alienating the traumatic speaker from their deep memories by co-opting the narrative.

Margalit (2002) credits the moral witness with the hope "that in another place or time there exists, or will exist, a moral community that will listen to their testimony" (155). While currently failing as moral witnesses, academics can work towards the realization of this hope by sharing material resources with marginalized communities of memory so they may continue to gather and proliferate their own testimonies. Beyond this, we must recognize that "ethics cannot be separated from politics" (Macías 2016, 38). We can and must refuse to elicit solely or primarily for our own purposes, stories of the Other. Instead, we must at last heed bell hooks' injunction (1992 151–152), first published almost three decades ago, and echoed above by Tina:

> Often this speech about the "Other" annihilates, erases: "No need to hear your voice when I can talk about you better than you can speak about yourself. No need to hear your voice. Only tell me about your pain. I want to know your story. And then I will tell it back to you in a new way. Tell it back to you in such a way that it has become mine, my own. Re-writing you, I write myself anew. I am still author, authority. I am still the colonizer, the speaking subject. and you are now at the center of my talk." Stop.

Notes

1. All names used in this chapter are pseudonyms.
2. Other members of the research team include Susan Strega (PI), Leslie Brown, Jeannine Carrière, Robina Thomas and Sinéad Charbonneau (RA), all from the University of Victoria.
3. Street sex work is qualitatively different from other forms of sex work and usually involves a combination of sex work for money and the exchange of sex for food, drugs, or shelter. It represents the smallest, though most visible, sector of sex work.
4. Despite being housed at the University of Victoria, British Columbia, the research team made the decision not to conduct interviews in Vancouver as the community was still deep in grief over the trial of serial murderer Robert Pickton and his subsequent appeal process, as well as the court's decision not to try Pickton for the murder of twenty other women. Many of the sex work–serving agencies we spoke with during the recruitment process reported that journalists and academics alike in recent years had exploited women in the DTES [Downtown Eastside] community.
5. In this chapter, we will be drawing only on the perspectives of women with direct experience in street sex work, as opposed to those of family members who have never worked in street sex work.

6. Following the work of Dean (2015), we use the term "disappeared" to refer to the many women abducted and murdered across Canada. As opposed to the more common "missing," "disappeared" conveys action on the part of a (male) perpetrator. By contrast, the term "missing" implies that the women are responsible for their own disappearance or simply vanished into thin air. As Dean (2009) eloquently explains, the term "disappeared" resonates with "*los desaparecidos*," a term for those "disappeared" by government forces in Argentina and under the Pinochet regime in Chile. For her sensitive and careful argument on the application of this term, see Dean's (2015) book *Remembering Vancouver's Disappeared Women: Settler Colonialism and the Difficulty of Inheritance.*

7. For more on this, read Pratt's (2005) use of Agamben's adoption of biopower in which she compellingly argues that the approximately sixty-nine women who were murdered after being disappeared from Vancouver's DTES experienced legal abandonment by the state. She extends Agamben's theory by attending to the gendered and racialized dimensions of rendering certain women "bare life."

8. Any doubt that the Inquiry was a site of history closed off from the gestures and plasticity of living collective memory is eliminated by the notice appearing in the centre of the commission's homepage. The notice reads: "This website is an archive and will not be updated" (www.missingwomeninquiry.ca). An archive that does not expand into the future, Derrida warns, entombs the memories it contains.

References

Agamben, Giorgio. 1999. *Remnants of Auschwitz,* translated by Daniel Heller-Roazen. New York: Zone Books.

____. 2005. *State of Exception,* translated by Kevin Attell. Chicago, IL: University of Chicago Press.

Ahmed, Sara. 2000. *Strange Encounters: Embodied Others in Post-Coloniality.* London: Routledge.

Amnesty International. 2004. *Stolen Sisters: A Human Rights Response to Discrimination and Violence against Indigenous Women in Canada.* London, UK: Amnesty International.

____. 2009. *No More Stolen Sisters: The Need for a Comprehensive Response to Discrimination and Violence Against Indigenous Women in Canada.* London, UK: Amnesty International.

Barman, Jean. 2007. "Erasing Indigenous Indigeneity in Vancouver." *BC Studies* 155: 3.

Brison, Susan J. 2002. *Aftermath: Violence and the Remaking of a Self.* Princeton, NJ: Princeton University Press.

Caruth, Cathy. 1996. *Unclaimed Experience: Trauma, Narrative, and History.* Baltimore, MD: Johns Hopkins University Press.

Clark, Natalie. 2016. "Shock and Awe: Trauma as the New Colonial Frontier." *Humanities* 5, 1: doi.org/10.3390/h5010014.

Crenshaw, Kimberlé, and Andrea J. Ritchie. 2015. *Say Her Name: Resisting Police Brutality Against Black Women.* New York: African American Policy Forum. static1. squarespace.com/static/53f20d90e4b0b80451158d8c/t/5edc95fba357687217b08 fb8/1591514635487/SHNReportJuly2015.pdf.

Culbertson, Roberta. 1995. "Embodied Memory, Transcendence, and Telling: Recounting Trauma, Re-Establishing the Self." *New Literary History* 26, 1: 169–195.

Dean, Amber. 2009. "Hauntings: Representations of Vancouver's Disappeared Women."

PhD dissertation, University of Alberta.

___. 2015. *Remembering Vancouver's Disappeared Women: Settler Colonialism and the Difficulty of Inheritance*. Toronto, ON: University of Toronto Press.

Delbo, Charlotte. 1995. *Auschwitz and After*, translated by Rosette C. Lamont. New Haven: Yale University Press.

Derrida, Jacques. 1976. *Of Grammatology*, translated by Gayatri C. Spivak. Baltimore, MD: Johns Hopkins University Press.

___. 1994. *Specters of Marx: The State of the Debt, the Work of Mourning and the New International*, translated by Peggy Kamuf. New York: Routledge.

DeVault, Marjorie L. 1999. *Liberating Method: Feminism and Social Research*. Philadelphia, PA: Temple University Press.

Dussault, René, and Georges Erasmus. 1996. *Report of the Royal Commission on Aboriginal Peoples*. Prepared on behalf of Royal Commission on Aboriginal Peoples. Ottawa: Canada.

Dwyer, Sonya Corbin, and Jennifer L. Buckle. 2009. "The Space Between: On Being an Insider-Outsider in Qualitative Research." *International Journal of Qualitative Methods* 8, 1: 54–63.

Felman, Shoshana, and Dori Laub. 1992. *Testimony: Crises of Witnessing in Literature, Psychoanalysis, and History*. New York: Routledge.

Fournier, Suzanne, and Ernie Crey. 1997. *Stolen from Our Embrace: The Abduction of Indigenous Children and the Restoration of Indigenous Communities*. Vancouver, BC: Douglas & McIntyre.

Freeman, Victoria. 2010. "'Toronto Has No History!': Indigeneity, Settler Colonialism, and Historical Memory in Canada's Largest City." *Urban History Review/Revue d'histoire Urbaine* 38, 2: 21–35.

Gordon, Avery. 1997. *Ghostly Matters: Haunting and the Sociological Imagination*. Minneapolis, MN: University of Minnesota Press.

hooks, bell. 1992. "Yearning: Race, Gender, and Cultural Politics." *Hypatia* 7, 2: 177–187.

Hunt, Sarah. 2013. "Decolonizing Sex Work: Developing an Intersectional Indigenous Approach." In *Selling Sex: Experience, Advocacy, and Research on Sex Work in Canada*, edited by E. van der Meulen, E.M. Durisin and V. Love (82–100). Vancouver, BC: UBC Press.

___. 2015/2016. "Representing Colonial Violence: Trafficking, Sex Work, and the Violence of Law." *Atlantis* 37.2, 1: 25–39.

Huyssen, Andreas. 2000. "Present Pasts: Media, Politics, Amnesia." *Public Culture* 12, 1: 21–38.

IACHR (Inter-American Commission on Human Rights). 2014. *Missing and Murdered Indigenous Women in British Columbia, Canada*. Organization of American States.

Janzen, Caitlin, Susan Strega, Leslie Brown, et al. 2013. "'Nothing Short of a Horror Show': Triggering Abjection of Street Workers in Western Canadian Newspapers." *Hypatia* 28, 1: 142–162.

Langer, Lawrence L. 1991. *Holocaust Testimonies: The Ruins of Memory*. New Haven, CT: Yale University Press.

Lawrence, Bonita. 2003. "Gender, Race, and the Regulation of Native Identity in Canada and the United States: An Overview." *Hypatia* 18, 2: 3–31.

___. 2008. "Regulating Native Identity by Gender." In *Daily Struggles: The Deepening of Racialization and Feminization of Poverty in Canada*, edited by M.A. Wallis and S. Kwok (59–72). Toronto: Canadian Scholars' Press.

Lozanski, Kristin. 2007. "Memory and the Impossibility of Whiteness in Colonial Canada." *Feminist Theory* 8, 2: 223–225.

Macías, Teresa. 2013 "'Tortured Bodies': The Biopolitics of Torture and truth in Chile." *The International Journal of Human Rights* 17, 1: 113–132.

___. 2016. "Between Violence and Its Representation: Ethics, Archival Research, and the Politics of Knowledge Production in the Telling of Torture Stories." *Intersectionalities: A Global Journal of Social Work Analysis, Research, Polity, and Practice* 5, 1: 20–45.

Margalit, Avishia. 2002. *The Ethics of Memory.* Cambridge, MA: Harvard University Press.

Million, Dian. 2013. *Therapeutic Nations: Healing in an Age of Indigenous Human Rights.* Tucson, AZ: University of Arizona Press.

Oliver, Kelly. 2000. "Beyond Recognition: Witnessing Ethics." *Philosophy Today* 44, 1: 31–43.

Oppal, Wally T. 2012. *Forsaken: The Report of the Missing Women Commission of Inquiry, Executive Summary.* Prepared on behalf of the Province of British Columbia. Victoria, BC: Library and Archives Canada. gov.bc.ca/assets/gov/law-crime-and-justice/about-bc-justice-system/inquiries/forsaken-es.pdf.

Pratt, Geraldine. 2005. "Abandoned Women and Spaces of the Exception." *Antipode* 37, 5: 1052–1078.

Razack, Sherene. 2007. "Stealing the Pain of Others: Reflections on Canadian Humanitarian Responses." *The Review of Education, Pedagogy, and Cultural Studies* 29: 375–94.

Regan, Paulette. 2010. *Unsettling the Settler Within: Indian Residential Schools, Truth Telling, and Reconciliation in Canada.* UBC Press.

Riessman, Catherine Kohler. 2002. "Doing Justice: Positioning the Interpreter in Narrative Work." In *Strategic Narrative: New Perspectives on the Power of Personal and Cultural Storytelling,* edited by W. Patterson (195–216). Lanham, MA: Lexington Books.

Ryan, Lorraine. 2011. "Memory, Power and Resistance: The Anatomy of a Tripartite Relationship." *Memory Studies* 4, 2: 154–169.

Strega, Susan, Leslie Brown, Marilyn Callahan, et al. 2009. "Working with Me, Working at Me: Fathers' Narratives of Child Welfare." *Journal of Progressive Human Services* 20, 1: 72–91.

Strega, Susan, Caitlin Janzen, Jeannie Morgan, et al. 2014. "Never Innocent Victims: Street Sex Workers in Canadian Print Media." *Violence Against Women* 20, 1: 6–25.

Taylor, Lisa, Umwali Sollange, and Marie-Jolie Rwigema. 2015. "The Ethics of Learning from Rwandan Survivor Communities: The Politics of Knowledge Production and Shared Authority within Community-school Collaboration in Genocide and Critical Global Citizenship Education." In *Beyond Testimony and Trauma: Oral History in the Aftermath of Mass Violence,* edited by S. High (88–118). Vancouver, BC: UBC Press.

Thomas, Robina. 2015. "Honouring the Oral Traditions of the Ta't Mustimuxw (Ancestors) Through Storytelling." In *Research as Resistance: Critical, Indigenous, & Anti-oppressive Approaches,* edited by L. Brown and S. Strega (177–198). Toronto, ON: Canadian Scholars' Press.

Turner, Phil. 2012. "An Everyday Account of Witnessing." *AI & Society: Knowledge, Culture and Communication* 27: 5–12.

Vancouver Sun. 2007. "Marnie Frey." December 10: A4.

Whitlock, Gillian. 2006. "Testimony, Memoir and the Work of Reconciliation." In *Re-*

thinking Settler Colonialism: History and Memory in Australia, Canada, New Zealand and South Africa, edited by A.E. Coombes (24–43). Manchester, UK: Manchester University Press.

Woolford, Andrew. 2009. "Ontological Destruction: Genocide and Canadian Aboriginal Peoples." *Genocide Studies and Prevention* 4, 1: 81–97.

9

Digital Racism

The Re-Shaping of Consent, Privacy, Knowledge and Notions of the Public[1]

Anne O'Connell

Research protocols require that informed consent is secured before a project is underway. In the collision of online and offline worlds, researchers continue to offer research participants forms of confidentiality and privacy that no longer exist. Our struggles with power, politics, and ethics in research settings are being further unsettled by the way digital worlds reshape the agreements and protections researchers and institutions attempt to uphold. The explosion of big data[2] and digital information has transpired with little attention to the ethical considerations of consent, privacy and confidentiality central to research ethics, as these data-gathering enterprises impinge upon the terrain once the preserve of scholars. I am concerned with the ethical, political and epistemological implications of the reorganization of knowledge production in the age of new technologies, big data and "informational capitalism" (Coll 2014). How are these forms of data collection impinging on the research ethics we employ in our scholarly research? How might critical debates about research ethics be harnessed to challenge the rigid, individualistic and corporate view of consent and privacy now being fashioned by privacy experts? In particular, participatory, decolonial and Indigenous research protocols that have named and challenged white supremacy and the violence of western research methods are critical to identifying the ethical problems with digital ethics. Yet where are these important dialogues occurring? How do university research ethics protocols that claim to protect privacy intersect with government and corporate privacy legislation? As a new biopolitical force, check box consent has become an instrument of corporate conduct that ignores or sidesteps scholarly and community protocols as it redefines consent for scholarly research and broader society. In this chapter, I am concerned with how digital worlds are disrupting our ethical commitments in research. I argue that check box consent is being reformulated alongside the reconstitution of the public, the introduction of new forms of privacy/surveillance, and knowledge(s) that adhere to hegemonic whiteness, neoliberalism and securitization.

In *The Imperial Archive: Knowledge and the Fantasy of Empire*, Richards (1993) examines how the British Empire collected and collated information as a way of ruling colonies that were too far away to control. In many ways, what resulted was a "paper empire" (Richards 1993, 4). As the state and private industry develop their knowledge-gathering capacities, my concern is with the digital empire, a growing empire that operates inside and outside of institutional rules and privacy legislation in ways that expand corporate and state power in Canada. In an information age that heralds empiricism and data points supposedly free of theory, I propose that big data reproduces colonial and imperial ways of thinking and ruling in ways that become more difficult to name. This concern reaches beyond the field of big data or data science, affecting both qualitative and quantitative projects and redesigning what constitutes ethical relationships.

Context

In the age of big data, endless amounts of information that account for our moment-by-moment offline and online engagements are stored by and sold to various stakeholders. In many occupations, workers have little input into the creation and management of databases that may affect their own job security and the lives of the people they work with (Reamer 2013a, 2013b). Amazon workers are under constant surveillance as the company effectively crushes attempts at unionization. Serious questions about confidentiality and the ethics of digital information find non-profit agencies, the private sector and government scrambling to design protective e-policies while the demand for e-services (online counselling and peer support groups, blogs) continues to grow. The impact of the Covid-19 global pandemic and the massive transfer of our work and social lives online compounds concerns about the parameters of privacy, security, labour practices and knowledge production. In academia, university research ethics boards employ research protocols and informed consent forms that claim to protect a form of privacy, confidentiality and anonymity that no longer exists. Government, corporate and academic practices continue to overlap, as corporate interests and emerging technologies have increasing power and sway in university and community settings. It has become increasingly difficult to distinguish between *conducting research* and *gathering data points*. Both are governed by separate legislation and different institutional norms in Canada, even as they impinge on one another's territory. Research projects increasingly create and access online data sources or rely on the outcomes they produce, from data managers who sidestep academic research protocols. The ethics of research has a set of ethical codes set out since the Second World War, including: the *Nuremberg Code*; *the Declaration of Helsinki*; the *Belmont Report*; other agreements from the World Health Organization (who) and United Nations Educational, Scientific, and Cultural Organization (unesco); and Canada's *Tri-Council Policy Statement*, which governs all research with human participants in Canada. The ethics of information gathering has a more recent tradition in Canadian Federal and Provincial Privacy and Freedom of Information Acts (1983), the Personal Information and Electronic Documents Act (pipeda 1994), and the Personal Health and Information Protection Act (2004). Legislation deals with issues of consent in anti-spam legislation, online privacy, surveillance and copyright concerns (C-30; C-13; S-4), including increased police powers through the Anti-Terrorism Act.[3] More recently, the Federal government's proposed Bill C-11: Digital Charter Implementation Act (2021) advances consumer interests instead of employing human rights–based principles.

I am interested in informed consent protocols, and more importantly, how the extensive critique of them is bypassed by data collectors. The tenets of informed consent in academia attempt to ensure that participants have a clear idea about: the purpose of a research project, the risks and benefits, their voluntary participation, and promises of confidentiality. As outlined later, these protocols operate out of academic settings built on colonial histories where hegemonic whiteness and racial hierarchies remain the norm (Mignolo 2009; Henry et al. 2017). The protocol to inform human subjects *before* research has been conducted has been replaced by a concern with the product — the proper management and security of human data. The lack of consent required on supposedly public data or the use of weak protocols, such as check box consent, are coupled with directives that we must learn how to manage our own data.

A responsibilized digital citizen is required. How do we understand ethics in this commercial formulation? What kind of ethics are we moving toward when our face-to-face encounters are non-existent or are computer mediated, while the body itself is increasingly compartmentalized, exteriorized, and commodified through a tissue economy that includes biobanks (O'Doherty et al. 2011; Sariola & Simpson 2011), transplant tourism (Jaycox 2012), the human genome project, and reproductive technologies (Haimes, Taylor & Turkmendag 2012)?

Given the colonial backdrop of western research protocols and the important critique of racial categories and other forms of "difference," data categories and classifications are often ignored or taken for granted in data science. If ignored, they "resurrect the liberal human subject" (Cool 2012, 27) as white, male, heteronormative and middle class. If racial difference is taken for granted in research or data science, as Badwall (2016) reminds us, a dangerous essentialism takes root. Data science can reinforce racial or gendered scripts that are quickly reproducible, and mass produced in ways that become linked to social policies, surveillance, terrorism and ways of ruling. For example, the data sharing permitted by the Anti-Terrorism Act or through predictive policing will not target all residents equally. The types of personal data on phones or government databases appear to be neutral while masking the racial bias upon which they rely (racialized and Indigenous bodies who are disproportionately surveilled) and the dominant logics they set in place (the criminalization of racialized and Indigenous bodies). With the growth of web-based surveys, large data sets, and biased algorithms, I am interested in how we recognize and respond to inequities and epistemic violence in research *and* data collection. My concern is about the ways in which colonial scripts and forms of knowledge become reinstated in the exact moment we adopt technologies promoted as productive and efficient, the revered tropes of neoliberal global capitalism.

As we know, our data exhaust (by-products of our online activities) is collected and traded by governments and corporate entities, the data barons of today. In the age of big data, ethics are often non-existent, muted, or occurring in the moment of engagement (or after). More than 98% of the world's information is now stored digitally. Mayer-Schönberger (CBC 2013) described this situation as the datafication of life, showing how one exobyte was filled from collecting data from the beginning of time to 2003. Yet in 2013, the internet gathered five exobytes in two days. Smolan (CBC 2015) stated that Facebook has uploaded fifty billion photos (now closer to 350 billion), while Walmart conducts one million transactions per hour. The future of the internet of things is already here, hoping to further integrate the connectivity of our devices, objects and services, while robotics and artificial intelligence encourage the further integration of flesh and machine. The sheer amount of data and the new programs and algorithms to make sense of it (at such little cost, according to Sullivan 2013), has created new forms of knowledge and new disciplines — such as behavioural advertising, massified research, computational social science, learning and people analytics. These shifts in data gathering and knowledge production expose new vulnerabilities in our understanding of informed consent and research ethics.

In the following section of this chapter, I lay out some of the debates surrounding research ethics and discuss how critical views are useful as we scramble to respond to questions of consent raised by online interactions and research. The next section looks at how the rise of online and digital data is reformulating consent in relation to the reconstitution of the public, the introduction of new forms of surveillance, and forms of knowledge(s) that adhere to neoliberal capitalism and securitization. While scholarly protocols need to respond more meaningfully to the digital world, decades of scholarly debate about informed consent can be harnessed to challenge the political and epistemological dangers of ignoring consent altogether.

Informed Consent: Western Regimes and Decolonial Research

The scholarly literature on research ethics and informed consent in the West point to the influence of Plato, the Hippocratic Oath and to the series of enlightenment theorists who explored and expanded upon liberal tenets, such as individual rationality, autonomy, freedom, choice and the social contract (Manson & O'Neill 2007; McStay 2013; Reimer 2013a). While some scholars accept these principles as universal and shared standards, many point to a number of concerning assumptions in these frameworks. Critical voices from participatory, feminist and critical race fields characterize informed consent as a tool embedded in the violence of universalized colonial epistemological regimes (Khan 2005; Mignolo 2009; Pateman 1988). Indigenous scholars, in particular, have critiqued the colonial knowledge base of research and have put forward an Indigenous philosophical, epistemological and methodological approach that upends western research practices (Battiste, Bell & Findlay 2002; Kovach 2009; Simpson 2007; Tallbear 2014; Tuhiwai-Smith 1999). In this view, alterations to informed consent will never dismantle the dominant power relations and colonial histories upon which it rests and through which it is authenticated. As Manson & O'Neill (2007, 57) argued, the "18th century Enlightenment tradition of the social contract and the principle of freely given consent lends moral legitimacy to actions which would otherwise be regarded as unacceptable." Informed consent is embedded in a western social contract or racial contract, as Mills (1997) would say, that recognizes white individuals as autonomous and free beings who create and participate in everyday practices and policies that oppress and marginalize non-white bodies. As feminist, critical race and Indigenous scholars have argued, ideas of freedom and autonomy remain western, liberal, colonial, individualist and universalizing (in name only). These dominant ideas about power run counter to Indigenous values of relationship, community, reciprocity, respect, experience and storytelling (Kovach 2009). Yet according to Tallbear (2014, 2) reciprocity or "giving back" still enforces borders between researcher and subject when research should be about "intellectual, ethical and institutional building projects." Notably, Simpson (2007) observes how the anthropological record of Indigenous peoples emphasizes ceremony and tradition while their political critiques of statehood, justice, rights and history are absent.

If we examine the common institutional origins of informed consent, the literature begins with the *Nuremberg Code*[4] (1947), set in place in response to the horrors of human experimentation in Nazi Germany, followed by the *Declaration of Helsinki* by the World Health Association (1964), which outlined ethical principles for medical researchers and was revised for the seventh time in 2013. While the *Nuremberg Code* and *Declaration of Helsinki* are not legally binding, they have been adopted by national legislations and across many disciplines, associations and professions, in and outside of clinical studies. Their main tenets uphold the view that research participants must know what the research is and why it is being done and must have the capacity to voluntarily consent to the parameters of the study without coercion. Another central document is the *Belmont Report* (1978), which articulated three core principles to consider when researching human subjects: respect for persons, beneficence, and justice. The *Belmont Report* arose out of the now-famous Tuskagee Syphilis Study (1932–1972), in which hundreds of rural and impoverished African American men, many of whom had contracted syphilis, were never made aware of or treated for their condition, and were actively prevented from attaining treatment, so that the U.S. Public Health Service could study the progression of an untreated disease (Jones 1993). The study continued despite the *Nuremberg Code* and *Helsinki Declaration*. A parallel study funded by Johns Hopkins and the Rockefeller Foundation transpired in Guatemala (1945–1956), where orphans, inmates, sex workers and psychiatric patients were infected with sexually transmitted diseases without their knowledge. An apology from Secretary of State Hillary Clinton in 2010 has been followed by two attempts at class action suits from survivors and their descendants (Ellis 2015). Further research atrocities included the forced malnutrition of Indigenous children in six residential schools (1942–1952) in Canada, whose families were never informed. Dental care was denied to those suffering. The study continued as children died. These research practices come from a colonial history of human experimentation and ideas of racial superiority that circulated during racial slavery, settler colonialism, the rise of racial sciences, and the eugenics movement (Goldberg 1993, 2001; Hartman 1997; McLaren 1990; O'Connell 2009, 2010a, and 2010b). As Sztainbok and Gajardo argue in this collection, contemporary expressions of systemic racism and an imperialist geo-politics continues to undergird knowledge production enterprises. In Canada, we have the *Tri-Council Policy Statement* of 1998, which governs all research with human participants under the principles of respect for persons, concern for welfare, and justice. Through the *Belmont Report* and the *Tri- Council*, Institutional Review Boards (U.S.) and Research Ethics Committees (Canada) have been established to review and approve research studies and informed consent procedures, often operationalized through the informed consent form. Each form is required to include adequate information about the risks and benefits of the research in ways that support comprehension and voluntariness. The requirement of informed consent and a review by a research ethics committee is an agreed-upon standard that is designed to reduce risk to participants and to protect their welfare.

The critiques of informed consent range far and wide, many of them offering important commentary about the problems with digital ethics.

Violations and failures of informed consent processes can be glaring or subtle, as they are often unable to respond to a variety of different research contexts and locations. Informed consent protocols reproduce a dominant medical model and a rigid view of power in clinical and non-clinical research (Bayer & Edington 2009; Fisher 2012; Mystakidou et al. 2009; Shah 2012; Shamin & Qureshi 2013). Universal research standards never uncover the material and cultural inequities of research itself (i.e., North-South funding inequities), the colonial epistemes underlying research studies and the institutional and organizational practices that pre-configure the researcher (often as white) and participant (often as non-white). Fewer protocols address the complications of multi-racial researchers and subjects, and native informant concerns driven by local and global geo-political pressures. In the clinical arena, researchers often neglect the social and institutional constraints on people's decisions (Degner 2002; Sinding & Wiernikowski 2009) and recycle a vision of autonomy at odds with human interdependence (Sherwin 1998). An extensive literature on research ethics in relation to medical research and HIV/AIDS clinical trials in "resource poor" countries explore the structural inequities, barriers and complexities. Resourced researchers from the North apply unfamiliar protocols in countries that cannot fund their own research, offering community involvement and collaboration (Angwenyi et al. 2013; Bayer & Edington 2009; CAHR 2008; Fang, Steen & Casadevall 2013; Mystakidou et al. 2009; Sariola & Simpson 2011; Shah 2012; Shamin & Qureshi 2013).

Researchers question how people and communities participating in research can make informed choices (if that itself is possible) when the material preconditions for decision making are absent (Haimes, Taylor & Turkmendag 2012; Jaycox 2012). Studies on the medical economy of transplant tourism and stem cell research, for example, reveal the ways in which impoverished women "consent" to selling their organs and participating in stem cell research (Haimes, Taylor & Turkmendag 2012; Jaycox 2012). The term medical colonialism captures the shift of bio-pharmaceutical clinical trials from the West to Brazil, China and India — trials that test for diseases not even prevalent in these communities (Kamat 2014). These international ethical violations persist and extend the types of violent human experimentation that our ethical guidelines have been designed to halt. In less severe cases, Hochhauser (1999) argued that research descriptions and consent forms are incomprehensible to many. Consent forms that outline research objectives and procedures are designed to protect the safety of institutions, operating as a legal contract with an assumed rational actor, that in the end has little effect on a research participant's decision-making process (Armstrong et al. 2012).

Qualitative researchers question the dominance of the medical model in research ethics when trying to attain informed consent (Bengry-Howell & Griffin 2012; Boulton & Parker 2007; Murphy & Dingwall 2007). Ethnographers argue that consent is not something that happens prior to research but is ongoing and embedded in the research relationship (Murphy & Dingwall 2007; Plankey-Videla 2012). Other qualitative researchers argue that informed consent prohibits trusting and respectful relationships and forms of inquiry that social scientists prefer (Bengry-Howell & Griffin 2012; Boulton & Parker 2007; Murphy & Dingwall 2007). In addition, the normative top-down expression of power that the medical model is built on imposes a singular standard for consent that assumes the researcher always has more power and takes less risk compared to the participant (Nordentoft & Kappel 2011). This dynamic does not capture how scholars of colour and research participants are marginalized by and negotiate a pervasive whiteness and systemic racism in scholarship and in university and research settings (Badwall 2016; Khan 2005). Some communities also hold researchers to a higher standard of accountability and relationality. Yet no research project can claim innocence, as ethical transgressions can occur while building relationships. As Janes argues in this collection, participatory models of research are already deemed to be equitable, such that power and harms are easily overlooked. Some scholars argue that institutions and universities ethics boards are over-protective while others are concerned their research protocols do not do enough to protect vulnerable groups (Barton 2011; Clement & Bigby 2013; Fisher 2012; Shorey, Cornelius & Bell 2011; Swaine, Parish, Luken & Atkins 2011; Tyldum 2012). These debates highlight the changing practices of consent and ethics in scholarly research, the obvious and subtle forms of pressure researchers and participants experience, and the ongoing exercise of institutional, disciplinary, economic and global power relations in research.

The literature on research ethics and informed consent attempts to find room for improvement by reducing risks and encouraging recruitment, inclusion, diversity, participation, and individual and community benefits. Broader understandings of ethical research asks that we move away from damage-centred research on marginalized populations (Tuck 2009) and the drive for supposed improvements. Informed consent as a biopolitical force (Foucault 1979, 1991) asks us to examine the subject that is being produced and the technologies that make consent real, normative and expert-led. The goal is to be less interested in a "better" informed consent process and to examine what kind of participant, researcher and knowledge is being constructed through these ethical agreements. Scholars in the health field have noted how improvement, openness, transparency and accountability puts increased pressure on participation and informed consent practices. Sariola and Simpson (2011) and Sinding and Miller (2011) have noted how a more participatory and open approach can exacerbate inequality. Power shifts from medical professionals to research participants, who become overburdened and responsible for decision making about research and their own health care (Reubi 2012, 2013; Sariola & Simpson 2011, 517). In these examples, the supposed informed participant is a neoliberal subject (white, male, straight, middle class) who has more resources to make informed choices about research and health care. The normalization of these expectations aligns with a consumer model in medicine or research that promotes openness, protection and progress in neoliberal capitalism.

Further challenges to research ethics and informed consent come from Indigenous scholars and communities that turn away from incremental improvement and instead disrupt the material and colonial epistemological foundations of research. The *Tri-Council Policy Statement* (TCPS 2) lays out the procedures for researchers who intend to work with Indigenous peoples in Canada. In addition, many Indigenous communities and organizations in Canada are adopting a variety of protocols, including the principles of OCAP (ownership, control, access and protection) developed to govern the First Nations Regional Longitudinal Health Survey (First Nations Centre 2007). Castellano (2004, 2010) noted how Indigenous ethics have a different set of ontological and epistemological starting points. An ethics of non-interference and an understanding of knowledge based on connections between land, family, spirituality, values and everyday living take precedent. Agreements do not only recognize and privilege human relationships, and view knowledge as originating from the individual. The centrality of oral traditions, the knowledge of Elders, ceremony and language place Indigenous philosophies in opposition to many forms of research and have been targeted to advance genocidal policies and practices. Ethics reviews do not only apply to working with human subjects given the importance of ancestors, the land, non-human entities, visions and a spiritual world. Dialogues between these entities are lost, and data are reduced to the observable phenomenon of human action. Indigenous research and science strives for a "holistic awareness and highly focused analysis" (Castellano 2004, 104) whereby individual stories are validated by communities, unlike studies that call for objectivity and distance. Indigenous research is tied to self-determination and ownership and control over data (Castellano 2004, 102–104). Many of these principles are central to OCAP, in which relational accountability and respectful representation are key. Indigenous communities must maintain the intellectual property rights to own their knowledge, while ensuring the epistemological and ethical values of holism, spirituality and interconnection are upheld. Tallbear (2014) and Tuck (2009) and Simpson (2007) emphasize a politicized decolonial framework that recognizes and builds institutional power and ethical knowledge. Critical, Indigenous and decolonial theorists offer broad historical, theoretical and economic critiques of consent and ethics in research, highlighting concerns with institutional and disciplinary power, as well as colonial knowledge production. While university ethics boards attempt to reduce risk and improve consent processes over time, attempts at openness and transparency can reinstate inequality through demands for the responsibilized self. How might these critiques and alternatives contribute to the ways in which digital ethics are being construed? At the same time, how are the broader forces surrounding the digital world transforming research ethics protocols?

Digital Ethics: Consent, the Public, Surveillance and New Knowledge(s)

For the most part, digital research and big data have sidestepped decades of deliberation about the complications of consent, while data is increasingly commercialized and linked to forms of surveillance. This is not just a problem for big data researchers. Qualitative and quantitative research relies on the findings of data science to situate their research questions, provide literature reviews and help analyze findings. We continue to practice informed consent in our research, but can we deliver on what we promise? How can privacy, confidentiality and anonymity be practised in the same ways when they are being transformed or ignored in the digital world? What does it mean to rely on secondary data of individuals in the public domain when clear protocols explaining the purpose of the research were never presented or expected to become data for unrelated research projects? Even if further possibilities for research were presented to participants, the future use of data sets cannot always been predicted and, when combined with other forms of data, can create new harms that human participants and researchers could not have imagined. This makes it even more urgent that we: 1. Think more deeply about consent; 2. Determine what constitutes "the public"; 3. Consider how we may be drawn into surveillance practices; and 4. Be aware of the reproduction of colonial and racist knowledge production.

More and more research is conducted using web-based surveys and collecting and linking data points and private information from health records, institutional and government records, phone and text records, public blogs, forums and social networking sites. Researchers need to think about how our research findings can be linked to identities or profiles tracked by Facebook or Google, and other data sets. How might consent be viewed and operationalized by scholars located in university settings quite differently from the consent processes of data collectors in government, non-profits and commercial bodies? Research protocols advise that if the site is reasonably understood to be public, then consent is not required (Boggio 2010; Foster & Young 2012; Wager 2012; Wilkinson & Thelwall 2011). Yet larger questions persist. Informed consent rules emerged in response to grievous harms and as critical theorists argued earlier, one's ability to consent to research is situated in extensive material inequities and damaging research (i.e. medical colonialism). A biomedical liberal model still dominates in academia, a framework exacerbated by the check box consent in big data research. The disembodied data set is in danger of reinforcing real outcomes on real bodies. In order to maintain a critical research agenda in online and offline worlds, I argue that examinations of consent need to be in conversation with shifting notions of the public, privacy and surveillance, and the new knowledge forms of data science. These conditions are increasingly shaping the conduct of researchers and participants in highly individualized, commercialized and responsibilized ways.

Shaping Consent — Check Box
Consent Is Not Consent

Researchers need to address the types of online consent practices used in their own research and the databases from which they may be drawing. Attempts at data protection in academic, commercial and government sectors includes online consent, de-identification measures, privacy guards and opt-in measures[5] (Cavoukian 2013). Opt-in consent legislation was introduced to make transparent the use of cookies and reign in commercial advertising. Canada's anti-spam legislation (CASL) for commercial messaging requires opt-in consent, clear identification and contact information about the sender, and unsubscribe options that lasts for at least sixty days (Geist 2014). Informed consent issues are particularly important in relation to the use of web-surveys, big data and secondary data in all sorts of sectors, such as health, education (learning analytics) and the labour market. However, those who remain critical of genomic privacy with biobanks, electronic health records and secondary data release are often silenced by dominant views that all health research benefits society (Foster & Young 2012). For example, the use of learning analytics that require opt-in (check box) consent, or that bypass consent altogether, harvests students' educational data with posts from Facebook and Twitter to optimize resources and improve programs, student advising, and decision-making processes. Concerns about these cases are overturned by arguments about efficiency or the greater good, technical solutions prevail to ensure that data are de-identified, given a short lifespan and stripped of demographic information. Expert technicians such as data stewards and custodians are appointed in organizations (Cavoukian 2013).

Concerns about big data sets have become a question of data protection, not a question about the ethics of the research question itself or consideration of the human subject. As a less direct form of data collection, issues of harm and confidentiality appear less critical, and the data are viewed as part of the public domain. A moral script regarding the security, health and knowledge of efficient institutions takes precedence over issues of justice, the shaping of consent and the conduct of researchers and participants. As mentioned earlier, patients and research participants become subjects who decide upon their own participation in studies through check box consent, an approach that encourages less dialogue about the research question. Similar to informed consent forms, online consent relies on an impenetrable and performative legalese that is reproducible, quick, and on an enormous scale can invite or bar participants from commerce, human services, or research projects while protecting institutions. Researchers begin to view data as unrelated to the human subject, yet a data subject is still being formulated. Participants glide over descriptions of research projects to click the "I agree" consent box. Opt-in conduct becomes a marker of an informed digital subject while scholars or government actors contend that the shaping of consent just needs improvement. As Janes points to the dangers of participation in community-based research in this collection, in the online world, danger lies in the rejection of participation. Residents must take legal action to be forgotten online if they do participate and change their minds (Gollom 2014; Mayer-Schönberger 2014) or remain on the margins of the economy if they are not plugged in. The magnification of this reality during the pandemic includes an overnight demand for an online work force, consumer goods and health information about vaccines and vaccine passports. The fundamental issues about ethics that critical and decolonial scholars stress are undermined by research or data collection that bypasses human subjects (yet still resurrects the universal liberal subject) and increasingly aligns with informational capitalism, global economies and even national elections, as seen by the Cambridge Analytica scandal. Those who are without digital goods and services are seen to be outside of the economy and outside of humanity, making the constant expansion and upgrade of digital goods and services essential to life itself. In the age of neoliberal capitalism, to be outside of the economy is to not exist. Digital worlds are critical to human progress. Colonial scripts of improvement and civilized opt-in conduct are alive and well in Zuckerberg's (2014) statement that the entire "developing" world must be wired if they are to be pulled out of poverty. These are the same countries that receive the bulk of global e-waste.

How Are We Defining the Public in Research?

The collection and surveillance of our data continues to challenge and alter what constitutes the "public" and the expectations of privacy in research and everyday life. When are we being private, and when are we *in* public versus *being* public (boyd and Crawford 2012)? As some in the data science field have noted, the collection of data points is problematically deemed to be unrelated to human subjects and therefore exempt from informed consent protocols (Metcalf & Crawford 2016; Zook et al. 2017). Metcalf and Crawford argue for the urgency of Big Data to define the human subject and to critically interrogate what is owed to "data subjects" (2016, 2). When thinking about individual data as being private or public, these two realms of society are also being reconstituted. Are government bodies deemed to be public compared to the corporate world? Universities in Canada are viewed as public institutions, yet seek out more corporate funding and survive on inflated tuition rates from international students in an era of reduced government funding. Private public distinctions, of course, are political and historical terrains sustained through a hegemonic whiteness in Canada, organized along lines of class, gender, sexuality, immigration status, disability, etc. Those with more power are afforded privacy and protection from institutions and more recognizable and legitimate as public actors, who in turn, define and surveil these very boundaries. The public–private distinctions continue to overlap as government panels convene to restrict the corporate power of Facebook, Google and Amazon, or make them public utilities. Even the highest corporate fine ($5 billion) for privacy violations in the history of the U.S. Federal Trade Commission pales considering Facebook's 16.9 billion-dollar profit reported to shareholders in the second quarter of 2019 (Vaidhyanathan 2019).

Increasingly, the differences between government and corporate terrains (public–private) are becoming opaque in a wide range of areas such as health, education, security, surveillance and the ownership of information. Informed consent should consider whether information gathering is done for marketing and private business purposes or is done to further health research in communities. Is one data gathering practice more in the public interest compared to the other, when the public and private are being reconstituted? University research ethics fit inside and outside of these political spaces. With such scale, Google can track flu outbreaks faster than public health departments; an app can predict the onset of depression or track your menstrual flow to enhance targeted advertising (CBC 2015). Health and fitness apps sell your personal data to multiple advertisers. Bennett, Haggerty, Lyon & Steeves (2014) argued that the conflation of these two realms is largely driven by the unquestioned principle of efficiency rather than the promotion of justice. These overlaps are critical to understand. Especially to Ellen Richardson when she tried to cross the U.S. border for a holiday but was turned away due to health information shared with border services about her suicide attempt two years earlier (Hauch 2013). Data she believed to be private was held by and shared across public institutions in the name of security. The overlap of public and private interests and the connection to state surveillance or commercial profit is only exposed through extensive public exposure after the fact. A class-action lawsuit was filed in June 2014, after 8,300 health data files of new mothers from Rouge Valley Hospital were sold for over a decade to a financial firm (Chown Oved 2015; Margison 2014). The City of Toronto (the largest Canadian city) is demanding Uber release information about their recent global data breach of 57 million customers (Beattie 2017). Lifelabs, a medical laboratory clinic, is currently responding to the largest data privacy breach in Canadian history. Cambridge Analytica manipulated over 87 million Facebook user accounts to build voting profiles that would help elect an American president (CBC 2018).

Concerns about the mass of information being collected and exchanged between public and private entities will continue to fill our courtrooms and legislatures, yet mask the inadequate informed consent procedures and the collection and protection of digital data. As Gandy (2000) wrote, "while our mediated world becomes increasingly transparent, those who seek to profit from our data are incredibly opaque" (cited in McStay 2013, 599). With new private–public entanglements, how do we remedy these issues? As the critical research literature shows, material inequities continue to shape who can receive and advocate for appropriate forms of privacy, autonomy and informed consent. Who has the financial power and expertise to collect and sell data, and how do individuals negotiate with real institutional forms of power that are public, private, or both? Researchers need to account for the changing conceptions of our public and private worlds and understand connections between consent and when human subjects view themselves to be in public.

The premise that human subjects are already in public when online assumes that the internet itself is a public setting. As Foster and McChesney (2011) noted, the internet would never have come into existence if it had been left to the private market. What started as a military and university endeavour has quickly devolved into the growth of monopolistic corporate powers that benefit from government deregulation (Mager 2012) and the elimination of competition evident in search engines, digital download companies, and the Wi-Fi market. Google has become the "ultimate user-exploitation machine," exploiting connections and networks of website providers and users' activities, dictating how website providers must build their sites, and punishing those who destabilize its system (Mager 2012, 781). It continues to control 92% of the market, making a mockery of economic and neoliberal notions of consumer power and cutthroat competition (Foster & McChesney 2011). As Vaidhyanathan (2011) added, we are not the customer of Google, we are its product, as every site we visit creates a profile sold to advertisers and back to us. Facebook not only sells our data but increasingly steers political campaigns and debates that use inflammatory, incendiary and divisive language to produce more clicks, more shares and more votes (Vaidhyanathan 2019). The absence of robust consent practices is particularly jarring given we are not only participants in these forms of data collection, but are also the product, consumer and voter. These concerns are closely linked to literature reviews, searches and academic research that relies on the internet and other large datasets. Similar to the internet, Vaidhyanathan (2011) maintained, Google should be made a public utility, given the expanse of their data sets and enormous archive are affordable to universities with the largest research budgets. As Foster and McChesney (2011, 4) added, we need to challenge a world of "digital feudalism, whereby a handful of colossal corporate mega-giants rule private empires."

Surveillance/Privacy: Digital Conduct

Online and offline data collection is being impacted by privacy legislation increasingly tied to new forms of surveillance. As we offer privacy and confidentiality to human subjects in our studies, these terms are being redefined by governments and the private sector that collect data we use in our research. Previous conceptions of privacy were adopted as a way to defend against outside intrusions and forms of surveillance. Coll (2014) points to how they now act in concert with one another. Coll's central observation challenges how we view privacy in our research, when it no longer guards against interference. While many call for fundamental digital rights protected by government, these rights are being trampled by governments in the name of security, as revealed by Edward Snowden and reports about the policing relationship between telecom companies and the federal government of Canada (Bolen 2014).

Displaying a circular logic, public–private actors must bypass consent and invade one's security in the name of security. The paradox of biopolitics is that protection for some is fully tied to harm for others; others who must be positioned as intolerable, outside of humanity. Since 2012, the Federal Government in Canada introduced three pieces of legislation that would override privacy measures in the name of security. The three intolerable others that society needed protection from included: the pedophile (Bill C-30), the cyberbully (Bill C-13), and the terrorist (Bill C-51). The more recent incarnation shifts focus to the economy, as the Digital Charter (C-11) is concerned with consumer privacy protection. Each bill has attempted to allow policing bodies to access private data without warrants and to offer full criminal and civil immunity to those handing over information to security officials. While C-30 failed, Bill C-13 was passed in October 2014, in spite of widespread criticism (Wingrove 2014). These increased powers of surveillance have spread to cellphones that, due to a recent Supreme Court 4–3 decision, can now be searched by police upon arrest (Payton 2014). The Anti-Terrorism Act (2015) extends the powers of surveillance and arrest in order to prevent plots and the promotion of terrorist activities. If we acknowledge that racialized communities and Indigenous peoples are disproportionately under state surveillance and over incarcerated, these tracking measures and loss of oversight are perilous to these same communities. As reported, the federal government requests personal information from telecom companies 1.2 million times each year (only three out of nine companies reported this). Canadian Border Services makes thousands of requests for customer data every year, without warrants (Bolen 2014).

While the privacy of residents is under threat, the ability for Canadians to access information from and about the government has diminished. The government's compliance with freedom of information requests has stagnated or regressed as paper-based mailed-in forms remain the norm (Beeby 2013); this situation has only worsened under the current Liberal government (Bronskill 2017). While the origins and definitions of privacy certainly vary, Coll (2014) asked us to be aware of how privacy is being shaped and by whom. Heeney (2012) suggested that we need a "reconceptualization of privacy and protection from information entrepreneurs and omnibus information providers" (316). Who should be at the table and how might these decisions be made? Do we hand over fundamental and enduring discussions about privacy, autonomy, self-determination and community to the private sector? Is Rogers Communications Inc. (Canada's largest communications and media company) the appropriate body to be establishing privacy policies and protocols outside of public scrutiny, yet be accountable to shareholders? Coll (2014, 1) argued that the idea of privacy has been taken over and "re-shaped by and in favour of informational capitalism, notably by being over-individuated through the self-determination principle." It produces "subjects of privacy who are supposed to take care of it according to the official conception of privacy advocates and of the legislature" (Coll 2014, 1). Once it is defined, privacy becomes only about data and remains the right and responsibility of every individual to manage instead of a collective value. As a form of self-conduct, users must demonstrate proper internet conduct over themselves and their children. New privacy experts take over calling upon the education of the masses in relation to the management of their own privacy and that of their children. As Coll (2014) maintained, "private companies and governments seem to be actually defending privacy values much more than the majority of consumers," although they are the very ones that represent a threat to privacy (8). The idea that we have control over our data is chimerical given weak consent models, the shifting public terrain of our data and the internet itself, and how our data are being surveilled.

Shaping Knowledge — New Forms of Colonial Categories and Digital Racism

Many critics have raised concerns about the ways in which data points and algorithms are viewed as knowledge. More concerning are the forms of racial bias inherent in data collection, facial recognition technology, algorithms, and the domination of white men in the tech labour market. As Bennett et al. (2014) argued, big data leads to a form of social sorting, as individuals become profiles sorted into hierarchies, whereby "certain kinds of profiles pass with greater ease than others" (6). Certainly, many recognize that "algorithms used by institutions invariably reflect and perpetuate current biases and prejudices" (Slade & Prinsloo 2013, 1517). Noble (2018) argued that the private monopolistic nature of search engines and algorithms remain rooted in whiteness, and deeply racist views towards people of colour, and especially women of colour. Harvested data are limited by time and demographic data should not be attached to predict one's chances at success (Slade & Prinsloo 2013). Even with the removal of personal information and de-identification practices, people become a set of categories that injure their autonomy in addition to propagating racist and misogynistic views about individuals and communities. As many theorists note, Indigenous peoples and racialized and marginalized individuals cannot transcend the classificatory hierarchies in which they are deemed to be located. This becomes dangerous as big data sets apparently produce unbiased correlations about groups and communities. The scale of these data projects is matched by their apparent ideological impartiality. As boyd & Crawford (2012) described, big data usher in a profound change at the levels of epistemology and ethics. While it certainly entails unprecedented levels of data collection and analysis, the idea that numbers speak for themselves glides over misleading claims to objectivity and accuracy. Racial bias for example, will be more difficult to pull out of an algorithm. In addition, data cleaning and errors, restrictive models that exclude "extraneous" data points, along with ideas of randomness and representativeness, are compounded by research that shows people often have multiple online identities, insert inaccurate information, and differentiate between being in public and being public (boyd & Crawford 2012, 672).

Big data inverts the research process we rely on (Kitchin 2014; Metcalf & Crawford 2016; Zook et al. 2017). Kitchin (2014) noted how big data sets are the "by-product of another activity" and do not arise from a specific research question. A series of algorithms can be applied to arrive at the best explanatory model, unlike researchers who choose a methodology or analytic approach to apply to the data based on their own knowledge of the topic (2; 5–7). Rather than testing a theory, Kitchin (2014) argued, "new data analytics seek to gain insights 'born from the data'" (4). As many have argued, this level of empiricism can present relationships and patterns that we do not know to ask. And while it can produce correlations, it cannot explain why — why things happen. But as Kitchin (2014) added, all classifications, histories, data points and disciplines are discursively formed, never exhaustive, and imbued with values, perspective, context and histories, some of which are favoured and others of which are erased. While big data are used less frequently in the humanities and social sciences, the types of knowledge they produce, along with their ideas about privacy, consent and treatment of human subjects, creeps into qualitative and ethnographic research.

The use of big data in social sciences run the risk of producing studies that result in an inescapable conflation between correlation and causation. People of certain races do a particular activity more than others, so the activity becomes something they do because they are of a certain race. Racial bias in big data is evident in who qualifies for insurance, university admissions, bank loans, risk assessment for Black prisoners, and predictive policing (Buranyi 2017). As Mayer-Schönberger noted (CBC 2015), this leads to punishing people for things they might do or suspecting someone of a crime because of who their friends are on Facebook. This form of policing is already well established in Toronto, through a carding system and subsequent massive databases that target young Black men. Categories of race, gender, class, disability and sexuality become fixed, leaving little room for interrogating the forms of power that create them and apply value to them in the first place, even when the categories are incorrect. Epistemological concerns and biases are compounded when "full" or somewhat full data sets owned by social media companies are sold to the highest bidder (boyd & Crawford 2012). Others note how our knowledge systems are already restricted rather than expanded by the way search engines are organized. Literature reviews for academic studies are increasingly shaped by commercial interests, such as Google Scholar or the hierarchy of pageviews. As many note, Google has become a proxy for cognition itself, one that sees the top ten sites accounting for 75% of pageviews (Foster & McChesney 2011; Vaidhyanathan 2011). As Foster and McChesney (2011) stated, "big sucks the traffic out of small" (4). This also affects our historical and archival research. The digitization of archives has become increasingly unequal, as the documents and events of the colonized are often overlooked or omitted from data sets (Koh 2014). Sullivan (2013) described the huge amount of institutional and corporate power in "an anti-democratic system of control that cannot be transformed because it can serve no other purpose than that for which it was designed — the rationalization and control of human existence" (227). In thinking through research ethics and informed consent, it is critical we attend to the ways in which digital consent is being harnessed for shifting ideas about the public, and how surveillance and knowledge are being reconstituted in the age of measurement. New technology and the uses of new technology remain rooted in racism and white supremacy in ways that are more difficult to name, given the supposed value-free data and pressure for responsibilized conduct.

Conclusion

Critical scholars have turned their gaze upon the western imperial canon that dominates forms of knowledge production by calling attention to the problematics of research itself. Scholars remark on the material preconditions required for equitable informed consent practices and how colonial forms of consent and knowledge are ever present. While biomedical models of consent rely on a liberal individualized view of the research participant, big data and other forms of digital research bypass the human subject in favour of the data profile. Online data that is deemed to be in the public realm does not require ethics approval. Human data is not considered to put human subjects at risk. When online consent is required, it is reduced to a form of check box consent that protects institutions. I argue throughout this paper that this starting point is dangerous and requires qualitative and quantitative researchers to re-examine their consent protocols, what constitutes the "public," and how their data may be connected to forms of surveillance and the entrenchment of colonial and racial categories and knowledge that appear to be neutral.

We need to do research in ways that allow for transparency, consent and participation while remaining critical of these terms and how they operate in service to, and can enhance, neoliberal goals. Researchers start with the idea that the internet is public, even though it is a massive private and corporate enterprise. We must be aware of who is leading the debate on protecting our privacy and how it has become aligned with surveillance tactics in the name of security for all. Indeed, racialized communities and Indigenous peoples disproportionately face surveillance measures, resulting in deeply uneven effects on communities. As argued, big data research appears as a neutral science despite the view that all classifications, histories, data points and disciplines are discursively formed and that all data are partial and limited. Again, these dominant practices become harder to name while they simultaneously increase harms to more vulnerable communities.

Whitehead and Wesch (2012) asked if digital worlds are part of reconfiguring what it means to be human. Given the proliferation of online worlds, gaming, multiple role plays and identities, and the further integration of flesh and machine, we need to trace how these worlds are made available to and shape particular subjects. Many are concerned about the ways in which online presences weaken our moral and ethical responsibility to one another. Certainly, examples of social isolation, anti-social behavior, online suicides, bullying, trolling, cyberbullying and cyberstalking are plentiful, and studies into them critical. But my concern is with how these problems about individual behaviour are being put to use, and the kinds of individuals, subjects and profiles (pedophile, cyberstalker, terrorist, consumer) that are being deployed in the name of our security and monopolistic corporate imperial power. Tufecki (2012) argued that the "human is always a contingent category and different regimes of 'humanity' have been deployed throughout history to produce the exclusions and inclusions so necessary for the construction of power through difference" (4). Perhaps it is not so much the different identities but the different ways that identities, ethics, data profiles, check box consent and opt-in conduct in research are now put to use for the privatization, commercialization and securitization of the public.

Notes

1   This chapter draws from the journal article "My Entire Life Is Online: Informed Consent, Big Data and Decolonial Knowledge." 2016. *Intersectionalities: A Global Journal of Social Work Analysis, Research, Polity and Practice* 5, 1.

2.   I draw upon boyd & Crawford's (2012) definition, which states that it is the "cultural, technological, and scholarly phenomenon that rests on the interplay of: (1) *Technology*: maximizing computation power and algorithmic accuracy to gather, analyze, link and compare large data sets. (2) *Analysis*: drawing on large data sets to identify patterns in order to makes economic, social, technical and legal claims. (3) *Mythology*: the widespread belief that large data sets offer a higher form of intelligence and knowledge that can generate insights that were previously impossible, with an aura of truth, objectivity, and accuracy" (663).

3.   C-51 increases police capacity for preventative arrest without warrants, cracks down on digital and hard copy "terrorist propaganda," makes encouraging or promoting a terrorist act its own criminal offence, increases sharing of personal information with government departments and gives CSIS new powers to interfere and disrupt plots. The broad definition of all terms sets dangerous precedents (see https://openparliament.ca/bills/41-2/C-51/).

4.   Ghooi (2011) argued that the *Nuremberg Code* has no legal force and drew heavily from the Guidelines for Human Experimentation (1931) already well known in Germany, yet these earlier guidelines are never referenced by the mostly American authors of the *Nuremberg Code*.

5.   The former Information and Privacy Commissioner of Ontario, Ann Cavoukian (2013), described how the de-identification of data is a principle now around the globe. She argued that the risk of data violations is small compared to the usefulness of secondary research. Privacy guards can provide differential treatment of information so that more distortion can be added when data are more intrusive

References

Angwenyi, Vibian, Dorcas Kamuya, Dorothy Mwachiro, et al. 2013. "Working with Community Health Workers as 'Volunteers' in a Vaccine Trial: Practical and Ethical Experiences and Implications." *Developing World Bioethics* 13, 1: 38–47.

Armstrong, Natalie, Mary Dixon-Woods, Ann Thomas, et al. 2012. "Do Informed Consent Documents for Cancer Trials Do What They Should? A Study of Manifest and Latent Functions." *Sociology of Health and Illness* 34, 8: 1230–1245.

Badwall, Harjeet Kaur. 2016. "Racialized Discourses: Writing against an Essentialized Story about Racism." *Intersectionalities: A Global Journal of Social Work Analysis, Research, Polity, and Practice* 5, 1: 8–19.

Barton, Bernadette. 2011. "My Auto/Ethnographic Dilemma: Who Owns the Story?" *Qualitative Sociology* 34, 3: 431–445.

Battiste, Marie, Lynne Bell, and L.M Findlay. 2002. "Decolonizing Education in Canadian Universities: An Interdisciplinary, International, Indigenous Research." *Canadian Journal of Education* 26, 2: 82–95.

Bayer, Ronald, and Claire Edington. 2009. "HIV Testing, Human Rights, and Global AIDS Policy: Exceptionalism and Its Discontents." *Journal of Health Politics, Policy and Law* 34, 3: 301–323.

Beattie, Samantha. 2017. "City Will Demand Uber Reveal how Many Toronto Users Were Impacted by Security Breach." *Toronto Star,* December 8. thestar.com/news/city_hall/2017/12/08/city-will-demand-uber-reveal-how-many-toronto-users-were-impacted-by-security-breach.html.

Beeby, Dean. 2013. "Access Commissioner Says Government Obstructs Freedom of Information Law." *Globe and Mail,* September 27. theglobeandmail.com/news/politics/canadas-info-czar-warns-against-federal-governments-new-obstructive-tactics/article14563504/.

Bengry-Howell, Christine Griffin. 2012. "Negotiating Access in Ethnographic Research with 'Hard to Reach' Young People: Establishing Common Ground or a Process of Methodological Grooming?" *International Journal of Social Research Methodology* 15, 5: 403–416.

Bennett, Colin, Kevin Haggerty, David Lyon and Valerie Steeves. 2014. *Transparent Lives: Surveillance in Canada.* Athabasca, AB: Athabasca University Press.

Boggio, A. 2010. "Biobanks and the 'Well-Being' of Humanity: Integrating Consent to Research with the Capability Approach." *Critical Public Health* 20, 1: 85–96.

Bolen, Michael. 2014. "Ottawa Is Spying on Us Without a Warrant and It's Time to Get Angry." *Huffington Post,* May 21. huffingtonpost.ca/michael-bolen/canada-spying-warrants-get-mad_b_5366782.html.

Boulton, M., and M. Parker. 2007. "Informed Consent in a Changing Environment." *Social Science and Medicine* 65, 11: 2187–2198.

boyd, danah, and Kate Crawford. 2012. "Critical Questions for Big Data: Provocations for a Cultural, Technological, and Scholarly Phenomenon." *Information, Communication and Society* 15, 5: 662–679.

Bronskill, Jim. 2017. "Canada's Access to Information Faring Worse under Trudeau Government." *Toronto Star,* Sept. 27. thestar.com/news/canada/2017/09/27/canadas-access-to-information-system-faring-worse-under-trudeau-government-audit.html.

Buranyi, Stephen. 2017. "Rise of the Racist Robots – How AI Is Learning All of Our Worst Impulses." *The Guardian,* Aug. 8. theguardian.com/inequality/2017/aug/08/rise-of-the-racist-robots-how-ai-is-learning-all-our-worst-impulses.

CAHR (Canadian Association of HIV/AIDS Research). 2008. *Ethics Issues for Canadian HIV/AIDS Researchers in International Settings.* Toronto, ON.

Castellano, Marlene Brant. 2004. "Ethics of Aboriginal Research." *Journal of Aboriginal Health* 1, 1: 98–114.

———. 2010. "Policy Writing as Dialogue: Drafting an Aboriginal Chapter for Canada's Tri-Council Policy Statement: Ethical Conduct for Research Involving Humans." *International Indigenous Policy Journal* 1, 2: ir.lib.uwo.ca/iipj/vol1/iss2/1.

Cavoukian, Ann. 2013. *Looking Forward: De-Identification Developments — New Tools, New Challenges.* Toronto, ON: Information & Privacy Commissioner.

CBC. 2013. "Spark: Viktor Mayer-Schönberger on Big Data." *CBC News.* measuringwhatmattersvt.wordpress.com/2013/05/28/spark-viktor-mayer-schonberger-on-big-data/.

———. 2015. "Datafication, Stock Market Trading and Open Knowledge." *CBC News.* cbc.ca/radio/spark/datification-stock-market-trading-and-open-knowledge-1.1532306.

———. 2018. "Ex-Cambridge Analytica Employee Believes Over 87 Million Facebook Users Had Data Compromised." *CBC News.* cbc.ca/news/technology/cambridge-analytica-nix-uk-committee-1.4622879.

Chown Oved, Marco. 2015. "Stolen Maternity Records Part of Larger Investigation, ITO Documents Say." *Toronto Star,* June 5. thestar.com/news/crime/2015/06/05/stolen-maternity-records-part-of-larger-investigation-ito-documents-say.html.

Clement, Tim, and Christine Bigby. 2013. "Ethical Challenges in Researching in Group Homes for People with Severe Learning Difficulties: Shifting the Balance of Power." *Disability & Society* 28, 4: 486–499.

Coll, Sami. 2014. "Privacy, Knowledge and the Subjects of Privacy: Understanding Privacy as the Ally of Surveillance." *Information, Communication and Society* 17, 10: 1250–1263.

Cool, Jennifer. 2012. "The Mutual Co-Construction of Online and Onground Cyborganic: Making an Ethnography of Networked Social Media Speak to Challenges of Posthuman." In *Human No More: Digital Subjectivities, Unhuman Subjects and the End of Anthropology,* edited by N. Whitehead and M. Wesch (11–32). Boulder, CO: University of Colorado Press.

Degner, L.F. 2002. "Ethics and Decision Making: Lessons from the 'Cancer Wars.'" *Canadian Journal of Nursing* 34, 3: 9–13.

Ellis, Ralph. 2015. "Guatemalans Deliberately Infected with STDs Sue Johns Hopkins." *CNN Americas,* April 14. cnn.com/2015/04/03/americas/guatemala-std-lawsuit/.

Fang, F.C., R.G. Steen, and A. Casadevall. 2013. "Short Takes: Informed Consent?" *Hedgehog Review* 15, 1: 56–59.

First Nations Centre. 2007. OCAP: *Ownership, Control, Access, Possession.* Sanctioned by the First Nations Information Governance Committee, Assembly of First Nations. Ottawa, ON: National Aboriginal Health Organization.

Fisher, Pamela. 2012. "Ethics in Qualitative Research: 'Vulnerability,' Citizenship and Human Rights." *Ethics & Social Welfare* 6, 1: 2–17.

Foster, Jon, and Robert W. McChesney. 2011. "The Internet's Unholy Marriage with Capitalism." *Monthly Review* 62, 10. monthlyreview.org/2011/03/01/the-internets-unholy-marriage-to-capitalism/.

Foster, Victor, and Alys Young. 2012. "The Use of Routinely Collected Patient Data for Research: A Critical Review." *Health* 16, 4: 448–463.

Foucault, Michel. 1979. *Discipline and Punish: The Birth of the Prison,* translated by Alan Sheridan. New York: Vintage Books.

___. 1991. "Governmentality." In *The Foucault Effect: Studies in Governmentality: With Two Lectures by and an Interview with Michel Foucault*, edited by Graham Burchell, Colin Gordon and Peter Miller. Chicago: University of Chicago Press.

Gandy Jr., Oscar H. 2000. "Exploring Identity and Identification in Cyberspace." *Notre Dame Journal of Law, Ethics & Public Policy* 14: 1085.

Geist, Michael. 2014. "The Fear-Free Guide to Canada's Anti-Spam Legislation: Answers to Ten Common Questions." June 10. michaelgeist.ca/2014/06/casl-guide/.

Ghooi, R. 2011. "The Nuremberg Code — A Critique." *Perspectives in Clinical Research* 2, 2: 72–76.

Goldberg, David Theo. 1993. *Racist Culture: Philosophy and the Politics of Meaning*. Oxford: Blackwell.

___. 2001. *The Racial State*. Oxford: Blackwell.

Gollom, Mark. 2014. "Google Looms as 'Censor-In-Chief' after 'Right to Be Forgotten' Ruling." *CBC News*, May 14. cbc.ca/news/world/google-looms-as-censor-in-chief-after-right-to-be-forgotten-ruling-1.2641714.

Haimes, E., K. Taylor, and I. Turkmendag. 2012. "Eggs, Ethics and Exploitation? Investigating Women's Experiences of an Egg Sharing Scheme." *Sociology of Health and Illness* 34, 8: 1199–1214.

Hartman, Saidiya. 1997. *Scenes of Subjection: Terror, Slavery and Self-Making in Nineteenth Century America*. New York: Oxford University Press.

Hauch, Valerie. 2013. "RCMP Collect Suicide Attempt Reports — And Share Details with U.S. Officials." *Toronto Star*, December 4. thestar.com/news/gta/2013/12/04/rcmp_collect_suicide_attempt_reports_and_share_details_with_us_officials.html.

Heeney, Catherine. 2012. "Breaching the Contract? Privacy and the UK census." *The Information Society* 28, 5: 316–328.

Henry, Fances, Enakshi Dua, Carl E. James, Audrey Kobayashi, Peter Li, Howard Ramos and Malinda S. Smith. 2017. *The Equity Myth: Racialization and Indigeneity at Canadian Universities*. British Columbia: UBC Press.

Hochhauser, Mark. 1999. "Informed Consent and Patient's Rights Documents: A Right, a Rite, or a Rewrite?" *Ethics & Behavior* 9, 1: 1–20.

Jaycox, Michael P. 2012. "Coercion, Autonomy, and the Preferential Option for the Poor in the Ethics of Organ Transplantation." *Developing World Bioethics* 12, 3: 135–147.

Kamat, V.R. 2014. "Fast, Cheap, and Out of Control? Speculations and Ethical Concerns in the Conduct of Outsourced Clinical Trials in India." *Social Science and Medicine* 104: 48–55.

Khan, Shahnaz. 2005. "Reconfiguring the Native Informant: Positionality in the Global Age." *Signs* 30, 4: 2017–2035.

Kitchin, Rob. 2014. "Big Data, New Epistemologies and Paradigm Shifts." *Big Data and Society* 1, 11. doi.org/10.1177/2053951714528481.

Koh, Adeline. 2014. "Inspecting the Nineteenth Century Literary Digital Archive: Omissions of Empire." *Journal of Victorian Studies* 19, 3: 385–395.

Kovach, Margaret. 2009. *Indigenous Methodologies: Characteristics, Conversations and Contexts*. Toronto, ON: University of Toronto Press.

Mager, Astrid. 2012. "Algorithmic Ideology." *Information, Communication and Society* 15, 5: 769–787.

Manson, Neil C., and Onora O'Neill. 2007. *Re-Thinking Informed Consent in Bioethics*. Cambridge, UK: Cambridge University Press.

Margison, Amanda. 2014. "Personal Data of 8,300 New Moms Sold to Financial Firm in Hospital Security Breach." *CBC News*, June 4. cbc.ca/news/canada/toronto/

personal-data-of-8-300-new-moms-sold-to-financial-firm-in-hospital-security-breach-1.2665503.

Mayer-Schönberger, Victor. 2014. "Omission of Search Results Is Not a 'Right to Be Forgotten' or the End of Google." *The Guardian*, May 13. theguardian.com/comment-isfree/2014/may/13/omission-of-search-results-no-right-to-be-forgotten.

McLaren, Angus. 1990. *Our Own Master Race: Eugenics in Canada, 1885–1945*. Toronto, ON: McClelland & Stewart.

McStay, Andrew. 2013. "I Consent: An Analysis of the Cookie Directive and Its Implications for UK Behavioral Advertising." *New Media & Society* 15, 4: 596–611.

Metcalf, Jacob, and Kate Crawford. 2016. "Where Are Human Subjects in Big Data Research? The Emerging Ethics Divide." *Big Data & Society*, Spring. papers.ssrn.com/sol3/papers.cfm?abstract_id=2779647.

Mignolo, Walter. 2009. "Epistemic Disobedience, Independent Thought and Decolonial Freedom." *Theory, Culture & Society* 26, 7–8: 159–181.

Mills, Charles W. 1997. *The Racial Contract*. Ithaca: Cornell University Press.

Murphy, Elizabeth, and R. Dingwall. 2007. "Informed Consent, Anticipatory Regulation and Ethnographic Practice." *Social Science & Medicine* 65, 11: 2223–2234.

Mystakidou, K., I. Panagiotou, S. Katsaragakis, et al. 2009. "Ethical and Practical Challenges in Implementing Informed Consent in HIV/AIDS Clinical Trials in Developing or Resource-Limited Countries." *SAHARA-J: Journal of Social Aspects of HIV/AIDS/Journal de Aspects Sociaux du VIH/SIDA* 6, 2: 46–57.

Noble, Safiya Umoja. 2018. *Algorithms of Oppression: How Search Engines Reinforce Racism*. New York: NYU Press.

Nordentoft, Helle Merete, and Nanna Kappel. 2011. "Vulnerable Participants in Health Research: Methodological and Ethical Challenges." *Journal of Social Work Practice* 25, 3: 365–376. doi.org/10.1080/02650533.2011.597188.

O'Connell, Anne. 2009. "Building Their Readiness for Economic 'Freedom': The New Poor Law and Emancipation." *Journal of Sociology and Social Welfare* 36, 2: 85–103.

____. 2010a. "A Genealogy of Poverty: Race and the Technology of Population." *Critical Social Work* 11, 2: 29–44.

____. 2010b. "The Pauper, Slave and Aboriginal Subject: British Parliamentary Investigations and the Promotion of Civilized Conduct (1830s)." *Canadian Social Work Review* 26, 2, 171–193.

O'Doherty, Kieran, Michael Burgess, Kelly Edwards, et al. 2011. "From Consent to Institutions: Designing Adaptive Governance for Genomic Biobanks." *Social Science & Medicine* 73, 3: 367–374.

Pateman, Carole. 1988. *The Sexual Contract*. Redwood City, CA: Stanford University Press.

Payton, Laura. 2014. "Cellphone Searches Upon Arrest Allowed by Canada's Top Court." *CBC News*, Dec. 11. cbc.ca/news/politics/cellphone-searches-upon-arrest-allowed-by-canada-s-top-court-1.2869587.

Plankey-Videla, Nancy. 2012. "Informed Consent as Process: Problematizing Informed Consent in Organizational Ethnographies." *Qualitative Sociology* 35, 1: 1–21.

Reamer, Frederic. G. 2013a. "The Digital and Electronic Revolution in Social Work: Rethinking the Meaning of Ethical Practice." *Ethics & Social Welfare* 7, 1: 2–19. doi.org/10.1080/17496535.2012.738694.

____. 2013b. "Social Work in a Digital Age: Ethical and Risk Management Challenges." *Social Work* 58, 2: 163–172. doi.org/10.1093/sw/swt003.

Reubi, David. 2012. "The Human Capacity to Reflect and Decide: Bioethics and the Reconfiguration of the Research Subject in the British Biomedical Sciences." *Social Studies of Science* 42, 3: 348–368.

___. 2013. "Re-Moralising Medicine: The Bioethical Thought Collective and the Regulation of the Body in British Medical Research. *Social Theory & Health* 11, 2: 215–235.

Richards, Thomas. 1993. *The Imperial Archive: Knowledge and the Fantasy of Empire.* London and New York: Verso.

Sariola, Salla, and B. Simpson. 2011. "Theorising the 'Human Subject' in Biomedical Research: International Clinical Trials and Bioethics Discourses in Contemporary Sri Lanka." *Social Science & Medicine* 73, 4: 515–521.

Shah, Siddarth Ashvin. 2012. "Ethical Standards for Transnational Mental Health and Psychosocial Support (MHPSS): Do No Harm, Preventing Cross-Cultural Errors and Inviting Pushback." *Clinical Social Work Journal* 40, 4: 438–449.

Shamin, Fauzia, and Rashida Qureshi. 2013. "Informed Consent in Educational Research in the South: Tensions and Accommodations." *Compare* 43, 4: 464–482.

Sherwin, Susan. 1998. *The Politics of Women's Health: Exploring Agency and Autonomy.* Philadelphia, PA: Temple University Press.

Shorey, Ryan C., Tara L. Cornelius, and Kathryn Bell. 2011. "Reactions to Participating in Dating Violence Research: Are Our Questions Distressing Participants." *Journal of Interpersonal Violence* 26, 14: 2890–2907.

Simpson, Audra. 2007. "On Ethnographic Refusal: Indigeneity, 'Voice' and Colonial Citizenship." *Junctures* 9: 67–80.

Sinding, C., and P. Miller. 2011. "Of Time and Troubles: Patient Involvement and the Production of Health Care Disparities." *Health* 16, 4: 400–417.

Sinding, C., and J. Wiernikowski. 2009. "Treatment Decision Making and Its Discontents." *Social Work in Health Care* 48, 6: 614–634.

Slade, Sharon., and Paul Prinsloo. 2013. "Learning Analytics: Ethical Issues and Dilemmas." *American Behavioral Scientist* 57, 10: 1510–1529.

Sullivan, John L. 2013. "Uncovering the Data Panopticon: The Urgent Need for Critical Scholarship in an Era of Corporate and Government Surveillance." *The Political Economy of Communication* 1, 2. polecom.org/index.php/polecom/article/view/23/192.

Swaine, J., S.L Parish, K. Luken, and L. Atkins. 2011. "Recruitment and Consent of Women with Intellectual Disabilities in a Randomised Control Trial of a Health Promotion Intervention." *Journal of Intellectual Disability Research* 55, 5: 474–483.

Tallbear, Kim. 2014. "Research Note: Standing with and Speaking as Faith: A Feminist-Indigenous Approach to Inquiry." *Journal of Research Practice* 10, 2: 1–7.

Tuck, Eve. 2009. "Suspending Damage: A Letter to Communities." *Harvard Educational Review* 79, 3: 409–427.

Tufecki, Zeynep. 2012. "We Were Always Human." In *Human No More: Digital Subjectivities, Unhuman Subjects and the End of Anthropology,* edited by N. Whitehead and M. Wesch (3–48). Boulder, CO: University of Colorado Press.

Tuhiwai-Smith, Linda. 1999. *Decolonizing Methodologies: Research and Indigenous Peoples.* London, UK, & New York: Zed Books.

Tyldum, Guri. 2012. "Ethics or Access? Balancing Informed Consent against the Application of Institutional, Economic or Emotional Pressures in Recruiting Respondents for Research." *International Journal of Social Research Methodology* 15, 3: 199–210.

Vaidhyanathan, Siva. 2011. *The Googlization of Everything (And Why We Should Worry).* Berkeley, CA: University of California Press.

___. 2019. "Billion Dollar Fines Can't Stop Facebook and Google, That's Peanuts to

Them." *The Guardian*, July 26. theguardian.com/commentisfree/2019/jul/26/google-facebook-regulation-ftc-settlement.

Wager, Nadia. 2012. "Respondents' Experiences of Completing a Retrospective Web-Based, Sexual Trauma Survey: Does a History of Sexual Victimization Equate with Risk for Harm?" *Violence and Victims* 27, 6, 991–1004.

Whitehead, Neil L., and Michael Wesch,. 2012. *Human No More: Digital Subjectivities, and the End of Anthropology.* Boulder, CO: University of Colorado.

Wilkinson, David, and Mike Thelwall. 2011. "Researching Personal Information on the Public Web: Methods and Ethics." *Social Science Computer Review* 29, 4: 387–401.

Wingrove, Josh. 2014. "Cyberbullying Bill C-13 Moves on Despite Supreme Court Decision." *Toronto Globe and Mail,* October 1. theglobeandmail.com/news/politics/cyberbullying-bill-c-13-moves-on-despite-supreme-court-decision/article20885941/.

Zook, Matthew, Solon Barocas, danah boyd, et al. 2017. "Ten Simple Rules for Responsible Big Data Research." PLoS Comput Biol 13, 3. doi.org/10.1371/journal.pcbi.1005399.

Zuckerberg, Mark. 2014. "Mark Zuckerberg on a Future Where the Internet Is Available to All." *Wall Street Journal,* July 7. online.wsj.com/articles/mark-zuckerberg-on-a-future-where-the-internet-is-available-to-all-1404762276.

Afterword: Researchers of Good Will

Sherene H. Razack

> What is one to do after understanding that one's empathy is compromised? (Bobis 2014, 241)

In *The Colonizer and the Colonized,* Albert Memmi discusses how he found himself writing about colonialism. Memmi writes of his early awareness that as a colonized Tunisian, he knew he was a second-class citizen without access to civil service jobs, but he also knew that privileges accrued to him as a Jew did not accrue to the Muslim colonized (Memmi 1965, xiii). For Memmi, Jews in Tunisia were more easily seduced into the game of passing, of trying to grab as much privilege as was possible, a condition he emphasized that afflicts all colonized peoples. Describing himself as a "half-breed colonizer" who belonged completely to no one, Memmi's interest in the colonizer of good will, the critic of colonialism who nevertheless finds it impossible to leave and to end his implication in colonialism springs from this in-between condition. Katherine Milley put Memmi's insight about colonizers of good will to good use in her work on white allies in Indigenous struggles who are critical of settler colonialism but who nevertheless find themselves unable to imagine a world in which they refuse the condition of being a settler, both materially and psychologically (Milley 2019).

Researchers are, by definition, in a similar state of in-betweenness as Memmi described. Regardless of whether we are insiders to the communities we study or critics of unethical research practices, we remain members of the university community, and in an elevated position to those we study. They are the objects of study and we are subjects who write about them. As critical as we are of the colonial structures in which we find ourselves, it is hard to leave our positions of scholarly authority and the material benefits of our scholarly perch, even when we occupy precarious positions in the academy. Many of the people we interact with for our research know well the contradictions with which we live. It puts us on the defensive. We call ourselves activist scholars, scholars for social justice, allies of the oppressed, and often insist that we are insiders to the communities we study, for one reason or another — sharing a race, a gender, a class, a history of oppression, solidarity and sisterhood. Yet, our structural in-betweenness also generates a deep commitment to being critically reflexive. We are committed to navigating what we already know to be a trap. Unwilling to believe that we are, as Malcom X insisted, either part of the problem or the solution, we embrace this in-betweenness where things can feel temporarily ethical, even as we never stop worrying that there is no pure ethical dwelling place.

The scholars in this book make it their mission to find an ethical place to stand in social science research even as they acknowledge its impossibility and never stop worrying. Displaying an attentiveness to the politics of knowledge production, and an uncompromising accounting of their own complicities, the contributors offer tentative paths out of the bind posed by their in-betweenness. Their proposed paths towards an ethical practice are more like aspirations. No one in this book claims to have a recipe for ethical practice and there are misgivings aplenty. It is these misgivings, however, that comprise the book's chief virtue. It was immensely generative to compile a list of the scholarly minefields the contributors describe in their research, and to recognize many of the dangerous places to which my own scholarship has travelled. In their own worries about their research, I found the energy to continue to struggle for an ethical place to stand and I am grateful to them for that.

Teresa Macías (Ch. 3) begins with critical reflections of her work on discourses of terror in post Pinochet Chile. The renowned anthropologist Michael Taussig wrestled with the problem of writing about torture and terror thirty years ago in his path-breaking book *Shamanism, Colonialism, and the Wild Man: A Study in Terror and Healing*. As he wrote then,

> Most of us know and fear torture and the culture of terror only through the words of others. Hence my concern is with the mediation of terror through narration, and with the problem of writing effectively against terror. (Taussig 1987, 3)

Macías confronts the problem Taussig named head-on, beginning with the recognition that the archive in which she finds accounts of terror has already tampered with victims' accounts, assembling their stories for our consumption in ways that continue the violence. It is important to remember, as Scarry (1985) emphasized, that torture is a story of power written on the body of the tortured and on the social body. Clarifying that her responsibility is not to find the authentic story of terror lying beneath the pastiche of archival narrations, Macías follows Taussig's injunction to account for the mediation of terror through narration. She acknowledges that the scholar's task is complicated by the uses to which the stories of terror are put in law. Human rights law requires a simpler story of violation than the story Macías tells about how terror is written on the social body, as a story of a nation whose suffering is deemed officially over.

It is hard to do the work of scholarly excavation when law demands an uncomplicated, spectacular narrative and the nation must be born again as innocent. The scholar of terror is immediately confronted by the unsettling possibility that some stories should not be told at all, as one reviewer suggests to Macías, because of what the story will do and the lines of power it will serve. The reviewer advises that Macías should not traffic in the horror, but how else to talk about the imprinting of power on a body? How else to do the research and writing? As all the scholars in this collection conclude, there is no one ethical place from which to do research. One can only hope to chart the least damaging path, which might sometimes mean not doing the research at all. To do as little harm as possible requires carefully threading one's way through the politics of knowledge production and the aesthetics of terror itself, hoping to arrive at an alternative psychological space to terror, an alternative empathy (Bobis 2014, 247). The scholar is called upon to examine terror with a clear eye, but who can do so untroubled and at a distance from the victims of terror? We traffic in the pain and suffering of the victims regardless.

Is the problem of engaging in what Bobis (2014) calls a critical creative empathy different when the researcher is of the community of the tortured? Are the risks different if the writer is among the community of the torturers rather than the tortured, a line that is often moving in any case? I have written, for instance, of the well-known filmmaker Errol Morris who set out to direct a documentary about the young American soldiers who tortured at Abu Ghraib, the film *Standard Operating Procedure* (2008 as cited in Razack 2012). Emphasizing the innocence of the soldiers who are described as dupes of unscrupulous leaders, Morris urges us to reserve our condemnation for the architects of torture as policy. Creating a moral community of Americans victimized by their leaders, he does not bring into the frame the suffering of the Iraqis who were tortured by American soldiers during the occupation of Iraq in 2003. Morris stands with the American rank-and-file soldiers, a position that can only be taken if the Iraqis (the tortured and their communities) remain outside the frame. We cannot hear their screams when the dogs attack the prisoners; Morris only shows us the drawings of these incidents of torture that the soldier Sabrina Harmon sends home in a letter to her wife, evidence in his view that she was troubled by torture. Was this distance from the victims of torture possible because Morris was not of the community of those who were tortured and whose country the Americans occupied? Was it racism that put the tortured out of the frame? Here is a classic example of the mediation of torture through narration.

Several of the contributors consider the dilemmas of the insider-researcher who stands with one foot in her community and one outside of it. The problem that the insider -researcher has is her impulse to sameness with her research subjects, a problem that looms large for Vannina Sztainbok and Lorena Gajardo (Ch. 2), who know intimately how Latinas are "heard through the accent." If the researcher wants to write about Latina political leaders, she first has to confront that the typical reader knows only of the Latina migrant worker and will be unaccustomed and unwilling to think about Latinas acting in the world rather than being victimized by it. While Stzainbok and Gajardo are researchers who must navigate through the racist imagination of their readers, one in which they too are trapped, they are clear that they cannot do so from a position of innocence. By virtue of being researchers (and situated in the Global North rather than the Global South to boot), they are not the same kind of Latina that they study. This is Memmi's dilemma and Stzainbok and Gajardo accept that they are complicitous in the structures of power even as they are marginalized in it. But, they insist, not all complicities are equal. Like Memmi, who was alert to privilege as well as penalty under a colonial system, they seek to find an ethical basis of resistance notwithstanding their compromised position. Drawing on

Gloria Anzaldúa, they propose an ethics of ambiguity. If the bodies of Latinas are bodies from which we extract stories, stories that are likely to make us feel good because we have indulged ourselves in their pain, then the researcher must resist this extractive relation. She must read for other things in the story and refuse to be trapped, as Anzaldúa advised, in any one story. The question remains, though, whether the limit point in the research is the moment when the stories implicate us. Will we then refuse to leave? Will we unconsciously omit the story of our privilege and emphasize our penalty, a "race to innocence" driving the analysis (Fellows and Razack 1998)?

When Leila Angod (Ch. 4) found herself in the field documenting an encounter between elite Canadian teachers and the South African school children they had come to help, she knew that the encounter would be overdetermined by race and history. The white elite teacher who endeavours to teach a Black child about computers is unprepared when the child refuses to be a site for the production of the teacher's good feeling. She is likely to read the child's refusal as deficit rather than refusal and resistance. Witnessing this event, Angod notes her own marginal position in the scenario as a Brown doctoral researcher, someone not accepted into the club of Global North white teachers. She is not the same as the Black South African children, and indeed is often urged by Brown South African elites to engage in anti-Black racism. Where is the path to accountability in this scenario? While accountability cannot be pursued through sameness, Angod chooses the path of calling out the white teachers' casual assumptions of racial superiority, refusing to normalize the violence of the encounter. Yet, she writes with brutal honesty, she didn't take this risk until her research was concluded. She leaves us traces of these intense moral dilemmas in the field so that we too can calculate how to respond to the complexities of the racial encounter. Is an ethical position even possible? Perhaps, as many researchers have concluded, Global North teachers and researchers should just stay home and leave the Global South alone. The researchers in this book do not accept this outcome. Instead, they insist that differences in power and privilege have to be negotiated. Like Angod, Gajardo and Stzainbok, Harjeet Badwall (Ch. 5) wants to arrive at a third space where paradox, ambiguity and ambivalence can reign, a space where the researcher claims neither sameness with the racialized social workers she interviews, nor distance from them as they recount the racial encounters that are familiar to researcher and research subject alike. Badwall sounds cautionary, as do the authors of other chapters, and hopes that a space really does exist between truth telling and the discursive work the researcher pursues. There are risks, she concludes, in doing research, and that's all there is to it. The lesson these contributors offer is an important one. In taking the risk to discuss their own struggle for accountability, they leave us with their unease but also with their insistence to work through it.

To work through the unease, and to inhabit a third space, a space LeFrançois and Voronka (Ch. 6) describe as "unruly," they propose mad methodology that emerges out of Mad Studies, a rejection of the biomedical psychiatric understanding of madness. Eschewing rational, logical understandings of ethical rules, these contributors suggest that we begin by understanding how much rationality is linked to scientific racism, where those deemed mad are evicted from personhood as ungovernable beings who simply cannot live within the world created by scientific reason. Importantly, those deemed mad are not the only ones evicted from personhood. As Toni Morrison suggested, contradiction, incoherence and emotional disorder fit when the subject is Black, a status in law where violence is authorized (Morrison 1997, ix). The researcher has no choice but to question rationality as a measure of humanity, a path that demands that she pay attention to the knowledge claims of those deemed unreasonable. As all the contributors argue, this is not a path that is acceptable to an academy that is hierarchical, competitive, and driven by neoliberal goals. How then does the researcher remain connected to those deemed mad and to grass roots organizing against the violence that springs from encounters with the medical/psychiatric system? In asking this question, LeFrançois and Voronka recognize the dilemma of the researcher embedded in two worlds, cautioning that it is easy to get caught in the pursuit of inclusion and improvement. Indeed, researchers are frequently held to account by the funders of grants, and required to lay out the policy implications of their research. They must participate in the governance of the unruly. We are co-opted into improving a system whose logic is profoundly anti-Black, anti-mad. The dilemma they name is one that is pressing upon us in 2020 in the wake of tremendous anti-Black police violence. As the Black Lives Matter Movement insists, we must pursue abolition of police and prisons, and refuse to fix a system premised on Black death.

Researchers sometimes understand our role as bearing witness to the violence that is inflicted on the communities we research. I myself have been drawn to this role, particularly when my research uncovers a relentless disposability of Indigenous populations (Razack 2015). The role of witness is a heroic one, and one to be avoided for the reason that it seduces the researcher into believing that she is the solution and not the problem. Janzen and Strega (Ch. 8), researching the lives of women in street sex work, warn that researchers are constrained in our capacity to bear witness to the pain of others. It is hard to admit that structurally, we are in the business not only of bearing witness to pain and suffering but of stealing it (Razack 2007). We are always doing something to other people's stories. It is not surprising that ethical research begins with the question of what we do with the stories of others. Janzen and Strega advance an unsettling thought. Regardless of whether they claim shared memory and shared struggle with their interviewees, they remain university researchers who rewrite their interviewees' stories. Writing recentres the researchers despite their intention to centre the voices of their interviewees. They remain colonizers. Is the only hope that researchers have is to come clean about the theft of voice that grounds all research? Researchers are obligated to begin with how poorly situated we are to hear stories in the first place, and how ill-positioned to honour our research subjects and to bear witness to their pain. Our interview subjects take their life in their hands when they entrust us with their stories and it is best that we prepare them for the theft that will inevitably occur. We should not entice them with the promise that they will be able to tell their own stories. The story we tell is always our own. As Janzen and Strega affirm, a structural distance between researcher and research subject always remains in place.

If there can be no ethical place to stand without the active participation of those declared unreasonable, collaboration and participation remain risky business. When the Social Science and Humanities Research Council insists that researchers demonstrate their links to communities, we should be forewarned that community/university partnerships are now fully commodified. There is little in it for communities themselves and researchers will be structurally positioned to grab as much of the spoils as possible. In Chapter 7 Julia Janes concludes that participatory research and an equitable playing field are at once impossible and essential. We can try to address things like compensation for research subjects, try not to promise too much, and avoid the fiction of common cause and community. Janes considers activist groups as epistemic leaders in contrast to the researchers who study them, but this position will send the grantors scuttling away as well as leave the researcher without a way to critique community. These problems are not solved by considering the community as possessing one kind of knowledge (even if that knowledge is not considered truer) and the researcher another, since neither group will be able to stay in the third space and practice the ethics of ambiguity. Each group will be essentialized. Janes leaves us with advice to respect and embrace the diverse interests, investments and resources of collaborators as we attempt to make our collaborations less dangerous for community collaborators. To this I add that we take our own in-betweenness seriously, never forgetting that we are knowledge producers of the university. In the book's final chapter Anne O'Connell reminds us that our ethical review protocols offer a confidentiality and privacy that no longer exists. Data collection is surveillance and not only in a literal sense that O'Connell describes, but also because to know the other has always been to control the other, the premise of all colonial and racial regimes. How can we be accountable under these conditions, O'Connell asks. We have no other place to begin than with our implication in the system.

Many years ago, at the beginning of my academic career, I wrestled with the reality that as a woman of colour in a nearly all-white academy I was inevitably hired to be the native informant. I was expected only to aid the authentic knowledge producers, gifting them with access to my own communities and providing culture not theory (Razack 2001). The conditions of communication were such that considering my privilege was a hard thing to do and I often sought refuge in the categories of activist, collaborator and sister in solidarity. I know today that these identities may shield me from practicing the kind of critical reflection that this book models. What is one to do after understanding that one's empathy is compromised? What does it mean to be a colonizer who refuses but who still stays? The contributors to this book do not shy away from the hard work of owning up to their privilege. They offer reflections on how they navigated the impasses of their research and strove to be accountable. The Filipino-Australian writer Merlinda Bobis offers a path to a creative critical empathy that sums up where I think the contributors to this book have ended up. We should understand that ethical research practice begins from the following positions: "I am your kin in mourning" and "I am and will always be an outsider" (Bobis 2014, 248).

References

Bobis, Merlinda. 2014. "'Weeping Is Singing': After the War, a Transnational Lament." In *At the Limits of Justice: Women of Colour on Terror*, edited by Suvendrini Perera and Sherene H. Razack (237–262). Toronto: University of Toronto Press.

Fellows, Mary Louise, and Sherene Razack. 1998. "The Race to Innocence: Confronting Hierarchical Relations Among Women." *Journal of Gender, Race and Justice* 1, 2: 335–352.

Memmi, Albert. 1965. *The Colonizer and the Colonized*. Boston: Beacon Press.

Milley, Katherine L.E. 2019. "The Colonizer and the Colonizer Who Refuses: Cultural Production and Colonial Crisis at Oka, Ipperwash, Burnt Church and Caledonia." PhD Thesis, University of Toronto.

Morris, Errol. 2008. *Standard Operating Procedure: The Escandal Was a Coverup*. Sony Pictures Home Entertainment.

Morrison, Toni. 1997. *Birth of a Nation'hood: Gaze, Script, and Spectacle in the O.J. Simpson Case*. New York: Pantheon Books.

Razack, Sherene. 2001. "Racialized Immigrant Women as Native Informants in the Academy." In *Seen But Not Heard: Aboriginal Women and Women of Color in the Academy*, edited by Rashmi Luther, Elizabeth Whitmore and Bernice Moreau (51–60). Ottawa: Canadian Research Institute for the Advancement of Women.

____. 2007. "Stealing the Pain of Others: Reflections on Canadian Humanitarian Responses." *The Review of Education, Pedagogy, and Cultural Studies* 29: 375–394.

____. 2012. "'We Didn't Kill 'Em, We Didn't Cut Their Head Off': Abu Ghraib Revisited." In *Racial Formation in the Twenty-First Century*, edited by Daniel Martinez Hosang, Oneka LaBennett and Laura Pulido (217–245). Berkeley: University of California Press.

____. 2015. *Dying from Improvement: Inquests and Inquiries into Indigenous Deaths in Custody*. Toronto: University of Toronto Press.

Scarry, Elaine. 1985. *The Body in Pain: The Making and Unmaking of the World*. Oxford: Oxford University Press

Taussig, Michael. 1987. *Shamanism, Colonialism, and the Wild Man: A Study in Terror and Healing*. Chicago: University of Chicago Press.

Index